Kinship and Killing

KINSHIP AND KILLING
The Animal in World Religions

KATHERINE WILLS PERLO

COLUMBIA UNIVERSITY PRESS   *New York*

COLUMBIA UNIVERSITY PRESS
Publishers Since 1893

NEW YORK CHICHESTER, WEST SUSSEX

Library of Congress Cataloging-in-Publication Data

Perlo, Katherine Wills.

   Kinship and killing: the animal in world religions / Katherine Wills Perlo.

      p.   cm.

   Includes bibliographical references (p.) and index.

   ISBN 978-0-231-14622-7 (cloth)—ISBN 978-0-231-14623-4 (pbk.)—

   ISBN 978-0-231-51960-1 (e-book)

   1. Animals—Religious aspects.   2. Human-animal relationships—

   Religious aspects.   I. Title.

BL439.P47   2009

205'.693—dc22   2008036403

BOOK & COVER DESIGN BY MARTIN N. HINZE

To my children, Sam, Sarah, and Angus;
grandchildren, Rachel and Vinny;
and dog, Blackie;
and to the memory of my mother Katherine Wills Perlo,
and of Heidi, Shane, and Rocky.

CONTENTS

ACKNOWLEDGMENTS

Thanks to editor Wendy Lochner, reviewer Dr Julian Franklin, and an anonymous reviewer for supporting the publication of the book.

Rafeeque Ahmed gave permission to quote from his letters to Robert Tappan. Much material under the headings of "Purveyors of Mystical Experience" and "Teachers of Morality" in chapter 8 previously appeared in my article "'Great Shamans and Great Teachers': Animals as Guides to Truth in Religious Texts," *Ecotheology* 7.2 (2003): 146–162, published by Equinox Publishing, copyright © Equinox Publishing Ltd 2003.

Thanks to the anonymous person who put extracts from Masri's out-of-print *Animals in Islam* on the web.

The staff of the internet hall, Elhovo Business Center, Elhovo, Bulgaria, gave valuable technical help and computer and internet facilities while I was temporarily without adequate resources of my own.

I am grateful to my fellow animal-rights campaigners for inspiration and for helping the animals. In particular, thanks to Annette and John Lagan who initiated the founding of what became Dundee Animal Rights (mark 2), Tegwen Brickley and Ruth Woods for helping it to flourish, and Norma George for keeping it going for so long.

Kinship and Killing

Introduction

> The hunter's effort to subordinate himself to his natural environment is disturbed by the need to kill. . . . this necessary slaying weighs more and more heavily upon his mind. It seems as though one of early man's major intellectual achievements is the attempt to become free from this burden. He finds a way of thinking death out of existence.
>
> —ANDREAS LOMMEL, *Prehistoric and Primitive Man*

> The idea that human beings have a special place in creation is so prominent, in so many religious traditions, that religion itself has sometimes been explained as an expression of man's desire to affirm his own worth.
>
> —JAMES RACHELS, *Created from Animals*

IT IS USUALLY ASSUMED THAT RELIGIOUS DOCTRINES have determined, or at least strongly influenced, their adherents' attitudes to animals. My purpose here is to argue that the influence runs, to a considerable degree, the other way round. From a secular perspective, Best observes that "animals have been key driving and shaping forces of human thought, psychology, moral and social life, and history overall."[1] My focus being on religion, I offer evidence from the texts of four major worldviews—Judaism, Christianity, Islam, and Buddhism (against the background of its neighboring faiths, Jainism and Hinduism)—as well as from their surrounding cultures (including our own) that conflicting feelings about human–animal relations have produced strategies of resolution, which have contributed to religious and philosophical beliefs. Once the beliefs are in place, of course, they in turn reinforce the strategies that have been developed to deal with the conflicts.

Conflicting feelings produce conflicting and diverse ideas. So I give a mixed picture of the religions, as containing both pro- and anti-animal teachings as well as some morally ambiguous ones. This account is offered in place of the frequently found claim that a given author's faith is overwhelmingly or essentially pro-animal. Fully accommodating diversity, the explanation of moral conflict can bring clarity to an apparently chaotic field of beliefs and assuage

the unease felt by religious animal advocates on encountering texts that con-
done animal exploitation.

Another feature of my account is that, in reversing the usually assumed
causality—"God's/the Buddha's word leads to human attitudes"—I endorse
projectionism, according to which, in the present context, human attitudes
toward animals are seen as the immediate source of the doctrines. The devotee could say, quite consistently, that those very attitudes come from God who
bestows free will and moral reasoning power, or from the workings of karma,
or, in the case of wholly benign inclinations, from the Buddha-nature in everyone. But, by concentrating on the human source, I deal with what we can
experience for ourselves, as opposed to metaphysical explanations.

I also reject arguments purely from authority, to the effect that we should,
for example, be vegetarian, or not, because scripture says so. In the case of
the animal advocate, such an insistence suggests that vegetarianism cannot
stand on its merits. There is, by contrast, a tendency to radical reinterpretation on the part of some modern religious animal supporters—more fully developed in chapter 6—showing confidence in our own (God-given/Buddha-
reflecting) reason and compassion. A tension can be observed here between
faith and politics.

Throughout history worldviews have moved away from anthropocentrism,
as the sympathy for animals that was evident to some degree in early texts
(although sometimes only potentially) became more explicit and insistent. By
the end of the twentieth century, all four worldviews possessed authoritative
spokespersons as well as grassroots campaigners for animal rights, arguing
not only in general terms but also as interpreters of their respective worldviews' values. Chapter 6 explores this development in detail, while, throughout the book, where it seems called for, the Animal Judge comments on the
doctrines being considered.

Geographical factors may have played a part in the development of religions. The "belief system and social structure of a culture are related fairly
closely to the type of economy and technology it enjoys, for example,
hunter-gatherer, pastoral, or feudal,"[2] and, while there is much debate about
what early people ate or were anatomically suited to eat, vegetarians favor
the view that

> in our primordial condition we were vegetarian, as the traditions of many
> societies (and some ... paleontological research) contend; ... [but] as cli-
> matic conditions changed, ... and as circumstance or adventure compelled

or encouraged us to find new habitats where there was an inadequate
year-round supply of vegetation, so we will have become at least occasional
killers.[3]

This progression, speculates Rod Preece, accounts for later moral conflict
and the attempt to justify killing, since "we will not immediately have lost . . .
the 'vegetarian elements of our psyche.'"[4]

We can also bear in mind such economic factors as that the New Testament
"was written . . . for an urban rather than an agricultural audience, and with
the expectation of the coming end of all things, so that much of the Jewish
tradition of wisdom about nature is deleted"[5] and that the nineteenth-century
Bible Christian movement "attracted a large following of the working class,
perhaps because the church offered food that was both nutritious and cheap."[6]
The latter phenomenon had the unfortunate corollary that when, in the following century, "meat became cheap and plentiful" because of agricultural
technology, "the Christian vegetarian movement was soon forgotten."[7]

But to whatever extent people's views derived from the facts of the environment, they were also inner reactions which were not inevitable but could have
been different, and thus represented choice, dictated by that much maligned
factor in the formation of ideas—emotion.

According to Flack and de Waal, sentiments are "the very building blocks
of morality in that they reflect the tendencies and capacities . . . with which
human morality as we know it would be unthinkable."[8] Since they determine
goals, they must come first in the process of deciding how to respond to the
physical and social environment; reason can then enter to determine means,
as Hume argued.

Reflection will tell you that you first react emotionally to certain acts or
policies, after which you seek justifications—preferably sound ones. Logic
will tell you that in the absence of wished-for goals, reason would serve no
purpose. (For example, my goal when appealing to logic in the previous sen-
tence was to help persuade the reader of the psychological basis of certain
religious doctrines.) This is why it seems to me to be not only ineffective but
irrelevant to claim that animal rights are objectively right or wrong, or that
they do or don't exist. It is a matter of values, which are not provable—but can
be tested against psychological plausibility.

Evidence to be offered in chapter 8 suggests that not only ethical choices,
but metaphysical interpretations of the world such as the various unitary
outlooks—monism, holism, pan(en)theism—have been shaped so as to fit the

values of the theorists, overlooking or explaining away problems that logic might find insuperable.

Where simple issues, such as meat eating, are involved, the connection between motive and justification can be consistent. People (or that aspect of the culture or the individual) in favor of it will point to the postflood permission; people (or that aspect of the culture or the individual) opposed to it will point to Eden; each will explain away the contrary text. But where vaguer, harder-to-define subjects such as the animal soul are involved, anything goes to justify the theorist's feelings about animals. So, on a matrix of *vertical*, animal advocate, speciesist, *horizontal*, yes animal soul, no animal soul, all squares would be filled. But, in all cases, the attitude to animals would come first.

In other words, I am adopting the view of religion that has been called projectionism, or "the theory that God and other supernatural entities are projected onto reality by human beings."[9] Originally a concept of Feuerbach's, it was given its English name by George Eliot, "who rendered Feuerbach's cumbersome philosophical term *Vergegenstaendlichung* in the arresting metaphor of *projection*."[10] It can represent a reconciliation of faith with sociology, as in the view of Mordecai Kaplan, founder of the Jewish Reconstructionists, for whom Judaism is "an evolving religious civilization in which rituals are folk-ways . . . and God a projection of human ideals reflecting a cosmic process making for salvation."[11] Alternately it can represent a total debunking of religion.

As humans have projected their attitudes and relations to animals onto their guiding worldviews, three aspects of human nature and experience have been at work in the process.

CONFLICT, CHANGE, AND SYMPATHY

CONFLICT

What I am concerned with is animal-related conflict among the various doctrines of each worldview, produced by conflict within the minds of the authors of the doctrines or between the opinions of different members of the culture (including scriptural authors) from which the doctrines emerged. It is an aspect of the "moral schizophrenia" regarding animals that Francione has identified, whereby "we claim to regard animals as having morally significant interests, but we treat them in ways that belie our claims."[12] It is true that no culture or individual lives up to the highest ideals held, but nowhere is the discrepancy so massive as in the case of animals.

~

The form of psychological conflict relevant to ethics springs from the paradox of the individual ego. To be altruistic, you must go outside yourself to identify with the other being's feelings. But without having selfish needs of your own, you could not understand what those feelings were, and so could not have any sympathy with them. Even the saint who has supposedly shed all personal wishes must *remember* what those wishes were like in order to have a motive for helping others or even to grasp the idea of "help." Also, the prospective beneficiary of the saint's actions must have egoistic needs, or the actions would bring no benefit.

Of course, in the view of the moral egoist, there is no conflict between self and others, because the service of others is in one's own best interest. In this respect, the conflict might be characterized as between "narrow self-interest" or "broad" or "enlightened self-interest." But, for simplicity's sake, I'll refer to "self" or "self-interest" versus "others" or "others' interests."

The ethic with which we are familiar places others first, sometimes at considerable expense to the self. There are other value systems (briefly reviewed in chapter 9), but, I argue, the one that prevails in the traditions examined is altruistic benevolence, as expressed by the Golden Rule. When it is violated, people experience conflict.

And the evidence offered below shows that conflict is nearly always present, even though the degree of necessity affects how one might judge the treatment of animals. Perhaps hunter-gatherers would starve or be seriously undernourished without killing animals, but still they apologize to their victims.

In other cultures, perhaps the only need that exists is the *perceived necessity* of, for example, blood sacrifice—which seems to modern Westerners to be a superstition as powerful as any psychotic compulsion—or the imaginary (in the modern world) necessity of meat eating, but still the sacrificial ritual is often surrounded with gestures of respect for the victim and present-day meat eaters still think of themselves as animal lovers because they love their pets. Explanations of sacrifice are as complex as the phenomenon is mysterious; its practice or abandonment varies from tradition to tradition.

Yet again, an oppressive practice could reflect what I call *manufactured necessity*: that is, a need that arises when a group has from the outset, without seeking alternatives seriously or at all, made itself dependent on the exploitation of another group and is convinced that it cannot do without that exploitation even when criticized later on. I have in mind slavery and animal experiments.

The attempt to relieve conflict, in all these situations, has produced three broad types of strategy.

STRATEGIES FOR DEALING WITH CONFLICT

Here are some examples of the means used to cope with guilt toward oppressed humans and toward animals, with the human cases described first since these, being familiar, will make the animal ones more understandable.

Aggression

Aggressive doctrines may not explicitly acknowledge any ethical problem involved in exploiting other beings, but nevertheless offer justifications for the practices in terms of their naturalness, inevitability, or inherent morality. Oppression of humans may be justified by claims of, for example, superior qualities of the dominant group or divine dispensation or social Darwinism. The divine right of kings, like Hinduism's God-given caste system, is an aggressive doctrine. In the West, Genesis 1:26 is the best-known example of a religious aggressive strategy toward animals: "Then God said: 'Let us make man in our image, in our likeness, and let them rule over the fish of the sea and the birds of the air, over the livestock, over all the earth, and over all the creatures that move along the ground.'" In both sacred and secular writings, the worship of reason has been used to downgrade animals.

We may see how religion follows, rather than precedes, speciesist attitudes, by noting the emergence from the Renaissance of the "era of excuses,"[13] in which "we find thinkers who no longer accept the Judeo-Christian account of animals, have come to the brink of philosophical vegetarianism, and then fall back on the safe domain of traditional gastronomy."[14] Strategies are still necessary, so that "images in our culture construct pigs and cows as appropriate victims"[15] whereas "horses are not generally meant to be killed and eaten in our culture"[16]—thus, mere habit, in the form of "what is meant to be eaten," becomes a form of aggression. The habit of animal experimentation, besides being backed by long tradition, uses the aggressive assumptions that the lives and health of human beings are more valuable than those of animals and that, therefore, it would be a betrayal of humanity to stop these experiments. The last assumption reflects the "logic of domination," according to which "that which is morally superior is morally justified in subordinating that which is not."[17]

Evasion

This most conflict-ridden strategy diverts attention from exploitative practices by introducing precepts of kindness within the power structure or emphasizing its benevolent aspect. Evasive practices provide the site of the early twenty-first-century controversy over "animal welfare" versus "animal liberation," the *versus* itself being subject to dispute.

Evasion of the oppression of human beings is found not only in the principle of charity but also, for example, in Russell's concept of the superior virtue of the oppressed,[18] who are seen as so simple-hearted, spontaneous, and childlike that one wouldn't want to deprive them of those merits by giving them equality. In a patriarchal society, chivalry toward women is an evasive strategy. The most prominent Christian example of evasion regarding animals is the "good shepherd" image, calling attention to that stage of usage in which the sheep are well cared for.

Clearly, aggression and evasion are inconsistent, reflecting a conflict in people's minds that requires compartmentalization. John Stuart Mill sheds light on such inconsistencies when he describes "how slowly these bad [i.e., oppressive] institutions give way . . . beginning with those which are least interwoven with the daily habits of life."[19] He is referring to the "daily habit" of oppressing women within societies that have shed other forms of inequality. In the animal context, the observation can be applied to people who will speak fondly of animals and possibly condemn cruelty to pets or cosmetic testing or circuses, but draw the line when it comes to such "daily habits" as meat eating and reliance on animals for medical research.

While adults may discourage children's vegetarian impulses by telling them "that they will not grow up big and strong without meat,"[20] they also, in a move Singer describes as "simple evasion," direct "the child's affection for animals . . . toward animals that are not eaten: dogs, cats, and other companion animals."[21] The result is that "rather than having one unified attitude to animals, the child has two conflicting attitudes that coexist, carefully segregated so that the inherent contradiction between them rarely causes trouble."

A similar coexistence of conflicting attitudes is found in a quite different society, that of southern African Bushmen, for whom "myth and art give emphasis principally to . . . sameness; in contrast the hunt places emphasis on otherness."[22] Yet one aspect of "sameness" among aboriginals, recalling our own society, is that there is "an amazing number of creation myths from primordial peoples portray[ing] God with a dog, not explaining the creation of the dog but merely assuming that God had a dog. . . . Pets are not a modern, Western invention."[23]

Defense

Here there is always recognition of an ethical problem, but the behavior in question is laundered rather than changed. Within human society there are defensive rituals connected with death, such as a hanging judge saying, "may God have mercy on your soul," Pilate washing his hands, or a postabortion ritual popular with women in Japan.[24]

In Aboriginal culture,

> The fact that [Aboriginals] have developed a sophisticated ideology to justify the "necessity" of such killings [of animals] reflects a "wish-it-were-otherwise" attitude, a recognition that in a perfect world the killing would not be necessary. The respectful prayer to the slain involves an apology for in principle unacceptable but in practice unavoidable reality.[25]

What the defensive strategy toward animals protects people from may be actual revenge or attack, symbolic revenge in the form of illness or other manifestations of a bad conscience, or one's own pain caused by identification with that of another. There are numerous examples of defensive hunter-gatherer rituals. From later civilizations, Rifkin gives these instances, among others:

> First, the priests purified themselves by bathing and donning clean ceremonial gowns. . . . At the foot of the sacred altar, the beast's head was sprinkled with holy water, which encouraged it to shake its head. The shaking was interpreted as a signal of assent, "a sign that the beast concurred with its own slaughter."[26]

"According to an ancient Babylonian text, the head priest would lean down and whisper into the ear of the dead animal, 'This deed was done by all the gods; I did not do it.'"[27]

Literal Defense

Guilt may be expressed in the fear of revenge (see the section on Buddhist defensive strategies, chapter 6), and there may also be rituals to deal with the realistic fear of predators: "'On the skin of the dead bear the Eskimos hung presents in an effort to pacify its soul. Dead seals too were treated with the utmost respect.'"[28] Preece questions the moral significance of such rituals, wondering whether they are "reflective of reverence and respect or of propitiation, fear and supplication. If one fears the power of the bear to inflict harm, or if one worries that the supply of seal will diminish, one might wish to offer propitiatory gifts . . . without any respect."[29] However, one would not fear revenge from the bear, or believe either species receptive to propitiation, if one did not identify with them.

Political Defense

Response to criticism from outside the worldview, especially from rivals, may be classified as *political defensiveness* and is found both in ancient Buddhist texts and in the present-day trend to assert the animal- and nature-friendliness of one's own worldview by contrast with that of others. The trend is encouraging from the standpoint of animals' interests, but the rivalry in itself seems irrelevant, since any increase in *ahimsa*, from whatever source, is to be welcomed.

A defensive phenomenon in modern scholarship is the attempt to justify animal sacrifice. Some theories regarding Israelite sacrifice will be described in chapter 2, but Patton reviews four benefits to the sacrificial animal through a wide range of traditions. First, he or she is "special, even unique; it is . . . ritually adorned and beautified for its death. It has a special relationship to God and in sacrifice is given back to Him."[30] Second, the "animal victim undertakes through the sacrificial process a role that is far from passive" but "is one of theurgic and social agency, accomplishing a whole, rich range of religious ends" (397). Third, because of an unblemished state and the pretense of willing participation, the animal is removed "from a life among countless other domesticated animals," "it is given ritual . . . thus also acquiring special cultural status" (397). Finally, in the "elevation and individuation of the victim" is the prospect of resurrection, since "apparent negations of the vitality of life" actually imitate "the gods' undying, unchanging state." (399). But one might note that all these benefits, or mitigations, of sacrifice are features of human moral conflict and imagery, not of the animal's experience.

Another type of political defense is that in which people attack animal advocacy, recognizing that it contains implicit criticism of themselves.

Effective Defense

Because of the problematization of killing, which points to the hope that the practices may eventually be given up, I have also classed, as relatives of the defensive strategy, pro-animal reforms—the *effective-defensive* strategy—and theoretical doctrines supporting those reforms.

~

The "defensive" strategy, as I define it, takes the specific forms described, which always contain some indication that the act of killing is problematic. Of course, all the strategies are defenses against conflict, and when seen together they illustrate the point by conflicting with each other—so that the biblical God appears at different times as stockbreeder, slaughterer, shepherd, and lamb. The following comment on Aboriginal defensive practices is equally applicable to aggressive or evasive doctrines: "If the harming of harmless beings were not in conflict with the dictates of our souls (our primordial instincts, if one prefers), it is highly unlikely that exculpatory myths would ever have developed, almost impossible that they could have become as pervasive as they are."[31]

EVIDENCE OF CONFLICT

You may look at the treatment of animals and doubt that most people have moral conflicts about them. But religious texts support the claim. The Bible "often seems to be telling two stories about animals simultaneously—God's divine plan and human use and abuse. . . . If the first story is not always kept in mind, the second story can seem to legitimate all sorts of practices that animal rightists would find abhorrent."[32] Islam, also, "looks at animals in two ways: 'As living creatures in themselves attesting to God's wisdom and omnipotence'; 'As creatures subjected in the service of man.' . . . In practice, it is sometimes difficult to reconcile these two views; and it is seldom that animals are given the benefit of this ambiguity."[33]

To address doubt that the inconsistent texts reflect inner conflict, ask this question: "*If* people felt guilt, uneasiness, or distress about killing animals, would doctrine X (for example, God giving permission to eat meat after the flood) help to set their minds at rest?" If the answer is yes, then, considering the obvious harm done to animals by killing them, it seems plausible that such feelings contributed to the development of the story.

Anthropologists, archaeologists, authors and philosophers have found evidence of, or surmised, guilt toward animals in early and modern societies.

Even in the ancient Indian Vedic tradition, which revolved around animal sacrifice, "as early as the *Rgveda*, sensitivity is shown toward the slaughtered beasts,"[34] and the later texts and classic epics, while still accepting the religious requirement of animal sacrifice, also contain attacks upon the killing of animals and the consumption of flesh.[35] "It has been suggested," writes Joseph Campbell of aboriginal cultures, "that the daily task and serious concern of . . . spilling blood, in order to live, created a situation of anxiety that had to be resolved on the one hand by a system of defenses against revenge, and on the other by a diminishment of the importance of death."[36] So, the "primary lesson" of the Buffalo Dance, whose participants act out an elaborate Blackfoot legend, is that "according to the way of nature, life eats life; and the animal is a willing victim. . . . But . . . where there is magic there is no death. And where the animal rites are properly celebrated by the people, there is a magical, wonderful accord between the beasts and those who have to hunt them."[37]

Art historian Andreas Lommel observes that the art of hunting societies may be characterized by the "animal style," in which the "animal glancing backwards" motif is prominent.[38] This motif encapsulates the conflict by which, on the one hand, the mythology of the hunter "makes no distinction between man and beast: men may be transformed into animals and vice versa,"[39] and, on the other hand, the shaman tries to "secure success in hunting expeditions." The animals shown in this motif "give the impression, not only of 'glancing backward,' but also of being startled and beginning to flee."[40] Predator and prey are locked together by the glance backward, and the whole figure—the face that is personhood, the body that is edible flesh, your friend who is nevertheless in mortal flight from you—summarizes the hunter's conflict.

In addition to scholars' disagreements over the history of human diet, the role of hunting in early societies has sometimes been exaggerated, as is now recognized. "In fact, in many societies, gathering has contributed more to the food supply than hunting."[41] Adams, also, comments on "the misconception that Native [American] people were all hunter types . . . rather than advanced civilisations that were mainly agricultural."[42]

But, where hunting did take place, it was often accompanied by guilt. Not all hunter-gatherer societies show conflict, just as, within any given culture, individuals will vary in their attitudes without impairing the prevalence of certain values. Some African forest dwellers kill endangered great apes without any apparent guilt.[43] On the other hand, according to Smart, "pygmy groups also celebrate a ritual of apology to the spirit of the animals that they have killed—something which is reminiscent of bear rituals in Northern Siberia. One cannot fail to be impressed by the echoes sounding from one hunting society to another."[44] The absence of placatory ritual among the Chipewyan of Canada is "superfluous in a system where every encounter between a man and a prey animal has so many characteristics of a sacrificial event";[45] the animal's consent is needed for it to be killed, and this is sought through *inkoze*, "an order of causality partially . . . revealed to humans through dreams of supernatural beings."[46]

It seems likely that hunters have more respect for free animals, seen as worthy antagonists, than animal farmers have for their captives. But conflict remained after the domestication of animals, as seen in the shepherd for whom "[a] shadow in his life had always been that his flock ended in mutton—that a day came and found every shepherd an arrant traitor to his defenseless sheep"[47] and in Isaac Bashevis Singer's reluctant ritual slaughterer who, having been urged not to show more mercy than God, declares defiantly, "I have more compassion than God Almighty—more, more! . . . I will not serve Him."[48]

A Hasidic story "dramatizes the tension contained in a way of life that both commands compassion for animals and designates a ritual of animal slaughter."[49] A community was seeking to replace the old *shochet* (ritual slaughterer), a "revered and saintly figure," who had died. When a candidate had finished his demonstration of the ritual, one observer

> gave a long sigh. "What's the matter?" asked the other. "Did he not do everything correctly? Was there something wrong with how he recited the prayer? . . . sharpened the knife? . . . moistened the blade?"
>
> "Our old *shochet*," answered the other, "moistened the blade with his tears."[50]

Not only did the old slaughterer feel regret, but the community expected him and his successor to do so. Unterman confirms, "Although Judaism accepts the eating of *kasher* meat as perfectly legitimate, there is considerable ambiguity felt towards the *shochet*'s work, and to the taking of life for the purposes of food."[51]

That such passages are not tendentious fantasy is suggested by Grandin's study of abattoir workers, which identifies three approaches—"mechanical,"

"sadistic," and "sacred ritual"—by which "the people who actually do the killing or who drive the animal up the chute" deal with their jobs.[52] In the mechanical attitude, "Serpell (1986) states that people who kill animals regularly become progressively desensitized. The first few killings are upsetting,
but then the person becomes habituated." The sadist devalues the animal and
so "justifies in his mind the cruel things he does to it"; while sacred rituals (a
feature of the "defensive strategy" found in religion) "serve a beneficial function by placing controls on the act of killing, and they also help prevent the
devaluation and detachment that leads to the mechanical approach or to sadism" (8). One slaughterhouse contains "an atrium built from columns with
carved cattle heads, a labyrinthine, serpentine loading ramp, and workers
reciting prayers" (8). Slaughterhouse management, for its part,

> tends to deny the reality of killing. The few times they [those with offices else-
> where] visit the plant they tend to avoid the kill area. . . . One manager told the
> author that he would not expand the stockyard because he did not want to see
> it from his office window. He wanted his plant to look like a "food factory." (5)

Consider also the name *Huntingdon Life Sciences* for an establishment
that kills five hundred animals per day. Both *food factory* and *life sciences*
draw attention away from the harm to animals.

Groves has studied means of coping with shame and guilt both in laboratory workers and in the animal rights activists who oppose them: the latter
being "worried that they were betraying the animals . . . if they accepted some
animal use but not others";[53] while laboratory technicians, as reported by
Arluke, "adopted some lab animals as pets, kept photographs of them, and
even deified them as heroes and martyrs to science."[54] The evasive belief that
animals do not suffer as we do has been particularly useful to "researchers
engaged in invasive work" who "needed a bail-out mechanism to help them
survive having to do to animals what, if done . . . to the family dog—would be
construed as monstrous sadism. To genuinely believe that the animals were
really hurting might force them to look into an abyss."[55]

If children are taken as examples of unmodified human nature, they provide evidence of our affinity with and kindness to animals—childhood abuse
of animals being rare enough to be regarded nowadays as a sign of emotional
disturbance predictive of later violence toward humans. Arluke disputes the
conclusiveness of such findings.[56] But no one can overlook the ubiquity of animals in children's books, films, and toys and depicted on wallpaper, bedding,

and clothing. Nevertheless, where the "daily habits of life" are involved, children's sympathy for animals may be discouraged; I have mentioned Singer's observation of evasive strategies in this context. Even if you agree with the discouragement of the child's instinct on grounds that that instinct is uninformed and unreflective, the point is that it is there.

In the face of such conflict, ultimately regret, ritual, euphemism, or rationalization prove inadequate. Sympathy prevents one from remaining at ease with these compromises; in that the compromise contains inconsistency, the intellect also is uneasy. This is especially true once the real or perceived necessity for the act has declined, for then people cannot go on saying, "It's just too bad; life is complicated." At that point the cases can be seen clearly as simple conflicts between self-interest and altruism, wherein the ethical requirement is clear but unwelcome. But even if the acts were necessary to meet vital interests, the regret and vicarious pain would push people on to find means of avoiding those feelings, leading to an effective-defensive strategy or changes in behavior.

CHANGE

In several ways, the factor of change influences the relation of worldviews to human-animal issues. First, underlying the subject is the evolution of human beings from animals and the continuing evolution of all beings and planetary conditions, both natural and human made. Our descent from other species is one source of our sense of kinship with them and, at the same time, of our sense of superiority insofar as human qualities confer power.

Second, an ontology of change may be part of the doctrines themselves. Such an outlook is potentially pro-animal in that it challenges fixed species identity and roles and dogmatic beliefs. It may support species egalitarianism from the outset (the Buddhist doctrine of impermanence), be invoked for its revisionist potential (Muslim reinterpretation by analogy with new circumstances), or be freshly introduced (the view of God as changing along with the experience of sentient beings, found in Judaism and Christianity).

With the help of such principles, doctrines evolve, their course driven by sympathy and facilitated by technological change, so that people stop seeing animal exploitation as necessary and are able to accept ideas more consistent with prevailing values of benevolence.

CHANGE AND ESSENTIALISM

But, in view of change, it might be contended that one cannot propose any particular moral norm as expressing the essence of a given religion. Writers often put the word *true* in quotation marks in this context, but examination of the essentialism-diversity problem offers the possibility that the word may be definable.

There are two senses of the word *true* in this context, the factual and the valuational. Factually, there is no doubt about what, with regard to vegetarianism (and much else), the true version of any religion *is*. It is a collection of mixed messages selectively endorsed and rationalized by different people calling themselves Jewish, Christian, etc. Valuationally, it is what each adherent thinks it *ought to be*, interpreting its varied messages in accordance with that ideal. And all adherents subscribe to what they sense as an essence of the faith; otherwise they could not feel committed to it. Schmithausen notes that, despite the different approaches of various scholars seeking authentic early Buddhism, "all of the papers . . . establish or presuppose . . . that it is possible to retrieve at least the essentials of the doctrine of the Buddha himself."[57]

Both diversity and (allegedly) discernible core beliefs, i.e., essence, can be found in any tradition. The question is whether any of the core beliefs can be considered decisive and morally imperative. If *true*, in this valuational sense, is defined as what God, Moses, Jesus, Mohammed, or the Buddha meant, varying interpretations can be found for any statement. Chapter 6 gives examples of the techniques of reinterpretation used by animal advocates, while humanists could use similar techniques to reinterpret animal-friendly statements.

We might profitably look at the fact that any religion embodies an aspiration: namely, the hope of moving from an unsatisfactory state of affairs to a perfect one. Through history the circumstances, the perceived deficit and the possible means of remedying it will change, and it will be this, rather than literary or historical authenticity (who said it, which document came first, or which translation was correct), that determines the view of a religion's core values. If this means imposing our own current values on the great religions, it is no different from what, as I contend, scriptural authors have always done, with or without (since that cannot be determined) the guidance of God or the Buddha-nature. And we can hope that altered circumstances and attitudes, such as those concerning animals, can lead to a belief in more beneficial essences than have prevailed in the past. As Foltz writes,

we need not be overly concerned with *which* of the many existing interpretations (e.g., eco-friendly or not, patriarchal or not, etc.) of Islam or any other
religion is historically or originally "the correct one," but rather, we should
acknowledge that among all possible interpretations available to us, it is the
eco-friendly, nonhierarchical ones that we desperately need to articulate and
put into practice today.[58]

Or we might ask the question, What kind of world do we want to live in?
Kemmerer uses a dystopian example to suggest an answer:

> Wouldn't it surprise and disappoint even those who object to protectionism if
> they should go to church (temple, synagogue or the mosque) and find that
> their minister (priest, rabbi, or imam) advocated exploitation of the weak, the
> infliction of unnecessary harm, or the taking of life for no better reason than
> to satisfy paltry pleasures?[59]

Assuming we choose the opposite of such as those listed in her example,
how is our choice of values to be linked to our particular religion, rather than
solely identified as a universal principle? Each religion expresses them in its
own way (as reviewed in chapter 6). It is through the combination of universal principles with religion-specific prophets, narratives, precepts, and imagery that animal advocates can claim Judaism, Christianity, Islam, or Buddhism as their own.

CHANGE AND MORAL EVOLUTION

A final type of change emerges from the evidence: the moral evolution of human beings from natural causes. While biological, environmental, and technological evolution all might have taken a different course, there is evidence
that, *given* the way these things have gone, and given favorable conditions in
future, humans are becoming more compassionate toward animals and
other humans. (Here we must distinguish between the public, on the one
hand, of whom the assertion is true, judging by the demand-driven increase
in availability of nonanimal foods and cruelty-free cosmetics, and, on the
other hand, industry and its governmental servants.) In this sense Kaplan's
"cosmic process making for salvation" need not be seen as supernatural,
since it comes from human reactions. Gradually, and to a limited extent, our
species has found social benevolence preferable: witness the rejection of
slavery and the adoption of democracy and of racial and gender equality, all

at least in theory, and this benevolence is now beginning to be extended to animals.

This too could change, of course, if environmental or genetic developments were to destroy the impulse of sympathy.

SYMPATHY

By sympathy I mean not only condescending kindness from above, but also identification and goodwill to those one identifies with. Within an altruistic morality, sympathy is the "is" of the "ought"; it is a compelling psychological fact. And the sympathy that can never be totally expelled from the mind of anyone capable of experiencing suffering or happiness herself is what has driven the improvements in behavior toward other humans and animals over the course of history.

I would like to see this approach used more often in arguments for animal rights. For the emotional reasons are the true ones: they are what the argument is about, namely, suffering and the wish to prevent, avoid, or cure it. The Buddha perceived this when he said (repeating the formula for several instances of cosmological speculation), "Whether there is . . . the view that the world is eternal or . . . is not eternal, there *is* birth, there is ageing, there is dying, there are grief, sorrow, suffering, lamentation and despair, the suppression of which I lay down here and now" (*M*.i.430).[60]

Equally, whether the Bible, Qur'an, Pali or Sanskrit scriptures promote such and such a policy, and however translated or interpreted the relevant passages are, whether there is a God and how *existence* or *God* is defined, if I am trying to promote that policy it is because I feel that it will prevent, reduce, or cure suffering, not because it is implied or even explicitly advocated in the text.

Thus, with due appreciation of those writers who have done so much to promote animal rights, I question the attempt at "proving" their case, either logically or theologically, when the motive is clearly emotional and policy oriented. If you believe in God, you can say that God ordained things in accordance with your policy, and that may be the case. But, as suggested earlier, this cannot be demonstrated, whereas the observable facts of the matter (e.g., to attack someone causes suffering) and your feelings about it (therefore you do not want it to happen) can be demonstrated.

Nevertheless, for the benefit of readers who may consider my subjectivist view a cop-out, I offer in the next section, and at greater length in chapter 9,

an objective justification for animal rights, on the narrow ground that denial
of them is inconsistent with the prevailing values of most human societies and
that the arguments given for the inconsistency do not survive examination.

THE ANIMAL RIGHTS DIMENSION

First it should be made clear that, although written from an animal rights
standpoint, my analysis of the worldviews can be accepted by the humanist,
that is, one who sees humanity as the measure of value. I shall sometimes,
when speaking of people rather than ideas, use the term *humanist* rather
than *speciesist,* but reject two of the former term's connotations: 1. that animal rights supporters are antihuman and 2. that humanists are necessarily
anti- or nonreligious.

WHAT IS SPECIESISM?

The term *speciesist* could be taken to mean "the attempt to draw moral
boundaries *solely* on the basis of biological considerations,"[61] implying that
superiority was not necessarily assumed for any one species. In practice,
however, the word assigns responsibility for boundary drawing to human beings. Thus, Regan continues, a "speciesist position . . . would take the form of
declaring that no [nonhuman] animal is a member of the moral community
because no animal belongs to the 'right' species—namely, *Homo sapiens.*"[62]
And, when Kemmerer defines speciesism as "the human tendency to make a
distinction with regard to how individuals ought to be treated *based solely on
species*, regardless of morally relevant similarities and distinctions,"[63] the
operative word is *human*; as it is in Waldau's working definition: "Speciesism
is the inclusion of all human animals within, and the exclusion of all other
animals from, the moral circle."[64]

   This reveals a difference between speciesism and its frequently offered ana-
logs, sexism and racism, as when, considering the former, Adams observes that
"Meat is a symbol for . . . patriarchal control of animals."[65] For, within intrahu-
man types of inequality, there could be unjust discrimination by members of
the normally less privileged group, such as women or black people, against
normally more privileged persons, such as men or white people. But speciesism
can only run in the one direction, namely, humans harming animals, because
although animals can indeed harm humans, speciesism, in its capacity as an

"ism," connotes not merely oppression and discrimination, but ideas justifying those practices; so far as we know, nonhumans cannot form such ideas. While animals may prefer their own kind, "loyalty to *all* members of one species . . . is a high-level abstraction" of which animals are incapable.[66]

The connection with oppression of humans lies in broader considerations: "Feminism should not embrace vegetarianism simply because it is a negation of the dominant world," but "because of what it is and represents. . . . I have faith that those humans who have been exploited can empathize with and help nonhumans who have been exploited."[67] And the same could be said of any human liberation movement.

Perhaps in an effort to make human privilege seem at least potentially fair, scholars have distinguished between "bare" versus "indirect" speciesism—LaFollette and Shanks's [68] terms—or in Rachels's terms "unqualified" versus "qualified" speciesism.[69] Bare or unqualified speciesism appeals to the factor of species alone, in itself, while indirect or qualified speciesism gives reasons for the discrimination. Inevitably, these reasons, being derived from the overvaluation of human qualities, take us back to the more blatant position.

When such human qualities are found to a marked degree in a nonhuman animal, we face the question, What if only one other species were admitted to the moral circle? "Inclusion of *any* nonhuman group would break [the speciesist] pattern, although . . . some 'ism' might still be being committed (indeed, the words 'chimpocentrism' and '*pan*morphism' have been coined)."[70] But since the rights of nonhuman primates are defended because of those beings' humanoid abilities and DNA readings, they are admitted to the moral circle as honorary humans, and if nonprimates remain excluded, the policy could still be seen as speciesist, even within Waldau's definition. In the same way, leaflets on behalf of hens, pigs, or whales will often describe the animals as "intelligent": does that mean that they too are to be admitted, and less intelligent animals not?

Of course, an activist for nonhuman primates might well insist that she wants moral equality for all species, but is concentrating on primates as an entering wedge—because their humanoid qualities carry more weight with the public. And, the campaigner's argument would go, any breaking of barriers is valuable in contesting attitudes like that of vivisector Colin Blakemore, who declared, in support of experiments on great apes: "I worry about the principle of where the moral boundaries lie. There is only one very secure definition that can be made, and that is between our species and others."[71] In our culture, even the denunciation of some acts as cruelty to animals is con-strained by the fact that "crossing the boundaries between humans and ani-mals is taboo in Western societies. . . . Those who are particularly anxious over such boundary blurring are likely to diminish the significance of cruelty, arguing that if taken too seriously, let alone on a level with violent crimes against people, it will degrade what it means to be human."[72]

In sum, whether inclusion of great apes or other favored nonhumans, such as pets, in the moral circle makes the position nonspeciesist depends on whether they are included in all their differentness from humans, rather than because of humanoid qualities or relationships, and on the intentions of the person including them toward the remaining nonhuman species. If the apes or pet dogs, as honorary humans, and no other nonhumans are included, I would say it is still speciesist. Waldau's working definition might cover the situation better by referring to the exclusion of *any* (rather than *all*) other animals from the moral circle.

What, then, about insects and other small creatures, which people in the West routinely exclude, even where they include the full range of other ani-mals? Are animal rightists being speciesist when they kill these beings? That would depend on whether the act is in self-defense—since small creatures can invade our territory and bodies more easily than large ones, on the seri-ousness or otherwise of the invasion, on whether there exists any other way of defending oneself, and on the extent to which a belief in the creatures' inferi-ority is held to justify the killing.

Whatever the particular animal whose status a human being is consider-ing, for the policy toward the animal to be speciesist, the willingness to harm must be present, together with reasons justifying the harm. When Richard Ryder introduced the word in 1970 or 1977[73] it was in the context of antivivi-section campaigning, and provided an analogy with the recognized evils of racism and sexism. It is a political rather than philosophical term. So my own definition of speciesism is the claim that it is morally acceptable for humans to use nonhuman animals to the latter's detriment, as by imprisoning, hurt-ing or killing them, in order to serve human interests other than self-defense, and that, in a competition for resources of any kind, including attention and concern, humans must prevail. The claim could be philosophical or theo-logical, or it could be the unreflective, automatic reaction of the person in the street, based on long exposure to various dogmas, but to be speciesist it would in every case justify humans harming nonhumans other than in self-defense.

Speciesism, then, is the aggressive strategy toward animals. It is not necessarily the same as humanism (which may simply extol humanity without justifying harm to animals), but humanists may also be speciesists; and it is to those in the latter category that I, nevertheless, often refer in this book by the more courteous term *humanists*.

While such humanists could accept my account of conflict-resolving strategies, they would be likely to interpret them differently. Where I call a doctrine an aggressive justification for animal usage, the humanist might call it a positive reason. Where I claim that uneasiness about killing animals could have contributed to the doctrines, the humanist might agree that that was the case, but maintain that the doctrines deal adequately and correctly with the matter, since any uneasiness, although evidence of a creditable sensitivity, was unwarranted. As to the case itself, however—the influence of conflict over animals on the doctrines—there would be agreement.

A BRIEF ANIMAL RIGHTS ARGUMENT

So the aim of this book is not to promote animal rights. Nevertheless, an explanation of my belief in that principle (which I define as the willingness to extend equal consideration to all sentient beings) may be useful. Throughout most of the book, my viewpoint will be expressed argumentatively only by occasional comments from the Animal Judge, until chapter 9 where it will be offered in detail.

Summarized for now, my argument is that speciesism contradicts prevailing cultural principles, particularly the Golden Rule or noninjury principle, with its implication of a sentience criterion of value; as well as society's prima facie acceptance of kindness to animals. Because of speciesism, the Golden Rule is not applied to nonhumans, while kindness toward them is, in practice, severely limited to cases where humans have nothing to gain from abuse. There are value systems outside the Golden Rule, such as social Darwinism, that have some representation in our culture, but consistency with these, if applied to the whole of life including human beings, would not pass the what-kind-of-world-do-we-want-to-live-in test. Speciesism is invalid because of its inconsistency *with what we consider good*.

The justifications for these inconsistencies do not hold water. The most commonly heard one is perfectionism, or according moral priority to possessors of certain valued qualities. Almost as prominent is the next-of-kin argument, to the effect that our primary obligation is to our own kind, even at the cost of gross cruelty toward others. Yet, since the qualities valued by perfectionism happen to exist most fully in human beings, that argument is circular. And the next-of-kin claim is used only against animals, not against humans outside our own family, ethnic group, or social class. To withhold moral status from these humans would be considered selfish and immoral.

Here I introduce the book's main proponent of this account.

THE ANIMAL JUDGE, AND GUIDES AND MESSENGERS

The Animal Judge was inspired by Henry Salt's Pig, who tells the Philosopher:

> Revered moralist . . . it were unseemly for me, who am to-day a pig, and to-morrow but ham and sausages, to dispute with a master of ethics, yet to my porcine intellect it appeareth that having first determined to kill and devour me, thou hast afterwards bestirred thee to find a moral reason. For mark, I pray thee, that in my entry into the world my own predilection was in no wise considered, nor did I purchase life on condition of my own butchery. If, then, thou art firm set on pork, so be it, for pork I am; but though thou hast not spared my life, at least spare me thy sophistry.[74]

In the same way, the Animal Judge's main function is to invite the reader to occupy the animal's place, in keeping with the Golden Rule. Besides appealing to emotion, this procedure tests how valid intellectually an argument or doctrine seems when you imagine it affecting your own interests. You might then more readily spot logical flaws, or lack of substance, that would be overlooked when it made no personal difference. It is immaterial that the animals themselves cannot formulate a concept of validity: they still suffer from human application of the doctrines, and the doctrines may still be flawed.

Besides measuring ethics, the animal perspective concerns truth seeking and is presented in chapter 7 in the sections on "spiritual attainment of animals" and animals as "guides and messengers." The same perspective may be found in a worldview's attitude to words, particularly in Buddhism and other forms of mysticism, wherein a downgrading of this uniquely human characteristic shows a relative lack of speciesism.

To look at the world through animals' eyes also represent a philosophical adventure, an escape from our human dissatisfaction, or a search for evolutionary roots. Stories about animals combine the projection of human wishes and characteristics with observed facts about the creatures. If they did not take the forms that they do, and behave as they do, the images could not be created.

To those most likely to dismiss the animal perspective as woolly minded or merely poetic, the following may be noted. First, the animals' different physical form and sensory equipment means that in the most literal sense they do not see the world quite as we do. A "bird's-eye view" must be different from that of a human being in an airplane. Second, whatever communication and symbolizing systems animals possess, they do not possess human language and are therefore not subject to "metaphysical blundering" (in Hartshorne's words; see chapter 7).

Third, and most important, whatever does go on in various animals' minds, we can never actually share their experience; and this fact of an unknowable other realm raises fundamental philosophical problems. We cannot speak of any fixed reality or world, when it exists through the perspective of myriad types of consciousness. Even if the word *reality* could, theoretically, be assigned meaning in the face of this problem, our species-limited perspective means we can never know what reality contains. Ignorance is a permanent fact of philosophy, and this is not a negative quality in the sense of reflecting our inadequacy: it is a necessary feature of a world in which things, including minds, are differentiated and, rather than being one great infinite blob, are thus limited. For practical purposes we can know things within our capacities, and we can know logical relations, but we cannot know things-in-themselves, if there are any such. This is the truth of the concept of God as unknowable, and it is brought out by consideration of the animal perspective.

Finally, the Animal Judge and the guides-and-messengers stories represent the wish to impress on the reader the fact of animals' experience, which is so easily distanced by human speculation, however sympathetic, about beings who are necessarily known from the outside. Noske has written of the need to try to enter into the Other's world, with particular reference to senses of smell, touch, sonar, etc. and to the animal's own brand of selfhood.[75] To each of the billions of animals on earth—battery hen, laboratory animal, dog, elephant, fish, or one of the "flies which only live for a few seconds" and "might have the bad luck to see only the trough of a wave"[76]—his or her experience, right now, is the entire universe, just as compelling as each of our individual human worlds is to us. That is an empirical fact to which supposed objectivity may blind us.

THE PROBLEM OF ONENESS

This dilemma emerges from the animal case because in one way a view that "everything is one and we are all part of it" supports animal rights, namely, it moves away from hierarchical values, including anthropocentrism, by stressing that we are all common clay or interrelated or God's creations.

But at the same time it works against these attitudes, as various writers have noted: "One must identify not only with the forest, but with the developer; not only with the starving, but with the oppressor; not only with the Jews, but also with Hitler."[77] EcoBuddhism's "adherence to the Hya-Yen principle of interdependence negates its social and eco-activist agenda, for if all depends on all, then the black rhino depends on the hydrogen bomb, the rain forest on the waste dump."[78] The problem is especially troubling in Mahayana Buddhism, where the emptiness doctrine coexists with the Bodhisattva ideal, as explained in chapter 8. But it also appears in the ecological holism (found in some, not all, green theory) that has been appealed to by modern Buddhists and Christians.

The classically theistic form of the problem is that "on the monistic or pantheistic view, evil, like everything else, must have its foundation in God; and the difficulty is to see how this can possibly be the case if God be absolutely good. This difficulty faces us in every form of philosophy in which the world appears as one flawless unit of fact."[79] Identification with the whole also requires abandonment of individuality and its paradoxical capacity for sympathy with other individuals, as mentioned earlier. Such neutrality can lead to outright amorality.

Even if doctrines of Oneness did not send contradictory ethical messages, but were totally benign in their implications, they would not compel our compliance with those implications. And even if they had an unambiguous message, and *did*, on some interpretation, compel our compliance, such views would not provide primary justification for ethical behavior. That justification lies in the impulse of sympathy, which is so inseparable from the prevailing ethic of the Golden Rule that the word *justification*, suggesting an outside advocate, seems inappropriate.

So although, at first sight, Oneness appears to support the moral inclusion of animals, on reflection it seems at best superfluous. What is the problem then? Why not simply accept that is and ought are separate?

That acceptance is philosophically unsatisfactory. Since both realms occupy the same universe, and occupy our minds, there must be some relationship. The solution, which I offer throughout, is that, of the various possible constructions of reality—all being words imposed on the things we experience—we choose those that make the strongest appeal to emotions, including those emotions that produce ethical impulses and conflicts.

STRUCTURE OF THE BOOK

In chapters 1 through 5 I review the attitude toward animals as found in the Hebrew Bible, Judaism, Christianity, Islam, and Buddhism. This last worldview is placed against the background of Indian thought from which it emerged, with particular reference to Hinduism and Jainism, and here and in later chapters is compared and contrasted with these.

"Change and the effective-defensive strategy" are combined in chapter 6, because the effective defense, consisting of arguments for the abandonment of animal-abusive practices, often changes the interpretation of traditional doctrines, relies on accounts of ever changing reality, or points to changing circumstances affecting animals and in any and all of these ways offers the possibility of changes in policy. These phenomena are reviewed as they occur in each of the worldviews.

Particularly helpful to animals in modern times is the emergence of mutual East-West influence, with a complex dialogue taking place between the oneness outlook and relative species egalitarianism of Eastern doctrine and the activism and individual rights values of the West.

Chapter 7 discusses the animal perspective, particularly the tendency of some schools of thought to value wordlessness; specifically, it presents some of the many narratives, found in all the worldviews, of animals as guides and messengers. More broadly, the largest meta-ethical question underlying animal issues, namely, the problem of Oneness, is explored in chapter 8.

A hopeful look at the future, with animal rights as the next stage in human moral evolution, is given in chapter 9. Here I offer my own view of a nonspeciesist future world.

The teachings of Judaism, Christianity, Islam, and Buddhism have been influenced by human beings' inner conflict over their relations with animals. The effort to come to terms with the killing and other exploitation of creatures whom people loved has produced strategies of aggression, evasion, and defense. Accordingly, as conditions made favorable treatment of animals more practical, and positive attitudes toward them came to the fore, the doctrines changed, taking the form of effective defense or abandonment of harmful practices. The universal values of sympathy and altruism, as expressed in various forms of the Golden Rule, but previously applied mostly to human beings, have contributed to this change.

In the philosophical sphere, narratives of animals as "guides and messengers," and texts with related themes such as the valuation of wordlessness, reflect people's wish to enlarge their own perspective. In addition, those doctrines that imply that reality is all one—a view that seems to support animal rights, but also works against ethics of any kind—raise problems regarding the is-ought relation. So the consideration of attitudes toward animals has brought important issues into relief, while changes in those attitudes may have promoted greater consistency with prevailing values, within all the worldviews.

All these claims conform to a picture of human emotions, particularly affection, identification, self-interest, conflict, and guilt as psychological facts occurring in reaction to environmental facts (including those known or plausibly inferred about animals), and being projected onto religious and ideological assertions. But, although my story focuses on our own species' attitudes, it cannot be defined as human centered, since the characteristics and (so far as we can infer it) experience of animals have generated the human ideas.

1. The Hebrew Bible

HERE ARE THE WEST'S AND THE MIDDLE EAST'S foundational justifications for speciesism, proudly asserting its supernatural sanction. Such claims are what people first think of in connection with the Abrahamic religions' views on animals. Here, in various ways, God is the great authorizer who gives humans a divine image, holds the power of life and death, permits the eating of meat, and demands obedience even against all moral sentiment.[1] But alongside these doctrines are numerous evasive passages in which people express their sympathy and affection for animals within the constraints of ways of life heavily dependent on animal usage.

Defense is less prominent: we find it in the ideal of vegetarianism contained in the account of Eden, and the ideal of nonpredation in Isaiah 11, passages that suggest there is something undesirable about killing without demanding its abandonment here and now. The Jewish Bible contains only some indirect allusions to defensive sacrificial ritual. However, Klawans's contemporary political defense of Israelite sacrifice[2] seems to hint at what might have been in the minds of practitioners thousands of years ago.

AGGRESSION

The God of the *Tanakh* reinforced human control of animals through narratives of dominion, of creation, of permission to eat meat following the flood, and of Abraham's sacrifice, through disparagement of free animals, and through the high valuation of human language, which prepares the way for logocentrism and its European descendant, rationalism.

THE IMAGE OF GOD, AND DOMINION

The very beginning of Genesis tells us that God created man in order to give him dominion over fish and fowl and all creatures. Of course, Genesis was written by a man, not a horse. There is no certainty that God actually did grant man dominion over other creatures. What seems more likely, in fact, is that man invented God to sanctify the dominion that he had usurped for himself over the cow and the horse.[3]

Kundera refers to Genesis 1:26—"Let us make man in our image . . . and let them rule over" the other animals. In keeping with other, more benign modern readings of this text, Murray points out that "the idea of a human being bearing the image of God originally belonged to the ancient ideology of kingship. In Sumer and Babylon kings claimed to be, and were regarded as, 'living images' of the patron gods of their cities."[4] But since

> Gen 1 was written when there were no more kings . . . by a process which modern scholars call "democratization" . . . the "Priestly writer" transferred the "image of God" from the king to the whole of humankind, saying that humankind, in both its sexes, is in a *vice-regal* relationship to God. . . . Thus there is an essential link between the "image" and the charge to rule over other creatures.[5]

The concept of vice-regency is found also in Islam, with the same connotations for modern thinkers (including Murray) of benign responsibility rather than tyranny. However, for royalty and its subordinate power holders alike, benevolence is an option rather than an imperative, a fact of which we are reminded by the harsher traditional application of Genesis 1:26–28, as well as by its practical consequences in the Torah.

For after the flood, the power conferred on humans is intensified: "The fear and dread of you will fall upon all the beasts of the earth. . . . Everything that lives and moves will be food for you. Just as I gave you the green plants, I now give you everything" (Gen. 9:2–3) This may reflect a historical increase in necessity following environmental change.

Differential laws are permitted by the doctrine. Humans can kill animals but not (except as a punishment) other humans (e.g., Gen. 9:5–6). Some killings of animals are unauthorized, but they are less wrong than those of human beings: "If anyone takes the life of a human being, he must be put to death. [18] Anyone who takes the life of someone's animal must make restitution—life for life" (Lev. 24:17–18). A bull who kills a human being "must be stoned to death, and its meat must not be eaten. But the owner of the bull will not be held responsible" (Ex. 21:18), unless the bull "has had the habit of goring and the owner has been warned but has not kept it penned up" in which case "the owner also must be put to death" (Ex. 21:29), but "may redeem his life by paying whatever is demanded" (21:30). The unsolved murder of a human being may be atoned for by breaking a heifer's neck (Deut. 21).

CREATION

God in his aggressive mode might be characterized as a stockbreeder and slaughterer, insofar as the portrayed relation of God to humans and to the rest of the universe mirrors and justifies the use of kept animals. People think of the Creator primarily in terms of the parental metaphor, but two features are equally or more consistent with the stockbreeding metaphor.

> 1. God is not of the human species, though (possibly) sharing their image, whereas a parent is of the same species as the child.
>
> 2. God (whether seen as personal or abstract) is unknowable in his totality by human beings, just as humans are incomprehensible to animals.

Considered from the animals' standpoint, the incomprehensible, arbitrary human who determines the circumstances, as well as the duration, of their lives is a counterpart to the mysterious God projected by humans as controlling them. A difference is that while animals have evidence of the stockbreeder's existence and know what he looks like, no more than the humans vis-à-vis their own perceived God do the animals know how the stockbreeder thinks, what he means when he makes a noise, why he makes them suffer, or why they are in his power. By contrast, children are mystified by parents for a while, but they grow up to gain some understanding of them and of the family situation.

The unconscious modeling of the divine ruler on the human stockbreeder is suggested by Levinas's observation, with regard to the "total adherence" of the practicing Jew in ritual, "the adjectives *tam* or *tamim* express this totality, which is also said of the lambs intended for sacrifice."[6] Klawans, too, notes that "in ancient Israel, sacrifice involves—in part—the controlled exercise of complete power over an animal's life and death. This is precisely one of the powers that Israel's God exercises over human beings: 'The Lord kills and brings to life' (1 Samuel 2:6, cf. Deuteronomy 32:39)."[7]

Yet this "is not the only aspect of sacrificial ritual that can be understood in light of *imitatio dei*" (since, for Klawans, sacrifice is a positive imitation rather than a construction of God, and certainly not a laundering of slaughter, toward which he feels little aversion).[8] The other aspects that he refers to, and that will be noted in the appropriate sections, contain both evasive and defensive concepts.

While offering an interpretation different from these, Atran also challenges the idea of the parental God, stating, "More recent experiments indicate that the idea of deities as surrogate parents is overgeneralized and, at least from the standpoint of folkpsychology, wrong."[9] He points out that

> social interactions with parents are customarily very different from social in-teractions with deities. . . . A child usually doesn't give thanks or sacrifices to his or her mother for a meal, and neither does a mother petition or give offer-ings to a child for a kiss. . . . Worship often involves an "authoritarian rank-ing" relationship.[10]

One that certainly characterizes the ranking between human and animal.

Creation also confers obligation on the created being. "I put to death and I bring to life, / I have wounded and I will heal, / and no-one can deliver out of my hand" (Deut. 32:39). Moses accuses Israel,

> *Is this the way you repay the LORD,*
> *O foolish and unwise people?*
> *Is he not your Father, your Creator,[11] who made you and formed you?*
> *(Deut. 32:6)*

People today continue to justify meat eating by saying, "They wouldn't have lived at all if we hadn't bred them for food."

THE POSTFLOOD PERMISSION TO EAT MEAT

> Everything that lives and moves will be food for you. Just as I gave you the green plants, I now give you everything. (Genesis 9:3)

Here is one of the biggest stumbling blocks for present-day religious vegetarians—although, as chapter 6 will show, they have had little difficulty in getting round it, largely through the "temporary concession" argument. But in earlier times, in the absence of much cultural support for vegetarian-ism, the passage was damning, so that Jacobs could introduce an argument similar to that of Salam (see the chapter on Islam), namely, that because of the permission given after the flood,

> for a Jew to adopt vegetarianism on the grounds that it is wrong to kill ani-mals for food is to introduce a moral and theological idea which implies that

Judaism has, in fact, been wrong all the time. . . . For this reason many traditional Jews look askance at the advocacy of vegetarianism as a way of life superior to the traditional Jewish way.[12]

Calvin used the biblical passage somewhat differently, but to the same effect, declaring vegetarianism to be "an insupportable tyranny, when God, the Creator of all things, has laid open to us the earth and the air, in order that we may thence take food as from his storehouse, for these to be shut up from us by mortal man, who is not able to create even a snail or a fly."[13] The vegan Eden, a frequently used counterargument, was in those days either ignored or offered as a utopian fantasy.

Yet from the perspective of psychological conflict regarding animals, there is no problem in the coexistence of Genesis 1.29–30 and Genesis 9.3. The author(s), as well as the society they came from, both liked and disliked the idea of meat eating, the balance perhaps tipped at times by geographical events, and both impulses found their way into the Torah. Even for the believer keen to avoid imposing her own feelings onto the word of God, there is nothing here that precludes a moral choice.

THE ABRAHAM STORY

The story of Abraham and Isaac (Gen. 22:1–17), while not the first representation of animal sacrifice in the Torah, suggests that the practice originated as a substitute for human sacrifice. God repeatedly warns the Israelites against the latter, evidently common among neighboring peoples. The Israelites believe that they must sacrifice their children to achieve complete propitiation, but being reluctant to, they devise an account of God accepting the will for the deed and being satisfied with a ram.

Besides more complex explanations of sacrifice sometimes offered, Hiebert suggests that the offering of first fruits, whether animal or vegetable, by the Israelites or the other societies practicing it, has "two interrelated motives: the expression of gratitude on the one hand and the interest in gaining the favor and aid of the deity on the other."[14]

But in the case of animal sacrifice, another motive can be discerned, for the Abraham tale provides a sacred justification for meat eating by the peoples of Judaism, Christianity, and Islam. Animal sacrifice, besides its function of appeasement, made "a religious ritual out of the embarrassing task of animal slaughter," thus resolving the "towering incongruity" of "a God who has mercy on all that lives permit[ting] the slaughter of animals for food."[15] Of course, the Israelites' priests had no property and relied on the products of sacrifice. According to Hyland, "the system of distribution of the dead animals exposes sacrificial religion as an obvious pretext for satisfying an unlawful lust for flesh: God got the suet and intestines while the people kept the most desirable body parts for themselves."[16]

The third-century vegetarian advocate Porphyry believed that sacrifice (in whatever culture) provided

> an excuse for eating meat. The deity would be offered a tiny or inedible portion of the carcass, with the remainder being consumed by the offerer or the priest. This view was also held by . . . Clement of Alexandria . . . who stated . . . "But I believe sacrifices were invented by men to be a pretext for eating flesh."[17]

Even the vegetarian Pythagoras had allowed his lower-level followers, the *akousmatikoi*, to eat "the hallowed flesh of sacrificial victims," but no other meat and not even the sacrificial meat all the time.[18]

DENIGRATION OF FREE ANIMALS

Because of the economic importance of kept animals, free animals are seen as threats to civilization, more specifically to the lives of the kept animals. God, likening the Israelites to sheep, promises: "I will make a covenant of peace with them and rid the land of wild beasts so that they may live in the desert and sleep in the forests in safety" (Ezek. 34:25). The Bible frequently portrays free animals as God's avengers: "I will send wild animals against you, and they will rob you of your children, destroy your cattle and make you so few in number that your roads will be deserted" (Lev. 26:22). God's judgment on Nebuchadnezzar is: "You will be driven away from people and will live with the wild animals; you will eat grass like cattle" (Dan. 4:32). Edom "will become a haunt for jackals, a home for owls. / Desert creatures will meet with hyenas, / and wild goats will bleat to each other; / there the night creatures will also repose" (Isa. 34:13–14).

As important exceptions to this pattern, the celebration of free animals may be found in Psalm 104 and especially in Job 38:39ff: illustrating a more mystical view of creation that is less concerned with the exigencies of everyday life.

BEGINNINGS OF LOGOCENTRISM

The later glorification of words could be supported by Adam's naming of animals (Gen. 2:19–20). Humans, made in the image of God, take on the role of vice-regents, so that (in Murray's monarchical account) "the *'adam* displays the kingly gift of *wisdom* and, by naming the animals, both defines their natures and establishes authority over them."[19] For Hyland, however, that act "was not an impersonal classification of genus or species: It was a personal encounter with individual creatures" and "a recognition that they, like him, were individual beings." But the idea that naming humans or animals represented dominion "has become a staple of conventional, scholarly wisdom."[20]

Writing, which had appeared in the Near East, and schematization, became essential to agriculture: "Above all, [man] had to perfect his technique for calculating time, the first discovery of which had already been made in the Paleolithic."[21] The period of the Exodus was also important to the growth of literature: "it is very possible—if not even probable—that the thirteenth century saw the first examples of Israelite written literature. . . . the Sinai desert has provided some of the earliest samples of Semitic writing (from about the time of the alleged exodus)."[22] The writing on the wall expresses moral judgments in terms of numbers, scales, and division (Dan. 5:26) and, in explaining it, as mentioned, Daniel recalls the condemnation of Nebuchadnezzar to animal form and expulsion from civilization.

In a more fundamental way, according to Hiebert, the book of Daniel expresses an apocalyptic worldview that moved beyond the Yahwist's "religion of the earth." The latter religion excluded all "philosophical or theological dualism . . . human and world, history and nature, spirit and body, mind and matter," whereas Daniel prefigured Christian/Greek dualism, in that it "despaired of life in this world and conceived of human salvation only through a complete transformation of the world's orders and/or as a new existence in another, supernatural sphere of reality."[23] The overvaluation of language, as an abstract, nonanimal function, is but one aspect of that all-encompassing dualism. It is further discussed in chapter 3 under "Logocentrism, Dualism, and Rationalism."

EVASION

While meat eating and animal sacrifice were entrenched features of the biblical economy and of the culture, the people were nevertheless very close to their animals, creating the potential for psychological conflict. Repeatedly things that happen in the stories, for good or ill, to a good or bad tribe, happen to the animals also. "Every living thing on the face of the earth was wiped out; men and animals and the creatures that move along the ground and the birds of the air were wiped from the earth. Only Noah was left, and those with him in the ark" (Gen. 7:23); "I will remember my covenant between me and you and all living creatures of every kind. Never again will the waters become a flood to destroy all life" (Gen. 9:15). The curses on the Egyptians affect animals as well as people. God tells Moses "You will bring water out of the rock for the community so that they and their livestock can drink" (Num. 20:8). In Jonah, the king of Nineveh tries to avert God's wrath by decreeing: "Do not let any man or beast . . . eat or drink. [8] But let man and beast be covered with sackcloth" (3:7–8). See also Joel (1), Zephaniah 1:2–3, Zechariah 14:12–15. Ecclesiastes 3:19–21 "cynically considers the kinship between people and animals. Both are described as sharing the common fate of mortality."[24]

Jeremiah (12:4) draws a moral distinction in commenting on God's indiscriminate punishments: "Because those who live in it are wicked, / the animals and birds have perished"; the consideration of innocence, absent from most biblical accounts of mass reprisals, is also introduced by Jonah (4:11): "But Nineveh has more than a hundred and twenty thousand people who cannot tell their right hand from their left, and many cattle as well. Should I not be concerned about that great city?" But elsewhere, more typically, Jeremiah writes, with approval, "Then say, 'O Lord, you have said that you will destroy this place, so that neither man nor animal will live in it'" (Jer. 51:62).

Most households apparently kept animals or had access to them: "on the tenth day of this month each man is to take a lamb for his family, one for each household. [4] If any household is too small for a whole lamb, they must share one with their nearest neighbour, having taken into account the number of people there are" (Exod. 12:3–4). It seems likely that if people had not lived in such propinquity to animals, the authors of Exodus (22:19) and Leviticus (18:23) would not have felt a need to warn against sexual intimacy with them.

Yet people regularly killed these close companions, without any explicit acknowledgment of guilt. Vegetarianism, as practiced by the Maccabees or

Daniel and his friends (Dan. 1:8–16), was undertaken to avoid eating the products of idol worship.[25]

Evasion of the conflict between killing and kinship is expressed in the following kinds of text:

1. ambiguous prophetic denunciations of sacrifice;
2. some details of dietary and sacrificial rules;
3. examples of human and divine concern for animals, within the narrow scope allowed by breeding for slaughter;
4. vegetarian implications in the texts;
5. the image of God as a shepherd.

AMBIGUOUS PROPHETIC DENUNCIATIONS OF SACRIFICE

When prophets and psalmists attack animal sacrifice, the ethical motive is unclear; Linzey can only say cautiously, "it is not altogether inconceivable that this cultic objection had a moral dimension."[26] This possible tendency may be expressed as disgust: "'The blood of bulls and of goats revolts me' ([Isaiah] 1:11). 'Prayer is vain, for your hands are covered with blood' (1:15)."[27] The blood here most likely refers to humans previously killed by the sacrificers—"the faithful city . . . was full of justice; / righteousness used to dwell in her— / but now murderers!" (Isa. 1:21). But alongside this meaning, and evoked as an image by the words, is the fact that the hands are literally covered with the sacrificial animals' blood. As given in the NIV, Isaiah 1:11 suggests repletion or indifference rather than disgust; the NIV's 1:15 however has the same sense as Eliade's quotation.

At 66:3 Isaiah begins in what seems like an even more ethical vein, which has been picked up by Jewish and Christian vegetarians: "But whoever sacrifices a bull / is like one who kills a man." The passage's continuation suggests mere disapproval of all sacrificial rites:

> and whoever offers a lamb,
> like one who breaks a dog's neck;
> whoever makes a grain offering
> is like one who presents pig's blood,
> and whoever burns memorial incense,
> like one who worships an idol.

> *They have chosen their own ways,*
>   *and their souls delight in their abominations.*

But Kalechofsky rejects such an interpretation: "Since the prophets' condemnation of the sacrificial system is often interpreted to mean a condemnation of 'empty sacrifice,' one must be grateful for Isaiah's succinct and unequivocal statement: 'He who kills an ox is the same as he who slays a person' (66:3)."[28] Much as one would like to see it this way, the subsequent lines do create a doubt. Schwartz has given three possible indirect meanings from a vegetarian standpoint:

> (1) By eating animals, we are consuming the grain that fattened the animal; this grain could have been used to save human lives. (2) In poor countries, the ox helps farmers to . . . grow food. Hence the killing of an ox leads to . . . more starvation. (3) When a person is ready to kill an animal for his pleasure or profit, he may be more ready to kill another human being.[29]

As modern reflections on the verse, these observations are sound, but as biblical interpretations they seem far-fetched. On the other hand, such departures are entirely in keeping with the Talmud's interpretive adventurousness.

That Isaiah's whole antisacrifice message is substitutive—calling for inner devotion rather than outward rituals—is established by the previous lines: "This is the one I esteem: / he who is humble and contrite in spirit, / and trembles at my word" (Isa. 66:2). Nevertheless, the language referring to violence toward animals implies an underlying aversion. Altogether, what the prophetic statements convey most immediately to the reader is a mixture of physical, cultic, and (perhaps unconscious) moral revulsion.

Equally strong evidence of evasion on this matter is perhaps found in Regenstein's observation that "when the Lord gave to Israel the laws of Sinai, including the Ten Commandments (Exod. 19 and 20), no mention was made of sacrifices."[30] He quotes Jeremiah 7:21–22, in his Bible translated "For I spake not unto your fathers, nor commanded them in the day that I brought them out of the land of Egypt, concerning burnt offerings or sacrifices."

The New International Bible, however, reads "I did not *just* give them commands about burnt offerings and sacrifices, but I gave them this command: Obey me . . ." (my emphasis). Yet Regina Hyland

> notes that in some Bible translations, the word "just" was added to Jeremiah 7:21–22, changing the meaning entirely: "For when I brought your forefathers

out of Egypt and spoke to them, I did not [JUST] give them commands about burnt offerings and sacrifices." She writes: "Obviously the addition of the word 'just' entirely changes the meaning of the text. It was deliberately inserted, with no pretense by scholars that the Hebrew supported such an addition. . . . It is the New International Version (NIV) of the Bible that altered the text, and this is the most popular translation since the publication of the King James Version in the 17th century. It is widely used by both scholars and laypersons and is the only translation of the seven leading versions of the Bible that has changed the meaning of Jeremiah 7:22."[31]

And it is certainly true, and important, that the Ten Commandments do not mention sacrifice.

SOME DETAILS OF DIETARY AND SACRIFICIAL RULES

Concern is shown for the mother-child bond, demonstrating an awareness that when animals are killed, something regrettable is happening from which that bond, at least, should be protected. For example, "Do not cook a young goat in its mother's milk" (Deut. 14:21, also Exod. 23:19, 34:26). This commandment is the source of the dietary laws that "milk and meat must not be eaten together; they must not be cooked together; and it is forbidden to benefit from food containing a mixture of milk and meat."[32] Since being cooked together could not matter to the dead mother and baby, this rule could only have been introduced from a sense of sorrow in the human being, which had to be symbolically assuaged before he could proceed to cook and eat meat.

"You must give me the firstborn of your sons. [30] Do the same with your cattle and your sheep. Let them stay with their mothers for seven days, but give them to me on the eighth day" (Exod. 22:29–30). The same seven-day rule is found in Leviticus 22:26–27 (including goats in my NIV translation), which continues at 22:28, "Do not slaughter a cow or a sheep and its young on the same day"—a regulation that "requires of all offerers of sacrifice, priestly and otherwise, to remain keenly aware of the familial relationships among the animals to be offered."[33] Maimonides (1135–1204) comments on this verse:

> people should be prevented from killing the two together in such a manner that the young is slain in the sight of the mother. . . . There is no difference in this case between the pain of people and the pain of other living beings, since the love and the tenderness of the mother for her young ones is not produced

by reasoning, but by feeling, and this faculty exists not only in people but in most living things.[34]

In a verse giving rise to rabbinical debate about God's motives, Deuteronomy 22:6–7 commands people to send a mother bird away before taking the young.

Another highly significant evasive theme is found in the prohibition on blood. "Any Israelite or any alien living among them who eats any blood—I will set my face against that person . . . and will cut him off from his people. [11] For the life of a creature is in the blood" (Lev. 17:10–11); "But be sure that you do not eat the blood, because the blood is the life, and you must not eat the life with the meat" (Deut. 12:23). This commandment, and the reason given—that the blood is the life—suggest a pretense that what is eaten was not a living thing, because it no longer lives. The fact of slaughter is washed away with the blood.

Other shades of meaning have been discerned in the rule. Referring to the above versions plus Leviticus 17:12, 19:26, Deuteronomy 12:16, 25, and 15:23, Schwartz glosses "Life must already have departed from the animal before it can be eaten."[35] Hyland, also, writes emphatically that "the point of the Scripture is not a concern with whether or not the carcass had blood in it. The meaning is much more primitive and direct: Human beings were being forbidden to eat creatures that were still alive."[36] That practice was specifically outlawed by the third-century Noachide law (see chapter 2), while the ritual blood prohibition was retained.

R. Samuel Dresner writes that the prohibition "is one of the most powerful means of making us constantly aware of the concession and compromise which the whole act of eating meat, in reality, is"; Moses Cassuto puts it more strongly: "This prohibition [was] an allusion to the fact that . . . all meat should have been prohibited. This partial prohibition was designed to call to mind the previously total one."[37] This last assertion might be supported by the fact that "although blood can be mostly drained from the major arteries of an animal, it cannot be removed from the capillaries. . . . Thus, the prohibition against consuming blood, if followed strictly, would prohibit the eating of flesh entirely."[38]. Berry, similarly, refers to the "sophistry of eating flesh that has been bled out when it is physically impossible to remove all the blood from flesh without destroying it."[39]

Somewhat differently, Berman writes: "Blood, believed to contain the essence of life, was ceremonially separated from the flesh. The blood was returned to the Giver of life."[40] Yet the wording of the biblical passages also enables the adherent not merely to be reassured that the animal is now dead, but to deny the consumption of an even *formerly* living being and perhaps, also, if Berman's interpretation be accepted, to imagine that the animal's essence lives on in the divine realm. All things considered, the prohibition is consistent with motives of denial and evasion.

For Klawans, however, the prohibition on blood was part of the purification process required of sacrificers, priests, and animals. Some scholars have regarded death as "the common denominator of the ritual purity system. . . . The purpose of the system . . . is to drive a wedge between the forces of death, which are impure, and the forces of life, which like God are holy."[41] One had to avoid and expel things associated with death.

Not only does this hypothesis conflict with the same verses from Leviticus, which associate blood with life, but also "why, if the ritual purity system is concerned with keeping death out of the sanctuary, does the sacrificial system involve precisely the opposite: the killing of animals, *in the sanctuary*?"[42]

EXAMPLES OF DIVINE AND HUMAN CONCERN
FOR ANIMALS

Phelps calls it the "Biblical Compromise," to be fully developed later by the rabbis, whereby "Jews could use animals for food, clothing, labor, transportation, and so forth, but they must treat them with kindness and compassion while they were alive and kill them as quickly and painlessly as possible when that time came."[43]

God's benevolence to all sentient beings is established as a general principle by Psalms 145:9, "His tender mercies are over all His creatures"; 145:16, "satisfying the desire of every living creature"; 147:9, "providing food for the beasts and birds"; and 36:7, "preserving both man and beast."[44] More particularly, "Who provides food for the raven when its young cry out to God and wander about for lack of food?" (Job 38:41); "He makes grass grow for the cattle and plants for man to cultivate" (Ps. 104:14); "The lions roar for their prey / and seek their food from God" (Ps. 104:21); "He provides food for the cattle / and for the young ravens when they call" (Ps. 147:9). Maimonides observes that verses of this type may (like God's promise at Gen. 9:8–17 not to destroy "all life") "refer to Providence in relation to species, and not . . . to individual animals."[45] But even where the verses do not mention an animal in the singular, a welfare component—applicable only to individuals, since collectives cannot suffer—may be discerned in the evocations of the animals "calling," "wandering about for lack of food," "roaring," and "seeking."

Cohen notes it as significant that "even the Decalogue shows consideration for dumb creatures and commands that they too should be allowed the Sabbath rest."[46] Indeed, Exodus 23:12 implies that sparing the subordinate groups is one reason why the main group should not work: "on the seventh day do not work, so that your ox and your donkey may rest and the slave born in your household, and the alien as well, may be refreshed." Also during the Sabbath year "let the land lie unploughed. . . . Then the poor . . . may get food from it, and the wild animals may eat what they leave" (Exod. 23:10, the same commandment occurring in Lev. 25:6).

The concern for animals projected onto the deity by humans who feel kinship with them is not in itself evasive. It is only the coexistence of such passages in the Bible with the aggressive doctrines also attributed to God that constitutes evasion. In an alternate world where there was no exploitation to be evasive about or aggressive doctrines to conflict with, the principle of kindness to animals would not embody conflict. But in the real world of the Bible, exploitation is always in the background.

Sometimes kindness is obviously for human benefit: "If you see the donkey of someone who hates you fallen down under its load, do not leave it there; be sure you help him with it" (Exod. 23:5). But elsewhere it is undiluted: "A righteous man cares for the needs of his animal, but the kindest acts of the wicked are cruel" (Prov. 12:10); "Do not muzzle an ox while it is treading out the grain" (Deut. 25:4);

> Let me not enter their council
>   let me not join their assembly,
> for they have killed men in their anger
>   and hamstrung oxen as they pleased. (Gen. 49:5–6)

Attending to the needs of pack animals is part of the formula for hospitality in Genesis. In an incident widely cited by animal supporters, Rebecca is chosen as Isaac's wife through meeting the condition, decided on by the servant-emissary, that she not only grant his request for water for himself, but offer to water the camels as well (Gen. 24:14ff). When the emissary asks to be put up at her father's house, she replies, "We have plenty of straw and fodder, as well as room for you to spend the night" (Gen. 24:25). Laban, confirming the invitation, says, "'I have prepared the house and a place for the camels.' [32] ... Straw and fodder were brought for the camels, and water for him and his men to wash their feet" (Gen. 24:31–2). The same formula appears at Judges 19:20–21, when the old man tells the traveling Levite, "'You are welcome at my house.... Let me supply what you need....' [21] So he took him into his house and fed his donkeys. After they had washed their feet, they had something to eat and drink."

There are two possible objections, based on instrumentality, to the belief that the Rebecca story shows concern for animals. The first, economic, objection would hold that working animals need to be kept in good condition for human benefit. The second, moral, objection is the "indirect duties" view, as held by Kant and Maimonides, and expressed by Schochet: "The point is not kindness to the animal per se. Eliezer merely assumes that a maiden who exhibits kindness toward his beast probably possesses other moral and ethical traits desirous in a wife."[47] To the economic objection can be opposed the more explicit expressions of concern in other biblical passages, attesting that a sense of duty to animals for their own sake was within the emotional capacities of the Bible's authors and their culture. To the second argument, that kindness to animals is only worth cultivating to promote kindness to human beings, Kalechofsky has the logical reply:

> We must also ask why Jewish (or any other) tradition would stress kindness towards creatures who have no inherent worth as a pedagogical value; should we not be urged to express our energies of compassion only towards creatures who have inherent worth? ... If Eliezer wanted trustworthy proof of Rebecca's fitness as a wife for Isaac, should he not have rather examined her treatment of ... other human beings, not his camel?[48]

My only departure from this argument would be to deny, as unverifiable, the "inherent worth" of anything and to refer instead to "creatures whom human beings value." The conflict, as I see it, is not between an attitude (instrumentalism) and a fact (inherent worth), but between two attitudes coexisting in the human mind.

VEGETARIAN IMPLICATIONS IN THE TEXTS

Food imagery, when positive, focuses largely on such things as corn, olives, grapes, figs, and bread and, when negative—for example, symbolizing aggressive or destructive behavior—refers to meat eating. These tendencies have been noted also by Schwartz,[49] who further cites the *Encyclopaedia Judaica*'s observation that "meat is never included among the staple diet of the children of Israel, which is confined to agricultural products, of which the constantly recurring expression in the Bible is 'grain and wine and oil' (Deut. 11:14) or the seven agricultural products enumerated in Deut. 8:8."[50]

Psalm 104:14–15, after the lines on grass for cattle "and plants for man to cultivate," goes on:

> *bringing forth food from the earth:*
> *[15] wine that gladdens the heart of man,*
>   *oil to make his face shine,*
>   *and bread that sustains his heart.*

In Isaiah 55:1–2, God says, "Come! buy wine and milk / without money and without cost. / [2] Why spend money on what is not bread." And at 55:10–11:

> *As the rain and the snow*
>   *come down from heaven,*
> . . .
> *so that it yields seed for the sower*
>   *and bread for the eater,*
> *[11] so is my word . . .*

Some other examples of extolling vegetable foods are at Jeremiah 31:5, Hosea 2:21–2, Amos 9:13–14, Micah 4:4, Zechariah 3:10. Schwartz also mentions Deuteronomy 8:7–10, 11:14, Jeremiah 29:5. Food deprivation may be illustrated by the same products: "I am like one who gathers summer fruit / at the gleaning of the vineyard; / there is no cluster of grapes to eat, / none of the early figs that I crave" (Mic. 7:1, see also 6:15).

Counterexamples may be found of positive references to animals as food:

> *they will rejoice in the bounty of the Lord—*
>   *the grain, the new wine and the oil,*
>   *the young of the flocks and herds (Jer. 31:12).*

"Jerusalem will be a city without walls because of the great number of men and livestock in it" (Zech. 2:4). But vegetable references prevail.

Images of meat eating used to make wrongdoing vivid may be found in Micah 3:2–3: "you who hate good and love evil; / ... / who eat my people's flesh, strip off their skin and break their bones in pieces; / who chop them up like meat for the pan"; in Amos 6:4: "You lie on beds inlaid with ivory and lounge on your couches. You dine on choice lamb and fattened calves."

Of course these verses refer to wrongdoing against other humans, not against animals. But imagery is not chosen at random. The first passage uses the brutality of animal slaughter to provide a metaphor and simile for violence against humans. The second, in the course of using meat eating to represent luxury, evokes the creatures themselves, not just "meat." Moreover, the luxuriousness of meat eating comes from the same circumstances as its moral questionability, namely, the greater difficulty (compared with plant cultivation) of breeding, confining, controlling, and killing living creatures.

Kalechofsky, quoting Numbers 11:18–20, interprets that episode as almost explicitly vegetarian:

Say to the people: Be ready for tomorrow and you shall eat meat, for you have kept whining before the Lord and saying, "If only we had meat to eat! . . ." The Lord will give you meat and you shall eat. You shall eat . . . a whole month, until it comes out of your nostrils and becomes loathsome to you.[51]

The ending of this passage suggests that possibly the punishment was not for meat eating per se, but for discontent: "because you have rejected the Lord, who is among you, and have wailed before him, saying, 'Why did we ever leave Egypt?'" (Num. 11:20). Nevertheless, the choice of meat as the subject of discontent cannot be dismissed.

Later on, at Numbers 11:33 "The meat was still between their teeth, not yet chewed, when the anger of the Lord blazed forth . . . and the Lord struck the people with a very severe plague."[52] Elaborating on the chapter, Kalechofsky explains:

The Bible tells us that there were "food riots" during the forty years in the desert, tensions caused by the lack of meat. It relates that these conflicts were caused by "the riff-raff": "The mixed multitude, or the riff-raff, that was among them, began to lust [for meat]; and the Children of Israel also cried out, 'Would that we had flesh to eat!'" (Numbers 11:4).

So,

Upon entering Canaan, the Israelites are given permission to eat "the meat of lust." . . . Rashi's comment on the food riots, "It was right for the Jews to cry for bread, but not for meat, for one can live without meat," reflects the derisive sentiment toward "meat of lust."[53]

Given the absence of a specific command not to eat meat, and given the Jewish tradition of meat eating, I feel that this episode falls into the "evasive" category, as an example of meat eating associated with bad characteristics—greed, disobedience, and ingratitude—rather than representing a rejection of meat eating in itself. But the prophets' negative metaphors of meat eating, the unreflective demands of the people, God's reluctant compromise, the ambiguous reasons given for divine anger, and Rashi's enlightened view together illustrate the complexity of Jewish response to the issue.

In another negative image, Zechariah (11:15; the same image being found at 11:4ff) writes: "Then the Lord said to me, '. . . For I am going to raise up a shepherd over the land who will not care for the lost, or seek the young, or heal the injured, or feed the healthy, but will eat the meat of the choice sheep, tearing off their hoofs.'" In real life, the sheep are going to be eaten eventually anyway, but the author, in using the shepherd as a symbol of worldly leadership, prefers to point out that his proper role is benign, of which more below. Hunted animals may be used sympathetically to represent human victims:

> *Her princes are like deer*
> *that find no pasture;*
> *In weakness they have fled*
> *before the pursuer (Lam. 1:6);*

> *As fish are caught in a cruel net*
> *or birds are taken in a snare,*
> *so men are trapped by evil times*
> *that fall unexpectedly upon them. (Eccl. 9:12)*

In addition,

there is no passage anywhere in the Bible that commends hunting or speaks of it as a virtuous activity. . . . When the Bible calls [Nimrod] "a mighty hunter before the Lord" (Gen. 10:9), that is not praise, but condemnation for the

arrogance that led Nimrod to flaunt in God's face his wanton killing of God's
creatures, the same arrogance that would soon lead him to attempt his infa-
mous construction project [the tower of Babel].[54]

While Hiebert points out that hunting is "this talent of Esau's that his father
Isaac particularly admires (Gen. 25:28)," he nevertheless surmises that
"Isaac's reference to Esau's living by the sword . . . (Gen. 27:40), together with
the characterization of him as a hunter, may signal J's conception of the
Edomites as potentially violent."[55]

By contrast, the conjunction of *favorably* described meat eating with sacrifice supports the claim that one of the functions of sacrifice is to endow the
killing and eating of animals with religious legitimacy: "the cooking-pots in
the Lord's house will be like the sacred bowls in front of the altar. [21] Every pot
in Jerusalem and Judah will be holy to the Lord Almighty, and all who come to
sacrifice will take some of the pots and cook in them" (Zech. 14:20–21). In this
manner, Zechariah's image of the bad shepherd who eats the sheep can coexist
with that prophet's favorable reference to sacrifice (see Zech. 9:11).

THE IMAGE OF GOD AS A SHEPHERD

Muhammad "used to . . . say proudly that 'God sent no prophet who was not a
herdsman . . . Moses was a herdsman; David was also a herdsman; I, too, was
commissioned to prophethood while I grazed my family's cattle at Ajyad.'"[56]
While there is no external evidence for the existence, let alone the biographi-
cal details, of "Moses, Joshua or any of the judges: we have none for David or
Solomon either,"[57] the biblical authors chose to portray Moses as a herdsman
(Exod. 3:1) and David as a shepherd (1 Sam. 16:11–12).

In the Bible, the shepherd with his sheep is the predominant model for
human-animal, God-human, and interhuman authority, because sheep—"a
major feature of ancient Israel's rural economy . . . of importance as a source
of food and wool"[58]—have features that support an evasive strategy by enabling the authority in question to seem benign. They are bred not only for
meat and milk (the latter mentioned in Ezek. 34:3) but also for wool, the production of which involves little or no distress to the animals (at least as people
imagine it, though Isaiah 53:7 links "a sheep before her shearers" with "a lamb
led to the slaughter") and lacks the gross associations of flesh eating. A person
contemplating a herd of sheep or an image of a shepherd carrying a lamb can
evasively focus attention on that innocent substance, wool. In contrast to pack

animals (who are, it is true, even more free from connection with food), sheep are not made to work, and are relatively small; while, compared with the full range of other kept animals, they have the advantages, for human psychological purposes, of woolly coats and appealing faces. Thus the evasive image of the kindly shepherd is supported by the harmless aspects of their use by humans and by their benevolence-inspiring features.

It is true that the image of the shepherd became romanticized in later times. But even the subsistence farmers of the Bible must have found it easier to harden themselves to the acts of slaughter (a psychological challenge that the modern urban meat eater is spared), and of flesh consumption closely following slaughter, by the thought that the animals had been well cared for in life.

We see here how the wish to evade guilt toward animals, combined with the nonanimal-related wish to believe that the stockbreeder God who kills and inflicts misfortune is really a shepherd who cares for people, becomes the foundation of a major religious image. The image, serving a different function, is noted also by Klawans.[59]

The Bible does sometimes equate humans with kept animals other than sheep, such as: "The ox knows his master / the donkey his owner's manger, / but Israel does not know" (Is. 1:3); "And you will go out and leap like calves released from the stall" (Mal. 4:2); "The Israelites are stubborn, like a stubborn heifer. / How then can the Lord pasture them / like lambs in a meadow?" (Hos. 4:16). Better known are the goats who are separated from the sheep (Ezek. 34:17).

But note that three of these references convey a nonbenevolent or judgmental authoritarianism toward the animals concerned, unlike that of the good shepherd toward the sheep, the contrast being drawn directly in Hosea's comparison of heifers with lambs. The calves' release from the stall calls attention to their confinement. In Numbers and Kings the shepherd analogies refer to worldly leadership; those in the Psalms and prophets refer to God: "But he [God] brought his people out like a flock; / he led them like sheep through the desert" (Ps. 78:52), "Then we your people, the sheep of your pasture, / will praise you for ever" (Ps. 79:13), and, of course, "The Lord is my shepherd" (Ps. 23:1). Some prophetic examples are at Isaiah 40:11, Jeremiah 50:6, Ezekiel 34:11–31, Micah 2:12, 4:8, and 7:14, and Zechariah 9:16.

Ezekiel (34) retains the favored image through several inconsistent applications. The shepherd-God has judged "between the fat sheep and the lean sheep. [21] Because you shove with flank and shoulder, butting all the weak sheep until you have driven them away, [22] I will save my flock, and they will no longer be plundered." Indeed, "the sleek and the strong I will destroy. I will shepherd the flock with justice" (34:16). In this image, confusing from a naturalistic standpoint, the prophet applies ideas of human social justice to the flock. Earlier (34:1–4) he uses the same image as Zechariah of the bad shepherd who exploits and eats but does not tend the sheep.

The bad shepherd in the two passages represents misused worldly power, and when, in Ezekiel 34:11ff., God assumes power and becomes the shepherd, the "sleek and strong" sheep represent the worldly leaders. They are different from the "choice animals" in Ezekiel 34:3, whom the bad shepherds eat and who at this point represent a luxurious commodity (as in Amos 6:4). Then, at 34:4, sheep are presented as helpless, the shepherd reproached for not caring for the weak and sick.

Dombrowski notes that Plato

> draws an analogy between Cronus's daemons and the men they ruled, on the one hand, and human shepherds and the animals they tend, on the other. The point to be made is that dominion is not a license for eating. It would be unfathomable for Cronus's helpers to eat men just because they were superior in intelligence.[60]

~

As the Animal Judge sees it, referring to evasions in the Hebrew Bible, "You breed us to be killed for meat, or for offerings to a god portrayed as a carnivorous glutton who, like yourselves, delights in the stench of our burning flesh: then you surround these acts with rules designed to show how kind you are. You kill our children, but not on the same day as their mothers; you cook them, but not in their mothers' milk. During the time you allow us to live, you refrain from cruelty and let us rest when you do. Those among us who are spared slaughter because we can carry heavy loads for long distances will be fed and watered at the end of one journey to ensure our fitness for the next; and you'll even help us to our feet when we collapse under the weight you've put on us. You write all this in your scriptures to convince yourselves of your kindness, but it also shows your guilt."

For if people had enough sympathy to be kind to animals, it is difficult to imagine that they felt no uneasiness about killing and otherwise harming them.

DEFENSE

UTOPIAN VEGETARIANISM

The vegetarian Eden is a stronger image than the favorable references to vegetables discussed under "Evasion." Together with Isaiah's peaceable kingdom, it is frequently offered as evidence that God did not intend people to eat meat. In both passages, not only the humans but the animals as well are vegetarian: "to all the beasts . . . I give every green plant for food" (Gen. 1:30); "The wolf will lie with the lamb, / the leopard will lie down with the goat, / . . . [7] the lion will eat straw like the ox. / . . . [9] They will neither harm nor destroy on all my holy mountain" (Isa. 11:6–9).

Actually, Genesis 2 is not quite clear about what Adam and Eve ate. They could eat from trees, of course, but there is also a reference to "livestock" (2:20). I can see the biblical author envisioning a vegetable garden, but having in the back of his mind (her mind, according to Harold Bloom's *The Book of J*) the grazing animals common at the time of writing: resulting in some confusion of imagery. This impression is supported by Hiebert's explanation that

> the environmental setting of the Yahwist's ancestral narratives is therefore the same setting presumed in his primeval narratives. Israel's ancestors following the flood are involved in the same agricultural economy established at creation in the primeval age . . . and reestablished by Noah after the flood. They practice the mixed farming . . . in which grain-based cultivation is supplemented with fruit crops and animal husbandry.[61]

Hence, "The animals are created to assist *adam* in his agricultural tasks. . . . The sense of domesticity . . . is highlighted by *adam*'s naming the animals (2:19–20) and by the Yahwist's mention of *behema*, 'livestock' (2:20; cf. 3:14, 6:7, 7:2–3, 8:20), along with the 'animals of the field' and 'birds of the air'."[62]

It is evident from these irruptions of J's actual environment that "this peaceful regime" is a fantasy, the vegetarianism of which might be kept as an ideal, but that after the flood "has to give way to the reality of a world in which humans and animals eat each other (Gen 9:2–6)."[63] Or one might say that in the later text contemporary people chose to define the meat eating world as the only possible reality in the circumstances.

Immediately after the account of the Fall, we are told that Abel kept flocks and Cain worked the soil (4:2), and that God actually preferred Abel's offering of meat to Cain's offering of "fruits of the soil" (4:3–5). But then that was after the Fall. It is possible that, by oral tradition, the biblical author(s) were aware of a historical change from original vegetarianism to omnivorousness: "From a primeval stage of simple food-gathering, man seems to have developed into a hunter, a process which we think began about 50,000 BC."[64] Whether or not there was speculation, in ancient times, about these now much debated claims, the choice was made to picture the lost paradise as vegetarian.

While recognizing Eden and the peaceable kingdom as exemplifying the near universal myth of "a primeval ideal state or 'golden age' . . . from which everything has declined, but which lives on . . . as an ideal . . . to be realized again,"[65] Murray also links the vision to the biblical theme of kingship. Isaiah 11:1–5 describes the emergence of a just ruler. Then "it is natural to expect the following section [11:6–9]"—that is, the peaceable kingdom lines—"to describe an ensuing state of prosperity, both of society and of the land," yet "if it has the function one expects, it must be metaphorical to a degree far surpassing what we find in the previous sections."[66]

In any case, "Jewish and Christian traditions have developed the paradise theme in this way," i.e., as Golden Age myth "weaving the Isaiah vision into their respective pictures of paradise restored in the messianic age."[67]

ALLUSIONS TO DEFENSIVE RITUAL

An important site of the defensive strategy is blood sacrifice and its attendant rules. This ancient tradition, which Islam still practices from long habit, is extremely difficult to understand nowadays. Referring to both animal and human sacrifice, Atran speculates:

> Emotionally hard-to-fake and materially costly displays of devotion to supernatural agents signal sincere willingness to cooperate with the community of believers. . . . Displays of commitment must be thoroughly convincing, and to be convincing people must be willing to make the ultimate sacrifice, however rare.[68]

When making such a traumatic sacrifice, however strongly motivated, as by the wish to legitimize meat eating, it would seem necessary to find means of coming to terms with it.

It is true that the ancient defensive words and gestures during sacrifice that I described in the Introduction are not present in the Bible. In Leviticus and Exodus, the standard gesture toward the animal before slaughter is for the offerer to lay his hand on the victim's head, but this does not necessarily imply any participation by or propitiation of the animal. However, Patton mentions "the sprinkling of water upon the animal's head in both the ancient Greek *thusia* and ancient Israelite *qorban 'olah* so that it appeared to nod its assent."[69]

Only after the fall of the Temple in 70 CE, when, in Judaism, "the dietary laws of the diaspora [replaced] the sacrificial system and the Temple priest was replaced by the diaspora *shochet*"[70] did defensiveness come in, this time during slaughter for food, as "Judaism sought to avert the brutalizing effect that killing may have upon the butcher by surrounding the Shohet's act with the softening and sanctifying influence of religion, requiring him to offer a prayer while he does the slaughtering and to cover the blood soon after the animal is killed."[71] The ritual cited by Rifkin, referred to in the Introduction, in which the priest whispers to the dead animal, "This deed was done by all the gods; I did not do it," is echoed in the Bible: but only in the human context. After killing a heifer in atonement for an unsolved murder, "all the elders of the town nearest the body shall wash their hands over the heifer . . . [7] and they shall declare: 'Our hands did not shed this blood, nor did our eyes see it done'" (Deut. 21:6). There is an obvious parallel with Matthew 27:24 in which Pilate "took water and washed his hands in front of the crowd. 'I am innocent of this man's blood,' he said. 'It is your responsibility.'"

The meanings of these biblical passages differ, and their animal associations only exist through proximity in the text. In the first case, the elders are concerned with guilt over the unsolved murder of the human being, not that of the sacrificial heifer, but the declaration is made just after the animal's death. In the second case, the human sacrificial lamb is to be offered in atonement for the sins of other human beings; and it is therefore the sacrifice itself for which Pilate disowns responsibility. But the resemblances display awareness of such traditions regarding animals.

Indeed, there is more than awareness of propitiation in the Israelites' belief, asserted by Regenstein, "that the sacrificed animal, when burnt, ascended to heaven, thus mitigating any feelings of remorse the offerer may have had toward these gentle animals. The Hebrew word for burnt offering is *olah*, which signifies 'that which ascends.'"[72]

POLITICAL DEFENSE

Inveighing against the "imbalanced moral disgust (that scholars often don't bother to conceal) towards sacrifice,"[73] Klawans contends that the "analysis of sacrifice too frequently focuses exclusively on the killing of an animal, which actually constitutes only one step of a ritual process that is much broader" (66).

That context is "the concern to imitate God" (72). For, apart from the requirement of purification, which "may well involve the separation of people from those aspects of humanity (death and sex) which are least God-like)" (72), "the sacrificial animal must be birthed, protected, fed, and guided—all things that Israel wished for themselves from their God" (74), so that "the key to understanding ancient Israelite sacrifice is to remember the analogy: as God is to Israel, so is Israel to its flocks and herds" (74).

In these and earlier-quoted comments we see all the conflict-resolving strategies. God is seen, aggressively, as stockbreeder and slaughterer, evasively as shepherd, and defensively as sanctifying recipient of the act of slaughter. The difference, with Klawans, is that he sees people as imitating God, whereas I see them as constructing God so as to resolve their uneasiness over killing animals, whether for food or out of superstition. To be sure, having constructed God, the Israelites would have liked to believe they were imitating him (or enacting some other spiritual metaphor) by sacrificing the animal, but the process had begun with an act of perceived necessity.

Waldau, commenting on arguments that sacrifice "is confirmation of the importance of other animals," cites versions of that argument from animal supporters Frear and Linzey. Nevertheless, he observes,

> positive views of sacrifice, and even the more reserved arguments of animal advocates like Frear and Linzey, are based on the argument that it is not the individually sacrificed animal whose interests matter. Rather, these views suggest that the whole process, and the implicit value of honoring God in traditional forms, have positive implications for the importance of other animals and life generally.[74]

Waldau doubts "that a parallel argument [to Frear's and Linzey's] would be made regarding sacrifice of *humans*."[75]

Whereas speciesists might try to defend the practice of sacrifice from their own perspective, pro-animal theologians are seen here as mitigating it in order to defend their religion against the charge of cruelty.

The Hebrew Bible provides much of the groundwork for the development of human supremacist beliefs. Its claims of divinely ordained dominion, its stockbreeder God who gives and takes life at will and extends permission to humans to do the same, and its establishment of animal sacrifice through the Abraham story, have all been used to justify exploitation. The anxieties of a pastoral culture are expressed through the denigration of free animals; we see also, in the high valuation of language, one root of what will become a fiercely anti-animal rationalism.

But the people portrayed in the Hebrew Bible, who ate meat and sacrificed animals, nevertheless lived with and had strong emotional ties to their victims. The resulting inner conflict is expressed evasively by the prophets' denunciation—albeit never unmistakably ethical in origin—of sacrifice, by the dietary laws, by descriptions of God's and the people's own concern for animals, by vegetarian indications in the Bible's food imagery, and by the metaphor of God in the benevolent authoritarian role of shepherd.

There is little defensiveness (with a clear acknowledgment of the wrongness of killing animals) in the Hebrew Bible. Utopian vegetarianism and nonpredation have provided the basis for modern Jewish and Christian animal advocacy, but the Bible presents them merely as past or future Golden Ages, rather than (explicitly at least) as conditions to strive for in practice. The actual rules of sacrifice do not contain any apologetic or propitiatory element: only the echo of such elements from other cultures is occasionally heard.

From this confused and conflict-ridden mixture, augmented by the animal-related economics and politics of their own eras, the sages of Judaism, Christianity, and Islam went on to shape their particular doctrines, as will be examined in the next three chapters.

2. Judaism

RABBIS AND OTHER JEWISH SCHOLARS HAVE PROMOTED the aggressive Hebrew Bible themes of the image of God, the importance of words, and divine permission to eat meat. Reinforcing these arguments we find an emphasis on the soul, allegedly confined to humans, the authoritarian theory that morality is to be defined by God's commands, and (in folklore) the occasional association of animals with demons.

Evasion in the Talmud takes forms overlapping to an extent with those of the Bible, namely, didactic precepts, vegetarian implications, and abandonment of sacrifice, together with stories of famous Jewish leaders and teachers who were kind to animals.

The defensive biblical doctrine of utopian vegetarianism has been kept in rabbinical descriptions of the afterlife, while rituals that sanctify slaughter for food emerge in Jewish practice. In addition, guilt toward animals is acknowledged in the ban on leather shoes at Yom Kippur and the withholding of blessings on garments made of leather or fur. We also see, in modern times, a self-conscious political defensiveness.

AGGRESSION

Here human superiority is unequivocal: "The Universe was created as the habitation of man and all that contains was provided for his benefit";[1] only God is above humanity. "With what object, then, did God form man and the world? . . . 'Whatsoever the Holy One, blessed be He, created in His Universe, He created but for His glory' (Aboth. vi. 11)."[2] Similarly, Unterman:

> The biblical account of the Creation in Genesis Chapters 1 and 2 is understood by Judaism to teach the central importance of man amongst all created beings. Such key ideas as men being created in God's image (1:26, 27), and command to man to fill the earth, subdue it, and have dominion over all earthly creatures (1:28), and the idea that man is separated from other creatures and can find no companionship among them (2:20) are developed in Jewish thought into a highly anthropocentric structure.[3]

To an extent, human superiority is qualified by responsibility.

> The idea of man's superior status . . . is thus bound up with man's responsi-
> bilities and duties towards God and the created world. . . . The *Zohar* . . . as-
> serts that man's control over the animal kingdom . . . is dependent on man
> manifesting his superior spiritual qualities. When the animals cannot per-
> ceive man's higher form, his soul, because he is not living a life of righ-
> teousness, then they lose their awe of him.[4]

While in this passage living up to human status is urged in order to secure
control of animals, Schwartz, contrastingly, urges it for their benefit: "It is because humans *are* a superior species that we should behave decently to animals."[5] Yet even this vegetarian Jewish scholar never comes down against human supremacy, but only attacks animal exploitation on humanist-compatible
grounds, for example, in regard to vivisection:

> In Judaism, as in most of the world's leading religions, animals are not consid-
> ered equal to human beings. The Jewish tradition sanctions animal experi-
> ments that benefit humans, as long as unnecessary pain is avoided. The ques-
> tion thus becomes one of whether or not people are really benefited and if
> other methods are available.[6]

But see chapter 6 for Schwartz's predominantly effective-defensive arguments,
notwithstanding those arguments' conformity to human requirements.

THE IMAGE OF GOD

The image-of-God claim "lies at the root of the Rabbinic teaching concerning
man. In that respect he is pre-eminent above all other creatures and represents the culminating point in the work of Creation."[7]

While various folklike texts convey a literally anthropomorphic view of the
deity, serious theology rejects such notions in favor of more abstract points of
resemblance between human and God. In Cohen's summary, the human soul is
what determines preeminence: "The possession of this Godlike feature is the
cause of his affinity to his Maker and his superiority over the other creatures."[8]

Maimonides gives a rationalist interpretation of the "image of God": "on
account of the Divine intellect with which man has been endowed, he is said
to have been made in the form and likeness of the Almighty, but far from it be

the notion that the Supreme Being is corporeal, having a material form."[9] To treat human reason as not merely admirable but Godlike undermines the value and, potentially, the moral entitlements of animals.

In the kabbalistic[10] version of the Godlike human, he, "like all the other created beings, only even more so . . . is composed of all ten *Sefirot* and 'of all spiritual things,' that is, of the supernal principles that constitute the attributes of the Godhead."[11] The *sefirot* are emanations of God.

An equally humanistic meaning was propounded by R. Hayyim Volozhiner (1749–1821), who drew on the Bible, the Talmud, and Kabbalah to define humans as in a sense even more important than God. In Volozhiner's hierarchy, "whose structure, deriving from Kabbalistic sources, still remains consonant with a Hellenic model,"[12]

> man's deeds, situated at the bottom, ring out to the top and guarantee or compromise the presence of *Elohim* [God] to the creature (or his departure from it), and the degree of his proximity or distance. . . . The presence of God to the world, in the form of its soul, and in the light of this, the coherence of the whole system and the presence of the soul to each world, all depends on man.
>
> Hence the likeness between *Elohim* and man.[13]

Here is a foreshadowing of the much later and secular anthropic principle, as the glorification of the human comes across more strongly than the implication of moral responsibility—"to practise the commandments is to ensure the being of the world."[14]

LOGOCENTRISM, DUALISM, AND RATIONALISM

The post-Plato Greek influence brings an explicit emphasis, which works against the status of animals, on the separation of body and mind:

> The Old Testament knows nothing of the contempt for the body and the excessive exaltation of the spirit which the Alexandrian Jews developed later under the influence of Greek philosophy. If Job likened the human form to a house of clay, he did so in order to illustrate human frailty as compared with God's omnipotence, not to depreciate the body against the soul.[15]

But the dualism of the Rabbis was qualified, the "idea that the soul as spirit is holy . . . and the body as matter is evil" being "foreign to Rabbinic thought."[16] One text compares body and soul to a lame man and a blind man, neither able to carry out the king's command alone, whereupon the king "ordered the lame man to mount the back of the blind man and judged them as one. Similarly the Holy One, blessed be He, will (in the Hereafter) take the soul, cast it into the body and judge them as one (Sanh. 91a, b)."[17]

On the other hand Cohen, having stated that the soul distinguishes humans from animals, also writes: "The Rabbis . . . credited the human being with a dual nature. 'Man's soul is from heaven and his body from earth' (Sifré Deut. para. 306; 132a)";[18] while, according to Solomon, "in the Middle Ages . . . the dualism of body and spirit prevailed, and with it a tendency to denigrate 'this world' and 'material things.'"[19]

Spinoza's rationalism, and the callousness toward animals it reinforces and justifies, are in notable contrast to his pan(en)theistic vision. He takes care to restrict to human beings his stricture that "hate can never be good"[20] and denounces "the law against killing animals" as

> based more on empty superstition and unmanly compassion than sound reason. The rational principle of seeking our own advantage teaches us to establish a bond with men, but not with the lower animals, or with things whose nature is different from human nature. . . . Men have a far greater right against the lower animals than they have against men. Not that I deny that the lower animals have sensations. But I do deny that we are therefore not permitted to consider our own advantage, use them at our pleasure, and treat them as is most convenient for us. For they do not agree in nature with us.[21]

We shall see how Maimonides' rationalism, noted under "Image of God," led to evasive judgments on animals, but that earlier scholar at least placed some value on compassion.

MEAT EATING

Tradition has upheld the postflood permission to eat meat, despite the vegetarian Eden and (so far as it affects animals) the peaceable kingdom of Isaiah. Jacobs attacks vegetarianism by dismissing the latter visions as "verses culled from here and there," giving priority to Genesis 9:

> When Noah and his sons emerge from the ark the animals are given to them as food. In any event, in Judaism attitudes are not formed simply on the basis

of biblical verses culled from here and there but on the way the teachers of
Judaism have interpreted the religion throughout the ages."[22]

As seen in chapter 1, he also argues that it would be positively wrong to reject
God's permission to eat meat.

Solomon would defend meat eating even in the event of its being "demonstrated that the *shehitah* [kosher slaughter] process is to some extent cruel":
"it is probable that the decision reached would be that *shehitah* be continued,
and the procedures improved as far as possible; otherwise, orthodox Jews
would be forced to be vegetarians. Judaism does not recognise cruelty to animals as an absolute value."[23]

While the apocryphal and apocalyptic vegetarian paradise is based on the
Eden of Genesis,[24] elsewhere Gan Eden, the heavenly abode of the righteous,
is shown as offering a feast on the flesh of the Leviathan as its main attraction. "'In the Hereafter the Holy One, blessed be He, will make a banquet for
the righteous from the flesh of Leviathan, and the remainder they will divide
and sell as merchandise in the streets of Jerusalem.' Its skin will be made by
Him into a booth for the pious."[25]

In the Talmud, "meat and wine are the means by which man 'rejoices' and
it is on this basis that it has long been customary for Jews to eat meat and
drink wine on the festivals."[26]

DENIAL OF SOUL

A translational issue arises regarding the various words in the Torah given as
"soul" or "spirit" and whether or not they differentiate the merely sentient
animal from the sentient-plus-spiritual or sentient-plus-cognitive human being. While some animal supporters have appealed to the Bible's use of *nephesh* for both humans and animals, Cohen notes several Hebrew terms for related qualities, and in particular the three "in common use in Rabbinic
literature": *Nephesh, Ruach,* and *Neshamah.* "Since the *Nephesh* is identified
with the blood, it denotes vitality and is applicable to animals as well as human beings," but "*Ruach* and *Neshamah* . . . denote the *psyche* of the human
being, which is his exclusively. It is the immortal part of his composition, the
'breath' infused into him by God."[27]

Ecclesiastes 3:19–21 is another source of debate on this point since it could,
depending on the translation, suggest that animals also have souls. Schwartz
gives it as "'who knoweth the spirit of men whether it goeth upward; / and the

spirit of the beast whether it goeth / downward to the earth?'"[28] Cohen quotes two different translations without commenting on the morally significant discrepancy: "Who knoweth the spirit (*ruach*) of man whether it goeth upward?"[29] and "Who knoweth the spirit of man that goeth upward ... And the spirit of the beast that it goeth downward to the earth."[30] R. José b. Chalaphta, the sage whose views are cited here, was interpreting "man" and "the beast" as referring respectively to "the righteous" and "the wicked."

There was, it is true, a belief, in contradiction to the denial of a hereafter to animals, that they "will be recompensed in the Hereafter for the sufferings they have to undergo on earth. This view is held by Saadiah but Maimonides believes it to be foreign to Judaism."[31]

In the kabbalistic interpretation of animal sacrifice, even though the animal is held to possess a soul or spirit, that very belief is used to uphold meat eating: "Because the evil powers in man are embedded in his flesh and blood, flesh and blood have to be sacrificed. More than that, the sacrifice frees the spirit of the animal, enabling it to rise to its divine root; the animals are symbolically connected with the animals described by Ezekiel in the throne-chariot."[32] Elsewhere, positing a benefit from the opposite direction, it is said that because of the vitality inherent in the *nephesh*, "any creature, animal or fish, which itself possessed vitality adds to the vitality of a person who eats it."[33]

VOLUNTARISM

The doctrine of divine voluntarism, according to which morality is defined as that which God commands, regardless of the content of the command, has been used to discredit vegetarian Jews to the extent of turning the permission given in Genesis 9:2–3 into an obligation, and claiming that to reject it was to imply, as quoted earlier, "that Judaism"—i.e., the God whose decrees defined Judaism—"has ... been wrong all the time."

Such blind obedience is encouraged by the Abraham story. "When God tests Abraham for the final time, it's less a test of Abraham's potential for compassion than his potential for discipline."[34] But although Judaism accepts obedience to divine decree, the implications of the principle have been variously understood, as will be discussed in the later section "Evasion" of this chapter.

ANIMALS AND DEMONS

In the folkloric demonology, which found its way into rabbinical writing,

> The men who planned to build the tower of Babel were divided into three
> classes. One said, Let us ascend to heaven and dwell there; another said, Let
> us ascend and practise idolatry; and the third said, Let us ascend and wage
> war (against God). The first class God dispersed; the third class was turned
> into apes, spirits, demons, and night-devils, and as for the second class He
> confused their language.[35]

We encounter speciesism as a template for all kinds of discrimination
among humans in the following kabbalistic identification of the Jews' enemies with animals: "The *goi* belongs to the kabbalistic sub-world of the demonic. . . . The *goi* was the tainted child of woman's [i.e., Eve's] carnal relationship with the serpent, the symbol of demonic powers. Since the gentile
had not undergone the cleansing experience of the revelation of God's *Torah*,
he remained half-human and half-demon."[36] It is typical of the confusions of
folklore that according to this literature animals themselves could be afflicted by and protected against demons. With equal inconsistency, on the
one hand it was believed that "'there is no evil impulse in animals' (ARN xvi),
since they have no moral sense,"[37] while, on the other hand, the trial of animals, appearing in the rabbinical judicial system, "was a common procedure
in ancient times and persisted down to a fairly modern period."[38]

EVASION

The Talmud has retained and promoted the evasive precepts and implications of the Bible, sometimes indeed finding meanings not at all apparent on
the surface. But it should be remembered that the rabbis did not always
agree—which leaves the door open for modern Jews to interpret both biblical
and Talmudic texts in keeping with their own values, as will be further discussed in chapter 6.

Despite Judaism's uncompromising humanism, an interesting sign of affinity with nonhumans is found in the Mishnah (Kilayim 8:5) where there is
a discussion whether ritual laws affecting dead human bodies also apply to

"adonei ha-sadeh ('the lords of the field') which some scholars have identified with chimpanzees."[39]

DIDACTIC PRECEPTS

As an example of rabbinical extrapolation from the Torah, although the latter "contains no explicit rule prohibiting cruelty to animals in general, there are so many commandments mandating humane treatment for them that the rabbis explicitly declared that consideration for animals is a biblical law."[40] The principle that "it is forbidden to cause pain to any animal" is, according to Maimonides and R. Judah ha-Hasid (1150–1217),

> based on the biblical statement of the angel of God to Balaam, "Wherefore hast thou smitten thine ass?" (Num. 22:32). This verse is used in the Talmud as a prime source for its assertion that we are to treat animals humanely.
>
> The *Code of Jewish Law* is more explicit and specific.
>
> "It is forbidden, according to the law of the Torah, to inflict pain upon any living creature. On the contrary, it is our duty to relieve the pain of any creature, even if it is ownerless or belongs to a non-Jew."[41]

Phelps, for his part, cites Deuteronomy 25:4, not to muzzle the ox while he was threshing, as the "primary Biblical basis for *tsar baalei hayyim*."[42]

Among many specific precepts of kindness are the obligation to help animals who are having trouble drawing a cart, a prohibition on tying animals' or birds' legs painfully,[43] the extension to any case of animals of unequal strength, involved in any activity, of the law against ploughing with an ox and an ass together (Deut. 22:10),[44] the obligation to feed animals first, derived from "'I will give grass in thy fields for thy cattle' and then 'thou shalt eat and be satisfied' (Deut. 11:15),"[45] hence, a prohibition on acquiring an animal unless one can feed it properly.[46]

That the Sabbath, and other religious obligations, are made for animals as well as human beings is found both in the permission to violate the Sabbath in order to help animals fallen into a pool[47] and in the Talmudic authorization "to interrupt the performance of a rabbinic commandment in order to ascertain" that the animals have been fed first.[48] As a general principle, Sabbath laws could be "relaxed somewhat to enable rescue of injured animals or milking of cows to ease their distress."[49]

You can see how sympathy influences doctrine when you consider the rather tenuous biblical connections from which the rabbis derived these rules. This was made possible for them by the tradition of the midrash,

> which solicits the letter of the text in order to seek out . . . the hidden and allusive meaning. . . . even when exegesis appears to be ignoring or neglecting the immediate signification of the text, it is in fact restoring the spirit of the whole to a purely "local" meaning. . . . At times, this hermeneutic, with its rules and tradition, separates the verse from its context and even isolates . . . a short sequence of words, like a piece of broken glass conveying meaning.[50]

So, in the example of Balaam's donkey, one protest by one animal in a particular situation—a protest that, in context, may be seen as a demand for authoritarian justice rather than compassion—led to a comprehensive principle of kindness to animals. Elsewhere, what might have been the purely fortuitous order assigned to God's statements at Deuteronomy 11:15 was taken as a command to feed animals before humans.

The "seven laws considered by rabbinic tradition as the minimal moral duties enjoined by the Bible on all men (Sanh. 56–60; Yad, Melakhim, 8:10, 10:12),"[51] known as the Noachide laws and dating from the early third century, end with "(7) not to eat a limb torn from a living animal."[52] Kalechofsky, following a different numbering of the laws, comments:

> Isaiah regarded the sixth law, that you may not tear a limb from a living animal (extraordinary as this seems, it was custom to consume living animals in this way . . .), as "the ancient covenant" and . . . declared that the "land would run with blood" in punishment for this treatment of animals. . . . Discussion of vivisection, within a Christian, Jewish, or Islamic tradition, should begin with this Noachic law, which Torah regards as binding on all humanity.[53]

As with the decalogic obligation to let animals rest on the Sabbath, this Noachide provision is significant in being one of a set of fundamental rules rather than an obscure bylaw.

Despite requirements to treat animals kindly, interpretation may impair the provisions' apparent humaneness. Deuteronomy 22:6–7 is the object of a dispute about God's motivation: "If you come across a bird's nest . . . and the mother is sitting on the young or on the eggs, do not take the mother with the young. [7] You may take the young, but be sure to let the mother go, so that it may go well with you and you may have a long life." Some scholars saw the reason for this command as "the preservation of species, rather than abhorrence of cruelty."[54] More damagingly, it has been seen as simply a test of absolute obedience to God—the voluntarist theory again—with the content of the rule considered irrelevant. The Mishnah "lists three occasions when a person praying must be silenced, one case being the worshipper who prays to God to show him (the worshipper) compassion because His compassion extends even to a bird."[55] Some Talmudic scholars maintain that the reason for the prayer being rejected is to emphasize that "God didn't give us His commandments because of compassion, but merely to place upon the Jews a set of decrees in order to inform them that they are His servants."[56] Maimonides rejected this view of God as arbitrary,[57] insisting that there is a purpose to all divine decrees, although he, like Kant, saw kindness to animals primarily as a means of developing a good character.

A further interpretive problem with the Jewish precepts of kindness lies in the fact that while "causing unnecessary pain to animals is strictly forbidden" in Judaism, "the fine line between the necessary use of animals and the avoidance of unnecessary cruelty is not always drawn successfully"[58]—a phenomenon all too evident in today's discourse. Jacobs, quoting the sixteenth-century R. Moses Isserles, offers a case, and explanation thereof, in which the line *is* adequately drawn:

> "Wherever it is for the purpose of healing or for some other purpose there is no prohibition against cruelty to animals. It is consequently permitted to pluck feathers from living geese . . . and there is no objection to it on the grounds of cruelty to animals. Nevertheless, the [Jewish (Jacobs's bracketed insertion)] world avoids this because it is cruel." Isserles . . . implies that whatever the law says, Jewish communities have not tolerated practices they perceive intuitively to be contrary to the spirit of Judaism.[59]

VEGETARIAN IMPLICATIONS

When food is blessed,

> Rabbi Yonassan Gershom, a modern chassidic rebbe ... states that "... meat is on the bottom of the hierarchy". ... on festivals and sabbaths, wine comes first. Otherwise bread comes first, and a blessing over bread covers *all* other foods except wine. If there is no bread, foods are blessed in the following order: (1) wine, (2) grains, (3) tree fruits, (4) vegetables, (5) all other foods, including fish, meats, etc.[60]

However, this could have been for economic reasons, since in rabbinical times "the bulk of the people must accordingly have lived mainly on a vegetarian diet, and the wholesomeness of vegetables is dilated upon" in the writings. But there was also some debate as to whether vegetarianism was indeed healthy.[61]

As background to such ambiguity, Kalechofsky suggests that "after the fall of the Temple, the Jewish association with a meat-centered diet was not inevitable, but developed in the West with the same response pattern of other Western or Westernized people. It is essentially a response of cultural assimilation."[62]

JEWISH LEADERS AND TEACHERS WHO WERE KIND TO ANIMALS

Besides the Bible's listing of kindly figures,[63] including Rebecca and Jacob, the Talmud gives further attention to this virtue. Carrying out the biblical shepherd theme, the establishment of Moses' leadership of Israel is described as follows:

> While our teacher Moses was tending the sheep of Jethro in the wilderness, a kid ran away from him. He ran after it until it reached Hasuah. Upon reaching Hasuah, it came upon a pool of water [whereupon] the kid stopped to drink. When Moses reached it, he said, "I did not know you were running because [you were] thirsty. You must be tired." He placed it on his shoulder and began to walk. The Holy One, blessed be He, said, "You are compassionate in leading flocks belonging to mortals; I swear you will similarly shepherd my flock, Israel."[64]

Tappan cites another midrash according to which "David was also selected to care for the Jewish people because of his kind treatment of his non-human flock."[65] Noah "was called a *tzadik* (righteous person) because of his extraordinary care of the animals on the ark."[66] He and his family were said to have emerged safely from the ark because

> "of the charity we practised there." "But what charity was there for you to practise? Were there any poor in the ark? Only Noah and his sons were there, so to whom could you have been charitable?" "To the animals, beasts, and birds. We did not sleep but gave each its food throughout the night." (midrash to Ps. xxxvii. 1; 126*b*)[67]

"Only one other Torah personality, Joseph, was given the designation *tzadik*. He too provided food for both humans *and animals* in a crisis."[68]

The principle, noted above, that compassionate acts take priority over formal religious practice is illustrated by the story of R. Israel Salanter (nineteenth century), who missed the Kol Nidre prayer on Yom Kippur in order to help a calf "lost and tangled in the brush. . . . His act of mercy represented the rabbis' prayers on that Yom Kippur evening."[69] R. Abramtzi forbade his coachman to whip the tired and mud-impeded horses for the purpose of getting home in time for the Sabbath celebrations. "'It is better' said the rabbi 'that we celebrate the Sabbath here than cause the death of these animals by suffering. Are they not the creatures of the Lord? See how exhausted they are. . . . The Sabbath Queen will come to us also here, for her glory fills the whole world.'"[70]

Schwartz also narrates how R. Zusya freed caged birds and quoted to their angry owner the words of the Psalms, "His tender mercies are over all His work."[71] In the Middle Ages a "long and strange tale of how the rabbi was rewarded for his kindness" to a frog was popular.[72]

But in this category the story most illustrative of moral conflict giving rise to evasion is that of Judah the Prince.

> A calf was being led to the slaughter and hid its head in the garment of R. Judah and bellowed. He said to it, "Go, since you were created for that purpose!" It was decreed in Heaven, Since he had no compassion, let sufferings come upon him. His sufferings eventually ceased because of the following incident. One day the maid was sweeping the house, and . . . was about to sweep away some young weasels. He said to her, "Leave them alone, for it is written, 'His

mercies are over all His works' (Ps. cxlv. 9)." It was decreed in Heaven, Since he has shown compassion we will show compassion to him.[73]

To the obvious inquiry, within Judaism's nonvegetarian tradition, "should we learn from this not to slaughter any animal and not to kill harmful animals?"[74] the tenth-century ga'on R. Sherira said no, declaring that "to save a calf that we *need* for nourishment is not required of us."[75] He offered a further argument combining aretaism, the idea that an act is good or bad according to what it says about the agent's character, with indirect duties to human beings and to those animals who were considered exempt from slaughter:

> If therefore that calf had fled before the knife of the slaughterer and buried its head between the knees of Rabbi in order to be saved, then the immediate delivery to the slaughterer appeared as a particular cruelty. If he had acted mercifully, he would at least have allowed the calf to stay for a while, and anybody who had seen him act in such a way, would have . . . learnt to be merciful himself. He, however, who saw that Rabbi delivered the animal immediately, and that no pity was stirred in his heart . . . , might have become more hard-hearted in his behavior towards other people and towards animals which are not needed and harmless.[76]

In his final point, the sage suggests

> it may perhaps also be that the sufferings came upon Rabbi because he had uttered the words: "Thou art created for this!" It is true that animals have been created for this destiny, and that men have been permitted to slaughter them; but the Creator did not deprive the animals of a due reward, and we may believe that all creatures, the killing of which has been permitted, will be rewarded for their pains. . . . The animal has, therefore, not been created in order that evil should be inflicted upon it but in order that good should be done to it; nor is it by any means created for the purpose of being slaughtered, although this has been permitted to man.[77]

As Kalechofsky truly observes, this argument is "fraught with moral wrestling."[78] "One can imagine" says the Animal Judge "the scene which gave rise to this story. It so strongly resembles contemporary newspaper reports of animals attempting to escape the abattoir. Forced for a moment to contemplate the actual horror of a living being resisting his or her fate, the meat-eating public is moved to tears and some of its members may even go vegetarian, while the rest reassure themselves with sophistry of diverse levels of accomplishment. Evasion par excellence!"

A vivid example is found in the cow who

> jumped a six-foot fence in Cincinnati in . . . 2002 to escape a meatpacking plant and then, until she was captured, ran free in a city park for ten days. The day after Easter, she appeared in a parade that celebrated the start of the baseball season. Now called, "Cinci Freedom," she received a key to the city. . . . She was then transported to an animal sanctuary to live out her natural life unmolested by meat packers, while many of the humans who celebrated her freedom headed to the ballpark to watch baseball and chomp down on some hot dogs.[79]

In this case, I suspect that it was American rugged individualism and admiration for "guts," rather than compassion, which inspired the mercy shown to Cinci Freedom. The other animals, too weak, too frightened, and/or too convinced of their helplessness to try to escape, received only indifference. The convoluted arguments of the rabbis represent true evasion, depending as that strategy does on an active and troubling conscience.

DEFENSE

UTOPIAN VEGETARIANISM

In addition to the utopias of Eden and the peaceable kingdom, in one thirteenth-century description of Gan Eden it contains no meat,[80] by contrast with the feasting on Leviathan.[81] The vegetarian version instead includes jewels, gold, water, roses, myrtles, milk, wine, balsam, honey, vines, trees, aromatic plants, angels singing, the Tree of Life, sages expounding the Torah, and various persons.

Species equality is also anticipated as a feature of the Messianic age:

> (vi) (Peace will reign throughout nature), as it is said, "The cow and the bear shall feed together" (ibid. [Is.] xi. 7). (vii) He will assemble all beasts, birds, and reptiles, and make a covenant between them and all Israel; as it is said,

"In that day will I make a covenant for them with the beasts of the field," etc. (Hos. ii. 18). . . . (Exod. R. xv. 21).[82]

RITUAL SLAUGHTER AND KASHRUT

Here is the most important defensive element in Judaism. The kosher method of slaughter that replaced Temple sacrifices required "a blessing prior to slaughter as a reminder that [the slaughterer] must have reverence for the life that he takes. Thus the laws of *shechitah* teach that meat-eating is a concession to people's weakness."[83] Prager and Telushkin also felt that "keeping kosher is Judaism's compromise with its ideal vegetarianism."[84] While the loss of the Temple is theoretically lamented,

> even Conservative Jewish *siddurim* suppress the traditional Orthodox prayers, found in the seventeenth blessing of the *Amida*, for the rebuilding of the Temple and the renewal of the sacrificial cult. Many modern Orthodox Jews, including rabbis, privately shudder at the thought of such a restoration . . . so thoroughgoing has been the . . . replacement of the sacrificial ideal by communal prayer, *mitzvot*, lived tradition, and Torah study.[85]

As with Islam, sparing the animal pain during slaughter is a further, related purpose of the ritual requirements. Inasmuch as "many ancient cultures commonly thought that meat would taste better if animals were tortured before their death, these slaughter rules . . . should be seen as nothing less than a revolutionary development in human history."[86]

LEATHER AND FUR

The fasting, prayer, and other observances of Yom Kippur (the Day of Atonement) offered people a direct means of reconciliation with God, replacing the symbolic blood sacrifice. On this "most sacred day of the Jewish year . . . it is forbidden to wear leather shoes. One reason is related to our behavior toward God's creatures; it is not proper to plead for compassion when one has not shown compassion toward other living creatures."[87] While this precept requires an actual change of behavior, I regard it as defensive rather than effective-defensive, in that it is only demanded on one particular religious occasion. In general, people were allowed to wear leather.

In another practice resembling the Yom Kippur rule, wrongness was acknowledged by withholding from leather and fur the prayer that was otherwise offered when wearing something new for the first time. According to the *Code of Jewish Law*: "It is customary to say to one who puts on a new garment: 'Mayest thou wear it out and acquire a new one.' But we do not express this wish to one who puts on new shoes or a new garment made of fur or leather . . . because a garment like this requires the killing of a living creature, and it is written: 'And His mercy is upon all his works' (Ps. 145:9)."[88]

POLITICAL DEFENSE

Solomon notes both Christian and Jewish sensitivity regarding the now largely rejected belief that the biblical God gives humanity a kind of tyranny over nature:

> So perverse is it to understand "and rule over it" (Gen. 1: 28)—let alone Psalm 8—as meaning "exploit and destroy" that many Christians take such interpretations as a deliberate attempt to besmirch Christianity, and not a few Jews have read the discussions as an attempt to "blame the Jews" for yet another disaster in Christendom.[89]

But the same author also introduces a note of competitiveness with Christianity, when he comments on the better-favored modern interpretation: "There has been discussion among Christian theologians as to whether the opening chapters of Genesis call on humans to act as stewards . . . or to dominate and exploit the created world. There is little debate on this point among Jewish theologians,"[90] who have always, he maintains, read the message as stewardship.

I detect defensiveness, also, in Aaron Lichtenstein's comment "Our approach is decidedly anthropocentric, and that is nothing to be ashamed of."[91] One might ask why—had there not been considerable debate and criticism on the point—anyone should think it was something to be ashamed of.

Judaism is not a proselytizing religion, overly concerned with membership. But when "after the destruction of the second Temple in 70 CE, a number of vegetarian sects . . . on the margins of Judaism began to attract followers from among Jews . . . many of the rabbis . . . were distressed at losing so many

meat-loving Jews to these reclusive and ascetic sects." They included "the Ess-
enes, the Therapeutae, the Ebionites, and the Nazoreans, of which there is
strong circumstantial evidence that Jesus himself may have been a member."[92]
Although these groups were also considered Jews, their increased popularity
could have motivated rabbis from rival tendencies to offer religious arguments
for meat eating (see chapter 6 for more on the role of asceticism in promoting
vegetarianism).

In modern times there might be some speculation, if not concern, within
the community as to the phenomenon noted by Berry when he asks, "Could
this"—the carnivorousness and warlikeness of the biblical God—"be why so
many Jews have gone over to . . . Buddhism, Hinduism and Jainism that
honor that first precept that all life is sacred?"[93] One explanation could be
that Judaism's own evasive traditions of kindness to animals incline Jews
toward faiths that bear out those traditions more consistently. Perhaps
"there is an ethical vegetarian in the Hebrew scriptures struggling to get
out."[94]

The Talmud and the Kabbalah take up aggressive biblical themes to develop
an increased glorification of humanity, albeit accompanied by an emphasis
on our unique moral responsibility. Evasive kindness remains subordinate to
aggression in conventional Judaism, with biblical vegetarian implications
ignored, dismissed, or even denounced. One writer even denies that abstention from cruelty to animals is an absolute value in Judaism. Although animals may be afflicted by demons they are also given demonic status.

Yet subordinate though the animals are, the injunctions to kindness toward them are many, as the rabbis, alongside humanist doctrines, continued
and extended through imaginative interpretations the humane traditions of
the *Tanakh*. Their methods (and those of post-Talmudic commentators) included direct prescriptions, emphasis on vegetable foods in some contexts,
and the elevation to mythic status of Jewish heroes, ancient and modern,
who showed compassion for animals. As in Christianity and Islam, the literature often stresses the priority of kindly acts over religious ritual such as
Sabbath observance.

Some Talmudic views of the afterlife have repeated the utopian visions.
With sacrifice given up, slaughter for meat is provided with a sacred context

through rituals containing a strong implication of regret. Further defensive ritual practices are the banning of leather shoes on Yom Kippur and the withholding from both leather and fur the blessings usually uttered when putting on new garments.

How differently Christianity has inflected these strategies will be examined next.

3. Christianity

AS WE MOVE INTO THE GREEK-INFLUENCED ERA, there is little direct positive support for animals (though Christian ethical precepts can be fruitfully extended beyond humanity) and much that undermines their interests, most prominently the indifference shown by St. Paul, the defeat of vegetarianism and of other early Christian concerns at the Council of Nicaea in 325, and the increase in logocentrism, that is, in the overvaluation of human language and reason, as the most salient feature of a dualism between mind and matter. Humanity created in the image of God is a Christian as well as a Jewish claim to moral superiority. Mystical writings, while more sympathetic to animals, have their human-glorifying aspect as well, and the Catholic Church has a particularly unfortunate reputation to overcome.

But sympathy for animals even within this speciesist culture emerges in several forms of evasion. The Gospels, like the Jewish Bible, contain vegetarian implications, and the image of Jesus both as shepherd and as sacrificial lamb reflect the closeness of biblical people to their animals. Popular culture has expressed kinship through legend and imagery, overlapping with partly factual accounts of animal-loving mystics and saints. As the centuries progressed, limited improvements of attitude, and limited practical reforms, were found among Catholics and Protestants alike.

Christianity has endorsed Eden and the peaceable kingdom as utopian fantasies, with the implication that they are not realistic goals at present. But unlike Judaism and Islam, it lacks defensive techniques of propitiation. In recent times, however, it has become politically defensive about its poor record on animal welfare.

Yet, is the Christianity as portrayed above the true one? For some scholars, it is not. Akers argues that the New Testament, despite

> provid[ing] important evidence about the historical Jesus and the history of early Christianity . . . is a highly edited, inconsistent document put together to support the viewpoint of a single party in early Christianity; namely the victorious party. It is the outcome of early Christian history, not just a record of it.[1]

Paul was in dispute "with the leadership of the mother church, and especially James" over vegetarianism and other issues.[2] 1 Corinthians 8:7–13 shows

Paul as indifferent to any ethical, as opposed to cultic and propagandic, aspects of meat eating:

> But food does not bring us near to God; we are no worse if we do not eat, and
> no better if we do.
>
> [9] Be careful, however, that the exercise of your freedom does not become
> a stumbling-bloc to the weak. For if anyone with a weak conscience sees you
> who have this knowledge eating in an idol's temple, won't he be emboldened to
> eat what has been sacrificed to idols? . . . [13] Therefore, if what I eat causes
> my brother to fall into sin, I will never eat meat again. (1 Cor. 8:8–13)

As a result of such considerations, as well as the patronage of Constantine, at
the Council of Nicaea

> the original Christian Bible was significantly altered to change or delete Jesus'
> humane teachings on animals. For example, the Edenites contend that refer-
> ences to Jesus and his followers as vegetarians and as having condemned meat-
> eating were deleted in order to attract more people to Christianity, and to ap-
> pease pagan converts and the appetite of Constantine and the bishops for meat.[3]

If the Edenites are correct, there could not be a clearer link between the wish
to eat meat and the adjustment of doctrine.

Part of the attempt to reconstruct Christianity as vegetarian consists of
identifying Jesus's ministry with Judaism, thereby distinguishing Christianity from the hellenized, Pauline version.

> Jesus was called Rabbi meaning Master or Teacher 42 times in the gospels. . . .
> He engaged in healing and acts of mercy. He told stories or parables—a rab-
> binic method of teaching. He went to the synagogue (Matthew 12:9), taught in
> the synagogues (Matthew 4:23, 13:54; Mark 1:39) . . . and it "was his custom"
> to go to the synagogue on the Sabbath (Luke 4:16).[4]

Jesus insisted that he had come to fulfill, not abolish the Law.[5] In promulgat-
ing the Golden Rule (Matthew 7:12), he "was merely repeating in the positive
what Rabbi Hillel had stated a generation earlier."[6] Akers maintains that an
original, Jewish, Christianity was corrupted by the later Church and particularly by Paul. In Vasu Murti's view, "I don't think it's possible to reconcile Paul
to vegetarianism, and Christianity without Paul would be Judaism."[7]

Against this account, another Christian vegetarian, Young, seeks to remain within a traditional framework. On grounds of selective bias and spiritual irrelevance, he criticizes attempts "to reject what the Bible implies and reconstruct a vegetarian Jesus,"[8] such as are found in the second- to third-century *Gospel of the Ebionites* and eighteenth- and nineteenth-century pro-vegetarian scholars. The alleged vegetarianism of John the Baptist, of apostles James, Peter, and John, of Matthew, and of the Church fathers Clement of Alexandria, Tertullian, Origen, Basil, Chrysostom, and Jerome, is described as limited or totally unsubstantiated, and, where it existed, ascetic in motivation.

Nevertheless Young shares the motives of the reconstructors. While rejecting absolute rules, preferring to identify "directional markers" in the biblical narrative "that serve as pointers for the journey, such as peace, community, resurrection, compassion, renewal, and the imitation of God,"[9] he ultimately finds that "the Bible neither commands nor condemns vegetarianism. It is left as a choice. However, as we locate our story in God's story, it is difficult to avoid the implication that vegetarianism is the best dietary choice for Christians."[10]

In view of such differences, can we, with Akers, regard the outcome of Nicaea and other post-Constantine developments as violations of true Christianity? Or did they reflect the will of God, in which case they must be accepted by Christians? Such questions, implying a genuine Christianity and will of God, are outside my projectionist approach; but for the moment, let us consider them within their own terms.

The problem with the will-of-God theory is the suggestion that whatever human beings decide upon in a religious context must be inspired. Yet a prominent theistic belief is that God gave humans free will, and with it the capacity to be wrong, even when they think they are carrying out God's wishes. If the winners were always right, God could be seen as supporting successful tyrants, rather than reluctantly tolerating them. And the fact that divine inspiration can be asserted in support of any viewpoint, whether that of the winners or of the losers, but never proved, neutralizes it as a means of settling disputes. We must rely on more independently assessable factors.

In the Introduction, under the heading of "Change and Essentialism," I argued that rightness, with regard to core principles and their application and interpretation in present circumstances, might be tested by asking, What kind of world do we want to live in? In Christian terms: How do you envision the kingdom of God? "The time was to come, with Constantine," writes Murray, when Christians ... would ... claim the hellenistic-Roman heritage of sacral kingship and "christianize" it into its Byzantine form. . . . The biblical royal ideals of justice, mercy, wisdom and peace had to survive cruel times, being more often trampled on than realized except by individuals, but witnessed to by brave prophetic figures, often at the cost of their lives. Yet the ideals and the world-view implicit in them were not doomed to be utterly lost.[11]

On this basis, if one accepts the view that early followers of Jesus were pacifist and vegetarian, Nicaea can be seen as a distortion of the religion, despite the Church's toleration of ascetic (but not ethical or gnostic) vegetarianism. And that is, of course, why most Christian animal advocates have promoted the authenticity of that picture.

With this in mind, let us look at received Christianity as it is.

AGGRESSION

ST. PAUL'S INFLUENCE

Paul excludes animals from moral consideration: "For it is written in the Law of Moses: 'Do not muzzle an ox while it is treading out the grain.' Is it about oxen that God is concerned? [10] Surely he says this for us, doesn't he?" (1 Cor. 9:9–10). Murray's argument, "Even if he did not think of God as caring for oxen, there is no reason to suppose either that he was unaware that other creatures suffer, or that he would have ascribed this to any other cause than the evil that had spread as a result of Adam's sin,"[12] invites the Animal Judge's response, "Where is the reason to suppose that he was aware of or concerned with it?"

Although Linzey,[13] like Young,[14] finds support for animals in Paul's words "the whole creation has been groaning as in the pains of childbirth right up to the present time" (Rom. 8:22), he acknowledges, "it may well be that Paul did not fully appreciate the implications of the view he was expounding."

Murray defends Paul on this point, observing that "the worst difficulties which have been ascribed to this passage have been created by those who insisted that the threefold mention of 'creation' (*ktisis*)" in Romans 8:18–24 "really refers only to humankind," for "it is now generally agreed that *ktisis* means the whole created universe or cosmos."[15] Preece mentions seventeenth-century churchmen Dr. Stradling and George Fox as also considering Romans 8:22 to apply to animals.[16]

Young offers further support for the apostle. The vegetarianism that Paul and the Church attacked, he observes, was not ethical, but antimatter. "The church wanted to guard against the heresy of gnostic dualism (spirit is good; matter is evil). While the Council of Nicea did not mention vegetarianism, several other church synods and councils of the period did—and they all approved it as long as it was not done out of abhorrence for God's physical creation!"[17] He points out that, "ironic as it may seem, the devaluing of animals"—as of the material world generally—"by the Gnostics led to a very strict vegetarianism, whereas the devaluing of animals today leads to an unrestrained eating of meat."[18] Nor does the complex reasoning of 1 Corinthians 8:8–13, quoted above, constitute an outright condemnation of vegetarianism, but rather a concern that the freedom offered by the Christian transcendence of dietary restraints should not lead to involvement in pagan practices.[19]

Above all, the issue should not create dissension among Christians. If Paul the visionary had had any ethical concerns about meat eating, Paul the apparatchik would have discarded them as soon as they threatened the cohesion and growth of the church. The fact that his rehabilitation may seem necessary for Christian animal advocates shows that his influence on traditional, received Christianity has been deleterious to the interests of other species.

NEW TESTAMENT SOURCES OF JUSTIFICATION FOR MEAT EATING

Acts 10:12–13 relates how "in a dream while hungry, Peter saw 'all kinds of four-footed creatures and reptiles and birds of the air,' and God's voice said to him, 'Get up, Peter; kill and eat.'"[20] Actually, the thinking behind this text was similar to Paul's in 1 Corinthians 8:8–13: "theologians generally agree that Peter's dream is an abrogation of tedious dietary laws intended to divide the faithful from the non-faithful."[21] Yet, Webb reminds us, "the story is used today, along with Matthew 15:11"—"What goes into a man's mouth does not make him 'unclean,' but what comes out of his mouth, that is what makes him 'unclean'"—"to justify the eating of animals."[22]

Apart from these complications, it is noteworthy that arguments about diet center around *meat*—reinforcing other scriptural evidence that people sense its inherently problematic nature.

LOGOCENTRISM, DUALISM, AND RATIONALISM

Three teachings affecting the Christian outlook may invite the label of *logo-centric, dualistic,* or *rationalistic,* in the sense of valuing the human mental realm above the animal physical realm. First is the opening of the Gospel of John: "In the beginning was the Word, and the Word was with God, and the word was God" (John 1:1–2); "The Word became flesh and made his dwelling among us" (John 1:14).

The second is the repudiation of the physical world by the Gnostics and Manichaeans, establishing a dualism between matter and spirit.

The third is the dualism of Aristotle, post-Manichaean Augustine, and Aquinas, who use human reason and language to justify hierarchies at the expense of animals and some humans.

It might seem that John, in his Gospel, wishes to elevate human language to the highest level. But as Jeffrey reads the passage, the author's emphasis is as much on "flesh" as on "word". John wishes to show that

> that which can only be seen as historical event—not just the covenant and broken history of Israel but also the physical life, ministry, death, and resurrection of Jesus—is nevertheless the ultimate demonstration of the *arche* (origin, principle), *dike* (justice), and *sophia* (wisdom) of the universe, so long the objects of philosophical reflection in the hellenized world.[23]

This analysis puts the passage closer to logomysticism, which I discuss in chapter 7, than to logocentrism, and it is unitary rather than dualistic. By contrast with Plato's "'cave' of mere shadowy appearances (this world's physical reality),"[24] John implies that "the light of truth is obtained not by great and perseverant intellects abstracting *from* the world but by the gift of God's redemptive grace in sending Jesus *into* our common world."[25]

A genuine dualism is found in the apocalyptic outlook expressed in the book of Daniel, by the influence of which "the doctrine of two worlds became foundational in the Christian West. Combined . . . first with Neoplatonic thought that separated soul from body and later with other forms of idealism, Christianity developed . . . a profound metaphysical dualism."[26] This type of dualism was spiritually motivated and sometimes led to ascetic vegetarianism. Its higher realm was associated with the logos of divine wisdom, as in John's Gospel. But its antimaterialism, which included, as noted above, a devaluation of animals, provides a link with the third logocentrism.

For the Church, while anathematizing the antiworld views of the Gnostics and similar groups (although it accepted asceticism when divorced from such beliefs), went on to adopt its own politically motivated, hierarchy-supporting dualism, as found in Aquinas, following Aristotle, which elevated human reason and language. "Now, of all the parts of the universe, intellectual creatures hold the highest place because they approach nearest to the divine likeness. Therefore divine providence provides for the intellectual nature for its own sake, and for all others for its sake."[27]

Today, such Aristotelianism may appear in more discreet, but still cognitive-based, garb, as in the process thinkers Birch and Cobb, for whom the use of animals "is permissible because humans, with richer experiences, have a greater knowledge of death, so their death is more important. . . . Domestic animals . . . can be traded for even trivial human desires because, with their more limited self-awareness, they are all (within a given species) alike."[28]

In sum, if we understand logocentrism to mean the overvaluation of human language, approach 1 is not logocentric, dualistic, or rationalistic. Approach 2 is dualistic, but not logocentric or rationalistic. Approach 3 is all of them. It is this third approach, to which the second approach contributed only the disdain for matter and nature, that the animal supporter and environmentalist deplores when mentioning logocentrism, dualism, or rationalism.

THE IMAGE OF GOD

Speciesism based on the *imago dei* is found in conventional Christian thinking, according to which the command in Genesis "to subdue [the earth] and to have dominion over these various animal groups . . . follows from the fact, clearly linked in the text, that male and female were created in the image of God (Gen. 1: 27,28)."[29] Using Augustine and Aquinas as his sources, Chereso applies the theme of imitation, found also in the Talmud, to support human superiority:

> "Image of God" is the theological definition of man that is the only basis for an authentic Christian anthropology.
>
> It belongs to the nature of an image to imitate . . . the being and activity of the thing imaged. Now the being and activity of God are those of a pure spirit knowing and loving itself. Therefore, of all the creatures of the material universe, man alone can be called the image of God, because man's soul and its

faculties for knowing and loving are spiritual (St Augustine, *Gen. ad litt.* 6, CSEL 28.1: 170–200; St Thomas Aquinas, ST 1a, 93.2).[30]

The 1994 Catholic catechism states baldly,

> God entrusted animals to the stewardship of those whom he created in his own image. Hence it is legitimate to use animals for food and clothing ... work and leisure. Medical and scientific experimentation on animals, if it remains within reasonable limits, is a morally acceptable practice since it contributes to caring for or saving human lives.[31]

MYSTICISM AND EASTERN CHRISTIANITY

The modern Christian zoophile's wish to find support from mystical and Eastern sources is compromised by the aggression found in some of those writings. The Byzantine Holy Saturday rite, which affirms "that 'the whole creation was altered by thy Passion; for all things suffered with thee, knowing, O Lord, that thou holdest all things in unity,'"[32] is acknowledged by Linzey to be "one of the comparatively few exceptions to an almost wholly monolithic anthropocentrism of East and West."[33] St. Gregory of Nyssa, listed elsewhere more favorably by Linzey, argued against human slavery on the grounds that "God gave humans dominion not over other humans but over the world and animals in particular.... One kind of slavery is therefore opposed on the grounds that another is self-evident."[34]

THE CATHOLIC CHURCH

While Catholicism is changing (see under "Evasion" in this chapter and see chapter 6), in the past the Church has been notorious for its hostility to animals—in contrast to the sympathy shown by individual mystics and saints. In the fifteenth century Pope Innocent VIII "ordered that pet cats be included when witches were burned at the stake. According to Gerald Carson, 'as late as the seventeenth century, it was risky for an old woman to have a cat as a pet.'"[35] It was believed that Satan could take the form of an animal. Pope Pius IX (1846–78) "forbade the opening of a proposed animal welfare centre in Rome on the grounds that it would divert attention from human welfare concerns."[36] In the mid-1960s, seventy-six-year-old nun Mother Cecilia Mary was threatened with dismissal for refusing to close a shelter for stray animals that she operated together with five other nuns. She was told that she must resume helping humans, but, following her argument that "charity is higher than any obedience," she "was later exonerated by the pope and continued to operate her shelter."[37] Priests have blessed the clubbing to death of baby seals off Newfoundland, and in 1979 the Jesuit magazine *America* defended the seal hunt, attacking those organizations that protested. Both Most Rev. Peter Sutton (Catholic) and Right Rev. Jack Sperry (Anglican) used the familiar "aboriginal peoples" argument during this controversy. In 1988 "the archbishop of Udine, Italy, is reported to have stated, 'It is not a sin to beat a dog or leave it to starve to death.'"[38]

As Regenstein observes,

> Sometimes the representatives of the church have gone to extraordinary lengths to justify acts of cruelty to animals, while attempting to maintain the principle that one should not engage in such acts as an end unto itself. The result of this moral and philosophical hair-splitting has been to condone almost any mistreatment of animals for which the slightest justification can be conjured.[39]

For example, the Jesuit father Joseph Rickaby's *Moral Philosophy* of 1888 or 1901 says: "It is wanton cruelty to vex and annoy a brute beast *for sport.* . . . But there is no shadow of evil resting on the practice of causing pain to brutes *in sport*, where the pain is not the sport itself, but an incidental concomitant of it."[40] If additional rationalizing were needed, it could be found in Descartes, whose mechanistic account of animals, according to which they cannot feel pain, "reconcil[ed] in one master stroke the prescription of Catholicism that animals do not have souls with the demands of the growing science of physiology"[41]—though the theologian would have to keep separate the claim that animals did not suffer and the claim that their suffering was justified.

One might be encouraged by the following paragraph in the 1994 catechism: "Animals are God's creatures. He surrounds them with his providential care. By their mere existence they bless him and give him glory. Thus men owe them kindness. We should recall the gentleness with which saints like St Francis of Assisi or St Philip Neri treated animals."[42] Yet following these same words we find the assertion, quoted earlier, of humans' right to use animals for any and all purposes, including vivisection. As Linzey notes, "The *Catechism* represents a major moral victory by the biotechnological establishment. It has received effective and official endorsement by the largest Christian organization in the world."[43]

The causal relationship between political motive and doctrine is subtle. It is not as though vivisectors stood at the elbow of the catechism's authors. But human demands have seemed so imperative to theologians as to have constituted a cosmic principle in themselves, rather than a need requiring supportive argument. Given such a theological dynamic, it is not surprising to find the paragraph justifying animal usage followed by the even more extreme statement: "It is contrary to human dignity to cause animals to suffer or die needlessly. It is likewise unworthy to spend money on them that should as a priority go to the relief of human misery. One can love animals; one should not direct to them the affection due only to persons."[44]

EVASION

In the past, Christians have mostly expressed their conflict over animals indirectly, through evasive imagery, symbolism, and folktales. The New Testament contains no direct commands to be kind to animals, either in general or with reference to particular species or situations. Indications of divine and human concern in the Gospels are mostly invidious, made to emphasize the greater worth of human beings. Nevertheless the animals benefit, and at least the concern is described as existing and, by implication, as a good thing. "Although Jesus is presented as underlining the special value of humankind over that of sparrows, the main point does seem to be that God is generous so much so that . . . sparrows 'sold for two pennies,' are in fact so valuable that 'not one of them is forgotten by God' (Lk. 12.6–7)."[45]

All three features—the benefit to animals, the approval of the benefit, and the speciesist conclusion—are present in Matthew 6:26: "Look at the birds . . . they do not sow or reap or store away in barns, and yet your heavenly Father feeds them. Are you not much more valuable than they?" and in Jesus's arguments about the Sabbath:

> If any of you has a sheep and it falls into a pit on the Sabbath, will you not take hold of it and lift it out? [12] How much more valuable is a man than a sheep! (Mt. 12:11–12)

> You hypocrites! Doesn't each of you on the Sabbath untie his ox or donkey from the stall and lead it out to give it water? [16] Then should not this woman, a daughter of Abraham, whom Satan has kept bound for eighteen long years, be set free on the Sabbath day? (Luke 13:15–16)

Akers, while acknowledging the species inequality of such passages, observes that they are examples of a fortiori argument: "an argument from the lesser to the greater, which goes from a statement that is accepted to conclude that it is all the more true in another case."[46] He also notes that "the principle of compassion for animals is therefore, a *presupposition* of all of Jesus' references to animals.... Jesus in the gospels does not ... *argue* the question of whether we should be compassionate to animals; rather he *assumes* it from the outset."[47]

A somewhat different case, the parable of the lost sheep (Mt. 18:12–14) offers an analogy with a human situation, but does not assert human superiority and describes convincingly the shepherd's anxiety over the sheep.

Having reviewed these rather weak claims to Christian animal support, I shall look at more promising, but indirect, indicators:

1. vegetarian implications in the Gospels;

2. the image of Jesus as a shepherd;

3. the image of Jesus as sacrificial lamb;

4. expressions of kinship in popular culture;

5. mystics and saints who were kind to animals;

6. limited reforms in Catholicism and in the Protestant era.

VEGETARIAN IMPLICATIONS IN THE GOSPELS

The New Testament contains two positive images of non sacrificial meat eating: the killing of the fatted calf in the prodigal son story (Luke 15:11–31), and the slaughter for a wedding feast at Matthew 22.4 (the same parable in Luke 14:15–23 does not mention slaughter). However, these celebratory slaughters may be seen as stand-ins for blood sacrifice in a culture, and a religious discourse, that is moving away from such ritual.

The Gospels contain very few references to sacrifice (Mk. 1:44; Luke 2:24, 5:14, 13:1), apart from the historically central Passover. Jesus is not described as eating the Passover lamb (whose slaughter is mentioned specifically at Mark 14:12 and Luke 22:7): the meal, yes, but not, in so many words, the lamb. As Linzey notes,[48] the Gospels nowhere show him as eating meat other than fish. The "body" that he offers the disciples at the Last Supper consists of bread, not meat; the "blood" is wine. At John 6:51 Jesus says, "If anyone eats of this bread, he will live for ever. This bread is my flesh." In response to his hearers' puzzlement, he says (6:53), "unless you can eat the flesh of the Son of Man and drink his blood, you have no life in you." Meat with the blood in it had been forbidden, but now that the death is voluntary (a crucial ethical distinction between Jesus's sacrifice and that of animals),[49] the blood (but in the vegetable form of wine) is allowable. The Lord's Prayer, of course, refers to "bread" (Mt. 6:11, Luke 11:3).

Finding problematic the pro-animal interpretation of the vegetable Eucharist, Adams and Procter-Smith observe that "this interpretation . . . assume[s] that animals are not being sacrificed in other, more quotidian, ways by our own unexamined actions."[50] Exactly—that is what moral conflict, resulting in evasion, is about: eating flesh at the table, but finding the idea of it rather distasteful in church.

Seeking reasons for the absence of meat in descriptions of Jesus's food, and dismissing actual vegetarianism as "a remote possibility," inasmuch as "it may be pondered whether Jesus was ever confronted with ethical vegetarianism such as we know it today,"[51] Linzey offers as the most likely explanation "the possibility that Jesus did indeed participate in the killing of some life in order to live. Indeed we may say that part of his being a human being at a particular stage and time in history necessitate that response in order to have lived at all."[52] Yet the Gospel authors chose not to picture him eating meat. This evasive preference might also explain apocryphal suggestions of his "special concern for, and affinity with, the animal world": "What may be significant is that this material, historical or not, exhibits a sensitivity to animals which some in the Christian community felt at one stage or another was—or rather should be—characteristic of the historical Jesus."[53]

THE IMAGE OF JESUS AS A SHEPHERD

In the Gospels, besides passing references to the shepherd–sheep relation (Mt. 9:36, 10:8, 15:24, 18:12–13, 25:32, 26:31; Mk. 6:34, 14:27; Luke 10:3, 12:32, 15:4–6), the fullest application of it comes at John 10:1–16 and 26–28, reinforced at the end of this Gospel by Jesus's threefold request to Peter to "feed my lambs" (21:15; "sheep" at 21:16 and 17). Instead of eating the sheep, Jesus says, at 10:11, "I am the good shepherd. The good shepherd lays down his life for the sheep," and, at 10:27–28, "My sheep listen to my voice; I know them, and they follow me. [28] I give them eternal life, and they shall never perish."

Evidently the authors wished to associate Jesus's benevolence to humans with benevolence to animals, and they could not have sustained such an ethic with a predominantly anti-animal imagery. (I say "predominantly" in

acknowledgment of such things as the invidious teachings mentioned earlier; the Gadarene pigs, Jesus's eating of fish, and the "fishers of men"
image—which, by contrast with the shepherd image, occurs only once in
each synoptic Gospel and is in any case a factual reference to the disciples'
occupation.) The impossibility of such a pairing is illustrated in Linzey's alternative portrait of Christ, such as might be proffered by a "hunter with
Jesus":

> Jesus would not just be eating some fishes, but feasting on calves and lambs.
> Jesus, according to the Predator Gospel, would be the butcher *par excel-*
> *lence*. . . . Instead of driving out the sacrificial animals from the Temple, the
> Jesus of the Predator Gospel would drive them in. The line that most charac-
> terizes his ministry would not be "the good shepherd lays down his life for the
> sheep" but rather "the good shepherd slaughters—with gratitude—as many
> sheep as he can."[54]

My point is not simply that Jesus was *in fact* a "good shepherd" rather than a
butcher, but that—as in Linzey's comment about apocryphal material attributing pro-animal attitudes to Jesus—the biblical authors wanted to express
their own values by portraying him in that light.

THE IMAGE OF JESUS AS SACRIFICIAL LAMB

The central event of Christian history and theology is the sacrifice of the symbolic Lamb. John the Baptist's "Look, the Lamb of God, who takes away the
sin of the world!" (John 1:29), and 1 Peter 1:18–19 "it was not with . . . silver or
gold that you were redeemed . . . , [19] but with the precious blood of Christ, a
lamb without blemish or defect," recall the sin-offerings and guilt-offerings
of the Hebrew Bible; 1 Corinthians 5:7 declares that "Christ, our Passover
lamb, has been sacrificed." Revelation 5:6 presents Jesus as a literal, albeit
fantastic, animal: "a Lamb, looking as if it had been slain, [with] seven horns
and seven eyes," to whom the living creatures and elders sing (5:9): "with your
blood you purchased men for God."

Since accounts of Jesus's death never acknowledge any wrongness of animal sacrifice, and Gospel statements about that practice (Mt. 9:13, 12:7; Mk.
12:33) merely emphasize ethical and spiritual substitutes, the sympathy expressed for the crucified human "lamb" is evasive. Yet the symbolism would
not reinforce sympathy for the martyred Christ if people did not already feel

sympathy for the lamb. For example, legend holds that "St Gudival of Ghent once brought back to life a sheep that had been killed 'because he saw in it Christ led like a sheep to the slaughter.'"[55]

For those who are skeptical of the animal meaning of Jesus's sacrifice, I would like to examine three elements of it more closely—Isaiah's prediction, the image of Christ as lamb, and the theologically motivated abandonment of animal sacrifice—and ask how necessary, considering the historical facts alone, each of the three would have been to the promotion of Christianity, had there been no animal dimension in the authors' outlook. Nowadays these elements are taken for granted, but the event stated plainly—that is, the martyrdom of a radical religious leader at the behest of the orthodox—does not entail them.

Why should one passage from an extensive prophetic literature be interpreted as pointing to Christ's story? According to Fox, who lists among false understandings of the Bible "the belief that bits of the Old Testament predict the New,"[56] "it was probably . . . the people of Israel whom . . . Second Isaiah . . . described . . . as a Suffering Servant in the tribulations of [the Babylonian] period."[57]

Why should the Christian authors choose to adopt Isaiah's imagery, by symbolizing Christ as a lamb? True, the death took place at the time of Passover, a festival recalling a major Jewish historical event. But that could have been ignored had its symbolism not seemed otherwise appropriate; alternately, the Passover connection could have been drawn with the martyred leader portrayed primarily as a future avenging angel, rather than primarily as a victim. The Hebrew word translated "lamb" can mean "lamb" or "kid";[58] Exodus 12:5 reads, "you may take [the animals] from the sheep or the goats"; so part of the reason for the choice of the image of the lamb in particular lies in the congenial features of that animal previously discussed. "The goat of God" would not have quite the same ring.

Last, would animal sacrifice have been abandoned in response to Jesus's death had the practice not already been falling into disfavor, as indicated by prophetic and Gospel statements? If the abandonment had been solely on grounds that people had been redeemed by the ultimate sacrifice of the crucifixion, as urged in Hebrews 7.27 and 9.12,[59] animal sacrifice could still have been retained—instead of the bread-and-wine Eucharist—as a symbolic reminder of his death.

In another twist, Akers argues that

if we accept the accounts of Jesus' baptism, then there was already in place an alternative method for purification from or forgiveness of sin *before* Jesus even approached his death on the cross. The rejection of animal sacrifice, or at the very least an alternative . . . , *must* have existed before Jesus' death, rendering the whole concept of the atonement superfluous.[60]

To unpack these different ideas: *individual* atonement may have been achieved through baptism, while the common Christian belief is that Jesus's death atoned for humanity globally. (This despite the fact that "the theology of the crucifixion was not fully developed . . . until the work of Athanasius in the fourth century. . . . Juridical, military, commercial, and moral-obedience images were used to describe Jesus' victory on the cross.")[61]

But either suggested substitute—baptism or the crucifixion—is compatible with the rejection of animal sacrifice, and (my main point) even in the accepted, nonvegetarian New Testament, the image of Christ as lamb reflects sympathy for the animal. I disagree that "identifying Jesus as an innocent and spotless 'lamb' can, as Adams and Procter-Smith suggest, lend credence to the idea that it is acceptable to sacrifice those who are blameless and voiceless."[62] On the contrary, Christian culture has historically *not* called this Friday "good," but has seen it—despite theological difficulties—as an outrage, at times justifying pogroms as attacks on "Christ-killers." Webb, too, questions the claim of "acceptability," stating, "The body of Christ, after all, was insulted, and through that trauma God identifies with the least among us, those who can feel but cannot defend themselves, those who suffer but cannot speak."[63]

What brings all these three elements together in conformity to an animal-related interpretation is Christ's message of compassion for the weak and humble: "If anyone wants to be first, he must be the very last, and the servant of all" (Mk. 9:35), while in Luke's nativity account, "the salvation of men and of the world are no longer awaited from the all-powerful Roman Caesars but from this powerless child."[64]

An agricultural economy relying also on animal usage and on the humanist justifications for it could not explicitly apply such a message to animals. But the message's relevance to animals permeates the choices made by the New Testament authors. This is what makes the image (harking back to Isaiah) of the sacrificial lamb, and the theology of giving up animal sacrifice, evasive.

EXPRESSIONS OF KINSHIP IN POPULAR CULTURE

Humans' love of animals has emerged among Christians who would not have considered questioning the habitual use of animals or the church's justification for it. Some of the following examples overlap with the subsequent section on saints and mystics, inasmuch as early European discourse was shaped by religion.

While the Gospel account of the nativity mentions the manger but not, specifically, animals, people have extrapolated both animal-relevant meaning and animal content to the place:

> Popular tradition has long pictured the infant Jesus lying on straw in a rough feeding trough (the earliest such representation is found on a sarcophagus that dates from 343). Time has added other details such as the ox and the ass at the crib. This very ancient tradition seems to depend in part on Is 1.3: "An ox knows its owner, and an ass, its master's manger," and in part on the LXX reading of Hab 3.2: "In the midst of two animals thou shalt be known."[65]

Bradley provides further evidence of lay instincts concerning the manger: "In 1655 the diarist Ralph Josselin dreamed that Christ was born in a stable 'because he was the redeemer of man and beast out of their bondage by the Fall.'"[66]

An example of people projecting religious significance onto animals lies in the predominant association of St. Francis with them, when in fact he "spent considerably more time surrounded by lepers and down-and-outs than by birds and squirrels."[67] The "danger in over-romanticising" the saint's communion with nature[68] shows the popular impulse to dwell on an area of moral neglect while expressing their affection for animals—all the more so as Francis's sometime vegetarianism resulted from his practice of "extreme asceticism and mortification of the flesh," and was abandoned when he had made himself ill from self-punishment. Then, "Once he had recovered, he would repent his 'lapse' and castigate himself publicly—not for eating the bodies of murdered animals, but for giving in to his body."[69]

Preece's observation, "there is an abundance of evidence that the culture was kinder to animals than was the dogma,"[70] is qualified by his awareness of the split, among ordinary people, between abusive habits and generous sentiments. Consider, for example, "the traditional Russian story of St Sergey and the bear," who became inseparable companions. Retold by Father Zosima in

The Brothers Karamazov, the story "is as well known, and as endearing, to Russian Orthodox youth as St Francis is to Catholic youth, and Androcles's lion is to Roman and medieval European youth."[71] Yet,

> what is reflective of Western ambivalence is that the Romans continued to delight in the story . . . while also continuing to attend the circus, and that medieval (and later) Europeans repeated the story ad nauseam to their children while continuing to bait bears and bulls. . . . The reality is, of course, that there are both higher and lower aspects to human nature.[72]

The lower aspect certainly characterized the professed ethos:

> What is remarkable, if not disturbing, is that his [St. Francis's] followers and later chroniclers found his actions and feelings toward nonhuman creation so extraordinary. St Francis once liberated two lambs, tied up across the shoulders of a farmer, who were bleating pitifully on their way to market where they would be slaughtered. St Francis removed worms from a busy road . . . so that they might not be crushed under the feet of passersby. . . . Such actions reveal much about St Francis and about those who regarded such behavior as extraordinary; others neither felt nor acted in these ways.[73]

In more recent times, an example of unconscious conflict on the part of congregations is given by Rev. V. A. Holmes-Gore in a Christian vegetarian leaflet: "At harvest festivals it is custom to thank God for the fruits of the earth. But who would think of laying upon the altar the carcass of a slaughtered bullock or lamb? The fact that any decent person would shrink from doing so is a clear indication that we know inwardly that God does not intend us to slay the creatures for food."[74] The leaflet's argument, of course, is in the effective-defensive category, as it promotes the abandonment of meat eating, but the popular habit Holmes-Gore refers to is evasive.

MYSTICS AND SAINTS WHO WERE KIND TO ANIMALS

In the early centuries of the first millennium, "the close relationship of beasts and saints was not a new theme in monastic literature."[75] Saint-and-animal stories number in the "hundreds, even thousands."[76] According to folk tradition, St. Francis was not the only one to include animals in his spiritual scheme. "Ailbe is the patron saint of wolves. . . . Blaise, patron saint of sick

cattle, lived in a cave in the woods to which wild beasts would come for sanctuary and medical treatment. . . . Eloy blessed a horse and rid it of demonic
possession. Gall, patron saint of birds, shared his cave-dwelling with a bear."[77]
Preece gives many more examples of saints who "can lay their claim to spiritual fame on their love and respect for other species"[78] and acknowledges the
ethical impulse behind the stories, since "If saints are rare, and if their exploits are sometimes in part a product of the imagination, they epitomize for
the people the life of honour and justice, which few lesser mortals are ever
able to achieve."[79]

Valuation of concern is found in Isaac the Syrian's description of a charitable heart as one "burning with charity for the whole of creation, for men, for
the birds, for the beasts, for the demons"; he prays "for the animals, for the
enemies of Truth, and for those who do him evil, that they may be preserved
and purified."[80] St. John Chrysostom, "more an exemplar than an exception
[whose] works remained required reading in the Russian Orthodox Church,"
argued: "Surely we ought to show [other species] great kindness and gentleness for many reasons, but above all because they are of the same origin as
ourselves"[81]—a statement anticipating Darwin, as Regenstein and Preece
have noted.[82] St. Basil (330?–379?) said of animals, even more radically, "May
we realize that they live, not for us alone, but for themselves and for thee, and
that they have the sweetness of life."[83]

Anxious to rehabilitate Western culture in regard to animals as well as
nature, Preece confronts the cases of "the customary villains," St. Augustine
and St. Thomas Aquinas,[84] by quoting remarks that seem to modify their
better-known aggressive doctrines. Augustine was "appalled at the suggestion that he should offer an animal sacrifice to gain a prize he covets. 'Though
the crown were of an undying lustre, I would not permit a fly to be killed to
gain me the victory,' Augustine tells us."[85]

He explains Augustine's rejection of vegetarianism as a reaction against
his earlier Manichaeanism.[86] The saint "was not so much arguing against
treating other species well as he was against what he saw as the vegetarian
excesses of his former fellow believers,"[87] excesses springing from an antiworld dualism.

Aquinas, for his part, "argued that charity was owed to all of God's creation, including 'the creatures without reason . . . fish and birds, the beasts
and plants.' . . . However, we are usually informed that Aquinas believed that
the only argument against cruelty to animals is that it may lead to cruelty to
people" (128). But considering that both thinkers put forward a predomi-

nantly human supremacist moral structure that has been determinant in the West, with kindness to animals regarded as supererogatory where it is not actually patronized or despised as sentimental, such comments can be placed in the "evasive" category.

A similarly brief turning toward animals is found in the mystic Margery Kempe, who wrote that "if she saw a man had a wound, or a beast . . . or if a man beat a child . . . or hit a horse or other beast with a whip . . . she thought she saw our Lord being beaten or wounded."[88] As it happens, this passage, quoted by Linzey and cited by Bradley, is the only clear reference to animal welfare in her book.[89] Still, such occasional pronouncements from earlier times indicate a basis for animal advocacy that was to increase in a more propitious ideological climate.

LIMITED REFORMS IN CATHOLICISM AND IN THE PROTESTANT ERA

CATHOLIC SYMPATHY FOR ANIMALS

Despite the Church's generally poor record, in 1095 Pope Urban II "extended the right of sanctuary to oxen, plough horses, and harrowing horses, as well as the men who worked them, because of their relationship."[90] The "Rituale Romanum contains services for blessing animals and stables, and the benediction for sick animals includes the plea, 'Be thou to them, O Lord, the defender of their life and the restorer of their health.'"[91]

In the twentieth century, marked improvements occurred. Cardinal Rafael Santos said in 1963:

> We are happy to dedicate a special day this year in order to remind our people of the great value of animals in our daily life and to give them whatever care and personal concern they deserve from us.
>
> But above all we should remember that animals are not only created by Almighty God to serve man's needs, but also to reflect God's goodness and wisdom.[92]

Regenstein observes that "the animal welfare movement within the church has been especially strong in Britain," the Catholic Study Circle for Animal Welfare having been founded in London in 1935, recognized by the authorities and blessed by Popes Pius XII in 1958 and Paul VI in 1967. There are other such organizations in Australia, Canada, and France.[93]

THE PROTESTANT ERA

No direct line leads from sympathy for animals to Protestant doctrine, but we can find parallel themes of fresh thinking and social reform that were propitious for the emergence of animal-friendly sentiment. At the very beginning of Protestantism,

> it is not known to what extent, if any, Luther's love for animals led to his break with the Catholic Church, but the church's attitude could have been enough to . . . alienate any humanitarian. In his commentary on Deuteronomy 22:6, . . . Luther wrote, "What else does this law teach but that by the kind treatment of animals they are to learn gentleness and kindness . . ."
>
> And English historian W. E. H. Lecky relates how "Luther grew sad and thoughtful at a hare hunt, for it seemed to him to represent the pursuit of souls by the devil."[94]

More radical than Luther, and persecuted by both Catholics and Reformers, was the Anabaptist Thomas Muntzer, a Lutheran pastor who supported "a large-scale peasants' revolt suppressed with cruelty,"[95] and who also "declare[d] it intolerable that 'all creatures have been made into property, the fish in the water, the birds in the air, the plants on the earth—all living things must also become free.'"[96]

From the seventeenth century onward, Protestant clergy and lay individuals began to express pro-animal sentiments, while in largely Protestant England and New England protectionist laws were enacted—limited both in extent and sometimes motivation from a modern perspective, but representing progress by contrast with earlier attitudes and indeed with some of the contemporary resistance that they met. They took place against a background that featured, "by the eighteenth century, . . . growing demands for drastic social reforms, including the abolition of slavery and the prevention of cruelty to children—and animals,"[97] many of these later causes inspired by the Methodism of John and Charles Wesley. John Wesley himself is described as vegetarian by Webb and Regenstein.[98] According to Phelps, however, he was only "vegetarian on-and-off for much of his later life . . . for reasons of health rather than ethics," despite his belief in a compensatory afterlife for animals.[99]

In December 1641 the Puritans of the Massachusetts Bay Colony adopted a code of laws written by Rev. Nathaniel Ward. Among other things it ruled that "no man shall exercise any Tirranny or Crueltie towards any bruite creature which are usuallie kept for man's use."[100] Cruelty was attacked by the founder of the Shakers, Ann Lee (1736–84), and that denomination's 1845 rules included a section on the treatment of animals (105); Mormons also advocated kindness to them (106).

Some seventeenth- and eighteenth-century laws existed "more to protect the interests of the owners than . . . the animals themselves,"[101] but there was an unsuccessful attempt in 1800 to restrict bull baiting.

As an example of the difficulties faced by these early animal supporters, a sermon in 1772 against cruelty to animals led to Church of England vicar James Granger going to prison. "Dedicating the sermon to a neighbor he had often seen whipping his horses, Reverend Granger admonished him . . . 'For God's sake and thy own, have some compassion upon these poor beasts. . . . Damnation will certainly come. . . . Ask God forgiveness for the cruelty.'"[102] The congregation's response is reminiscent of current attacks on PETA: "The foregoing discourse gave almost universal disgust to two considerable congregations. The mention of dogs and horses was censured as a prostitution of the dignity of the pulpit, and considered as proof of the author's insanity."[103]

Other significant eighteenth-century events were the publication in 1776 of Humphrey Primatt's *Dissertation on the Duty of Mercy and Sin of Cruelty to Brute Animals* and a prosecution in 1790 for an atrocity against a horse, a similar prosecution following three years later.[104] In 1822 another breakthrough occurred with the passage of Richard Martin's "Act to prevent the cruel and improper Treatment of Cattle," which applied to a variety of farm and working animals.[105] Here again there was ridicule; nevertheless, Martin could claim that "every preacher in London has spoken in support of the bill."[106]

Another two years saw the foundation of the RSPCA by Rev. Arthur Broome. In 1868 Rev. Thomas Timmins helped George T. Angell found the Massachusetts SPCA. Angell started the "first periodical in the world devoted to animal welfare" and with Timmins organized Bands of Mercy in primary schools, their young members vowing "to be kind to all living creatures, and try to protect them from cruel usage."[107]

DEFENSE

Apart from its endorsement of the biblical utopias, I find in Christianity no defensiveness in the sense of acknowledging a wrong but seeking to launder it. The most noticeable form of defensiveness in Christianity is the political kind such as the aforementioned ridicule and hostility toward early anticruelty crusaders, plus, in modern times, the search for mitigation of or evidence counterbalancing Christianity's past dominionism and ill-treatment of animals.

POLITICAL DEFENSE

Much of this defense takes the form of blaming the Greek influence—with some justification—for the church's human supremacist views. "Greening Christianity . . . means stripping off . . . alien layers that have accumulated to reveal the original greenness of the Garden of Eden and the cross on Calvary."[108] As Bradley expounds these layers,

> the idea of a radical separation between human beings and the world of nature was totally foreign to Hebrew thought but it is deeply embedded in Greek philosophy. The Stoics . . . preached the superiority of man over nature. The effect of this alien Hellenistic strand in early Christianity was greatly compounded by the influence of the Gnostics with . . . their insistence that all matter was corrupt and sinful. . . . It has been confirmed by the dominance of Cartesian dualism between mind and matter.[109]

The Greeks themselves, although largely responsible for Christianity's speciesism, were not always anti-animal:

> Some of the less rationalist of the Presocratic philosophers saw their goal as the re-creation of a golden age of peace and vegetarianism. Vegetarianism, which was a practice of the cult of the Orphic mysteries, remained a prominent and respected part of Greek life at least until the time of Plato. It was not until Diodorus Siculus in the first century BC that we encounter an entirely negative view of the retrospective golden age and of principled vegetarianism.[110]

In fact, later Western philosophy itself—derived to a great extent from the later Greeks—has sometimes helped to counter the rationalist influences, the irony being, as Preece points out, that "while environmental and animal rights criticisms are directed against the predominant tendencies of Western society, they are predicated on inherent but sometimes unpractised values of that society."[111]

Yet traditional Christianity has felt less threatened by negative criticism than by the positive attraction of rival creeds, since "many of those who in recent years have come to care deeply about . . . animals, plants, rivers and mountains have turned to eastern religions or gone back to old pagan beliefs for spiritual succour."[112] Christianity is trying to bring itself into greater harmony with present-day feeling. Linzey's arguments, however, are aimed less at other religions than at secular animal rights supporters like "Peter Singer, immersed in utilitarian calculations,"[113] Christian human chauvinists like Barth,[114] and other Christian defenders of animal abuse.[115] But Bradley wants to prove to actual and potential adherents of other faiths that "Christianity is in fact the most concerned of all the world's great religions about the fate of the non-human as well as the human part of creation."[116]

Christianity's attitude to animals has long been identified with St. Paul's rejection of concern for the ox and neglect of any ethical aspects of meat eating, with the political motives (recruitment, appeasement of Constantine) for rejection of the vegetarianism attributed to the earliest Christianity, with Greek intellectualism, and with the hostility to animal welfare displayed by the Catholic Church. Even in figures appealed to by modern pro-animal Christians, such as some of the mystics and the Eastern Orthodox Church, doctrines of perfectionism and an absence of vegetarianism can be found. And the vegetarianism often attributed to Jesus and to some apostles and Church fathers has been challenged as unsupported by evidence.

The New Testament, lacking direct conventions of divine or human concern for animals except as examples of the superior claims of humanity, nevertheless offers certain evasive vegetarian implications in the Gospels, and, more importantly, the symbolism of Jesus as shepherd (continuing the earlier Hebrew theme) and as sacrificial lamb. In later Christian culture, people showed their affection for animals by introducing them to the nativity scene and by incorporating stories of zoophilic saints within their folklore. The deeds and pronouncements of such saints and other religious figures, plus the limited but promising improvements in attitude and practice, beginning in the seventeenth century, with the help of some Protestant clergy and some Catholics as well, confirm an evasive strand within what nevertheless remained an overwhelmingly humanistic creed up until the late twentieth century.

Like Judaism, Christianity accepts the vegetarian Eden and the peaceable kingdom and in the same spirit of utopianism. While the New Testament contains no defensive rituals affecting animals, one can see a recollection of them in Pilate's disowning of responsibility toward the symbolic Lamb. More significant is the political defensiveness of modern Christians as they speak up for their religion in the face of its earlier-acquired reputation for hostility to animals.

With its identity determined more by the New Testament than by the relatively green Jewish Bible, and with the Greek influence correspondingly stronger than on either Judaism or Islam, Christianity stands in something of a contrast to those faiths as regards animals. But Islam is in its own way the odd one out—its particular practices and theology reflecting somewhat differently both benefit and harm to nonhumans—and these characteristics will be explored in the next chapter.

4. Islam

JUSTIFICATION OF ANIMAL USAGE COMES FROM THE Islamic God's absolute authority, which overrides kindness where this would interfere with the culture's prevailing practices. Abraham's sacrifice (a symbol of divine authority outweighing natural sentiment in the human context) is celebrated by the continued practice of animal sacrifice; and ideas of dominionism and human superiority, held in common with Judaism and Christianity, are given an Islamic coloration by the emphasis on human submission to God. There is also an element of logocentrism, though it is much less significant than in Judaism and Christianity.

Evasion is necessary because Islam characterizes God as above all compassionate. The Qur'an and Hadith affirm the importance of animal welfare, introducing rules that make meat eating, animal sacrifice, and usage for work more humane.[1] We find a prevalence of vegetable food imagery. Many Hadith report Muhammad's sympathy for animals, that of the religion as a whole being embodied in the story of the Thamud people who were punished for cruelty to an animal.

Sufi literature often continues the tradition of kindness, and in modern times the Sunni imam Hafiz B. A. al-Masri has argued for humane farming and prestunning in ritual slaughter. Insofar as he does not call for the total abandonment of meat eating, however, Masri (himself a vegetarian) displays evasion.

Defense occurs in Islam, as in Judaism, through rules and rituals attending slaughter for food, but, unlike Judaism, Islam practices animal sacrifice to which defensive prescriptions are applied. The relevant Qur'anic verses, and translator Ali's commentary, acknowledge the value of animal life and come close to apologizing for the "necessary" killing.

So it is not surprising that political defense is found in Islam also.

AGGRESSION

THEISTIC SUBJECTIVISM AND THE SALAM ARGUMENT

A prominent aggressive strategy in conservative Islam is the doctrine of "theistic subjectivism," the term applied by Hourani to the view, also known as divine voluntarism, that "makes values ultimately dependent on the will of God rather than on any facts in the natural order of the world."[2] Quoting 33:36 of the Qur'an, "'It is not for any believer . . . when God and His Messenger have decreed a matter, to have the choice in the affair. Whosoever disobeys God and His Messenger has gone astray into manifest error,'" Hourani comments, "Here is an unusually sharp command to Muslims to surrender their moral judgements to the decisions of God and the Prophet."[3] In keeping with this authoritarianism, the conservative Ash'ari (873–935) "does not shrink from the extreme consequence . . . that lying and other conduct generally considered wicked would have been good acts if God had declared them so and obligatory if He had commanded them."[4] Smart describes Asharism as the "Sunni or mainstream tradition."[5]

The doctrine has been used to suppress instincts of sympathy, just as an authoritarian, sympathy-suppressing message has been found by Christians and Jews in the Abraham story. Medieval proponents of the Asharite account used concern for animals negatively in their arguments.

> God can make harmless animals, children and insane persons suffer and not compensate them . . . because he does it all the time. And He is under no necessity not to, because necessity . . . does not apply to Him. Nor is such action opposed to His wisdom, understood as His knowledge of the harmony of the world. Nor is He a wrongdoer in doing it, because wrongdoing is wholly inapplicable to Him.[6]

An example of the principle is found in the following argument against vegetarianism: "Muslims may not choose to prohibit themselves food that is allowed by Islam. Accordingly, vegetarianism is not permitted unless on grounds such as unavailability or medical necessity."[7] This amounts to saying that permission—the middle, neutral area of Islam's five grades of divine prescription (command, encouragement, neutrality, discouragement, prohibition)—constitutes a command.

In fact, the Qur'an does not command people to eat meat. We read in 6:142: "Eat what Allah hath provided / For you, and follow not / The footsteps of Satan," which seems rather to warn people to ignore pre-Islamic dietary laws when they do eat it. Forward and Alam say merely, "Few Muslims are vegetarian."[8] It is possible that Muhammad was largely vegetarian, but, if so, it was out of asceticism. "His biographers attest that as his faith deepened, his asceticism increased. Professor Charles J. Addams asserts that he was a *hanif*,"[9] since "Syrian Christianity, with its mystical-ascetic bent, held a particular attraction for Muhammad, as it did for many other Arabs . . . who emulated the Syrian Christian monks by swearing off meat and drink and becoming wandering ascetics, or *hanifs*."[10]

Al-Salam (1182–1262) offers a speciesist argument against ethical vegetarianism: "The unbeliever who prohibits the slaughtering of an animal [for no reason but] to achieve the interest of the animal is incorrect because in so doing he gives preference to a lower, *khasis*, animal over a higher, *nafis*, animal"[11]—which Izzi Dien places on the authoritarian plane, writing: "Vegetarianism is not allowed under the pretext of giving priority to the interest of animals because such decisions are God's prerogative."[12]

Noting that Salam "used the word 'unbeliever,'" Izzi Dien suggests that he might, like the Mu'tazilites and their opponents quoted earlier, have been referring "to adherents of Eastern religions who believe in the sanctity of animals."[13]

Voluntarism is here invoked to uphold a daily habit of life pitted against a contrary impulse, which must also have been present in the culture to account for any need to suppress it. Besides discrediting positive vegetarian tendencies, divine authority could ease the minds of those who chose to eat meat but still suffered from uneasiness.

ABRAHAM'S SACRIFICE

An Islamic turn to the story is given it by the fact that in the Qur'an, unlike in the Bible, the son (in this case Ishmail) is told he is going to be sacrificed and agrees to it. Apart from such doctrinal justification, the retention of animal sacrifice very likely "derives from the norms and conditions of pre-Islamic Arab society, and not from Islam itself."[14]

Besides maintaining an ancient custom even predating the Hebrews, the practice preserved identification with the Abrahamic tradition, of which the pre-Islamic Arabs considered themselves part. In both these aspects of continuity, keeping animal sacrifice was a natural move in gaining support for the new religion.

The ritual element of sacrifice is defensive, but the principle is aggressive: God demands this type of killing, and you needn't regret it because, like Abraham, you have abdicated moral responsibility in God's favor.

DOMINIONISM

Dominion over animals is seen as one of the benefits to human beings in a scheme of things to which they must submit for good or ill; and their own obedience to Allah—who, like the stockbreeder of the Jewish Bible, gives life and death (45:26, 53:44) and determines ageing and the time of death (40:67)—justifies the submission which they forcibly exact from animals. The Qur'an tells us:

> ... all creatures
> In the heavens and on earth
> Have, willing or unwilling,
> Bowed to His Will. (3:83)

By compensation to the human beings,

> It is He who produceth
> Gardens ... (6:141)
> Of the cattle are some
> For burden and some for meat: (6:142)

Other such statements include: "It is He Who hath made /You (His) agents, inheritors / Of the earth" (6:165); "It is We Who have / Placed you with authority / On earth, and provided / You therein with means / For the fulfilment of your life" (7:10); and "Allah has subjected / To your (use) all things / In the heavens and on earth" (31:20).

PERFECTIONISM

Perfectionism—the belief that a dominant group deserves its powers because of some superior qualities—is sometimes found in the Qur'an's grounds for human supremacy: "He has created man: (55:3) / He has taught him speech / (And intelligence)" (55:4). Allah "breathed /Into him something of / His spirit" (32:9).

But for the most part, human dominance is credited to Allah's benevolence rather than to the superior qualities of humans. When some modern writers imply the latter, as in "man—the prize of creation,"[15] or "The life of conviction is man's great distinction from the animal kingdom,"[16] their comments seem to reflect the influence of Western humanism; but see some Sufi perfectionist comments, below. It is "the relationship between Allah and humanity" that has been the focus of Muslim thinkers, so that this religion, "like Christianity and Judaism, has for the most part been manifestly 'theanthropocentric,' to use Karl Barth's somewhat unwieldy term. Iqtidar Zaidi implicitly confirms this when he states that 'we are seeking a religious matrix which maintains man's position as an ecologically dominant being.'"[17]

Although Islam does not confer a divine image on human beings, animals may be denigrated for no particular reason. Nonbelievers are likened to dogs (7:176) or beasts (8:22, 8:55). At 22:31 a bird of prey is a simile for a false teacher; Israelite dietary laws are mocked by a metaphor of rats who will not drink camel's milk but will drink sheep's milk.[18]

While "some animals may be kept to give pleasure,"[19] the Prophet warned that "whoever keeps a (pet) dog which is neither a watch dog nor a hunting dog, will get a daily deduction of two Qirat from his good deeds" (bk. 65, ch. 4, no. 1918).

The Qur'an contains two identical references to apes, used as terms of abuse of human beings, since apes are what Sabbath-breakers will be turned into (2.65 and 7:163–6). Verse 5:60 also refers to persons "transformed into apes and swine," the ape part of which Ali says may reflect the other two references, or may be allegorical.[20] There is a derogatory Tradition in which "those who incited discord will emerge from their graves as monkeys."[21] Baboons are known in Yemen, where they were regarded as agricultural pests and were mostly destroyed by leopards or humans;[22] they thus incurred the denigration applied to all free animals in farming economies.

As with Christian mysticism, to see in perspective the Sufi literature, which sometimes supports animals, it is necessary to acknowledge its aggressive features as well. In contrast with Sufism's unitary side, its doctrine holds that "the love of God for man proves the uniqueness of man in all the world of creation."[23] There is an acceptance of meat eating (except by ascetics) and of hunting, although, as in the Qur'an, neither is mentioned often. Bell explains that the trees of Sidreh and Tuba in Paradise will give you fruit or cooked birds to choice.[24]

In an argument for heredity over environment, applied to a slave who is adopted by a vazir but turns bad, Sa'di (1210–1290) first presents the "nurture" view in lines about the dog in the cave of Ephesus: "And the cave-sleepers' dog sometimes remained / With good men, and the rank of man attained";[25] then refutes it with: "The wolf's whelp will at last a wolf become, / Though from his birth he finds with man a home."[26] More extremely, he writes: "The most glorious of created things, in outward form, is man; and the most vile of living things, is a dog; yet . . . a grateful dog is better than an ungrateful man."[27] Reflecting Muhammad's personal aversion to dogs, this passage's speciesism is little impaired by its second half, which expresses the value of gratitude rather than of dogs.

Shah invokes human supremacy to reject the standard interpretation of *Sufi* as meaning "wool": "Equally important lexicographers, however, stress that 'wool is the garb of animals' and emphasize that the Sufi objective is toward the perfectioning . . . of the human mind, not the emulation of a herd; and that the Sufis, always conscious of symbolism, would never adopt such a name."[28] And he dismisses as false Sufism "a publication in which it is claimed that Sufis prefer a vegetarian diet and that students must be 'free of caste, colour and creed' before developing 'occult powers.'"[29]

Rejecting human-animal identification, El-Misri denies any transmigrational implications in a statement of the Prophet "that man on the Day of Restoration is raised up in the form of one or other animal, corresponding to his leading characteristic." Instead he reads it as meaning that "man . . . may . . . see himself, according to his dominant tendency, as a sheep, a monkey, or a hog."[30] El-Misri may have been concerned to resist Buddhist influence.[31]

Perfectionism becomes literal in the Sufi ideal of the Perfect Man. In a summary of ibn 'Arabi's ideas, Arberry writes: "Just as the Reality of Muhammad was the creative principle of the Universe, so the Perfect Man was the cause of the Universe, being the epiphany of God's desire to be known; for only the Perfect Man knows God, loves God, and is loved by God. For Man alone the world was made."[32]

Recall, from chapter 2, the views of Kabbalah and of Volozhiner, who similarly identify humanity as a cosmological agent.

LOGOCENTRISM

In the Qur'an, the Beast is pitted against the Word on the Last Day (27:8).
Muhammad's "call to mission" consisted of the angel Gabriel's command to him
to "Read!"[33] The word Qur'an "means 'recitation' and is derived from the same
root as the first word [Muhammad] ever heard descending out of heaven."[34]

Aggressive rationalism is found in El-Ghazali's comment "A camel is stronger than a man; an elephant is larger; a lion has greater valour; cattle can eat
more than man; birds are more virile. Man was made for the purpose of
learning."[35]

Chapter 7, however, will discuss Islam's more distinctive logomysticism
and antiwords tendency.

EVASION

Islam's all-powerful God is described as gracious and merciful at the opening
of all but one of the Qur'an's chapters, which can lead to awareness of inconsistency in divine rulings that go against compassion; and, following that
awareness, to evasive compromises.

The sympathetic side of God emerges in improvements of conditions for
animals and assertions of their importance even apart from human use,
while that use itself is unchallenged. Evasion is also found, as in the Bible, in
food imagery, principles of kindness, and evidence of God's concern. The
Thamud story advances kindness to animals as a test of morality in general
as well as of correct belief. Sufism offers examples of animal imagery and of
sympathy, especially for pack animals. For, despite the harsh implications of
divine voluntarism, Islam, like Judaism but unlike the New Testament, contains clear principles of kindness to animals.

Such precepts are found in the Qur'an and Hadith. But evasion was perhaps even more marked in the animal campaigner and vegetarian Imam
Hafiz B. A. al-Masri, who argued for humane slaughter without condemning
meat eating itself.

FOOD IMAGERY

Like the Bible, the Qur'an frequently omits meat when listing good things. It
is not that meat is considered bad, but that images of nonmeat foods might be

considered more appealing. Favorable references to meat do occur, as at 26:133–34, where cattle are mentioned first, 16:5–8, where meat and other uses of animals are listed ahead of vegetable and inorganic gifts (16:10ff, seafood occurring in verse 14, about the sea), and 6:142 (cattle for burden and some for meat). But passages without animals for use are also prominent. The word *fruits* is used as symbol of worldly and spiritual goods—we are not promised "the meat of the Hereafter"! A plea to Moses to ask God for food refers to "what the earth / Groweth—its pot-herbs, and cucumbers, / Its garlic, lentils, and onion" (2:61).

Of several detailed descriptions of the pleasures of the Garden, only two include meat: 52:22 and 56:21. An example of a long meatless account, 76:12–21, lists garments of silk, raised thrones, a climate neither too hot nor too cold, fruit, "vessels of silver and goblets of crystal," "a Cup (Of Wine) mixed / With *Zanjabil*" [ginger], a fountain, "youths / Of perpetual (freshness)" compared to pearls; green silk and brocade garments, silver bracelets, and again wine. The "Parable of the Garden" (47:15) lists water, milk, wine, honey, and fruits.

KINDNESS

The Hadith contain many examples of Muhammad's kindness to animals. General principles are found, for example, in book 71, chapter 10: "(What is said regarding) being merciful to the people and to the animals. . . . No. 2019. The Prophet . . . said, 'If any Muslim plants any plant and a human being or an animal eats of it, he will be rewarded as if he had given that much in charity'"—and in book 41 (The Book of Watering), chapter 5, no. 1094. In the latter, 1. grounds of empathy are offered for giving water to a dog: "The man said, 'This (dog) is suffering from the same problem as that of mine'"; 2. kindness to other species is endorsed as a principle: "The people asked, 'Is there a reward for us in serving (the) animals?' He [Muhammad] replied, 'Yes, there is a reward for serving any animate.'" Masri translates this: "'O Messenger of Allah! Is there reward for us in animals?' He said, 'There is reward in every [creature with a] moist liver' (i.e. in acting kindly towards every living creature)."[36]

There is evasion in the effort to establish slaughter as an ethical practice by making it painless: "Muslims believe that [halal slaughter] is the quickest and least painful. . . . Muslim law forbids slaying an animal in the presence of other creatures, so as not to distress them unduly."[37] Thus kindness to animals includes "respect for their feelings";[38] one is forbidden to sharpen the knife in the animal's presence. Islam, like the Jewish Bible, "recognizes the bonds of motherhood and childhood"[39] through a prophetic condemnation of taking nestlings in the presence of the mother bird, and through "the prohibition of killing a nursing animal."[40] Muhammad said, in regard to a she-camel's first-born:

> The slaughtering of the newborn is allowed, but if you leave it until it becomes young and full of body—until it reaches the age of two or three years—it is better. [If you slaughter the newborn] . . . its meat will be attached to its fur [i.e., you will get very little meat], you will not get much milk, and you will drive your she-camel mad.[41]

A few more of the numerous examples of compassion are "The Prophet forbade beating (animals) on the face" (bk. 65, ch. 12, no. 1927). Allah forgave a prostitute's sins when she watered a thirsty dog (bk. 54, ch. 11, no. 1398), and, as in similar Jewish and Christian cases, religious observances were made flexible to allow the watering of camels:

> Those who observed *Saum* (fast) did not do any work and those who did not observe *Saum* (fast) served the camels and brought the water on them and treated the sick (and wounded). So, the Prophet said, "Today, those who were not observing *Saum* (fast) took (all) the reward.'"(bk. 53, ch. 33, no. 1249)

Kindness to camels is, again, shown as being more important than ritual in another Hadith: "Anas says: 'When we stopped at a halt, we did not say our prayers until we had unburdened the camels.'"[42]

Haykal relates how Muhammad "used to rise and open the door for a cat seeking to enter. He attended with his own hands to a sick rooster and rubbed down his own horse with his own sleeve. When Aishah rode on an obstinate camel and began to pull him hardly, he said to her 'Softly and gently please.'"[43] When a Muslim woman told Muhammad of a vow to sacrifice to God a camel which had brought her home from captivity, "the Prophet answered: 'What a terrible reward you propose to the camel which served you and carried you to freedom! That is clearly an evil act and no vow to perform an evil is valid'."[44] The Hadith contain many ethical limitations on trading practice (bk. 34, pp. 463ff), not all of them favorable to animals, but number 1023 (bk. 34, ch. 34) is: "The seller is not allowed to keep camels, cows, sheep or any other animal unmilked for a long time (so as to get more price by cheating)."

GOD'S CONCERN

We find in the Qur'an 29:60 that Allah looks after all creatures; at 67:19: "None can uphold them [birds in flight] / Except (Allah) Most Gracious: / Truly it is He / That watches over all things." At 11:6 we have: "There is no moving creature / On earth but its sustenance / Dependeth on Allah: He knoweth / The time and place of its / Definite abode." Similarly to Psalm 104:14–15, humans are linked with their animals at 20:54: "Eat (for yourselves) and pasture / Your cattle": 32:27; "Crops, providing food / For their cattle and themselves"; and 25:49: with rain We "slake the thirst / Of things We have created— / Cattle and men in great numbers." In these last three, it can be noted that Muhammad, in portraying animals as companions to human beings, temporarily evades the prospect of eventual slaughter.

If some of the verses quoted seem to celebrate God's power rather than his concern, a less ambiguous illustration is noted by Izzi Dien, quoting a Hadith (which he points out, however, has been described as "weak" by one scholar): "'Had it not been for the elderly worshippers among you, suckling babes, and animals grazing . . . , God would cause his torment to fall on you like boiling liquid."[45] Powerless and vulnerable animals are often mentioned as the reason why God sent rain to townships despite the sins that their inhabitants might commit."[46] Consider, by contrast, the Bible where, as Jeremiah 12:4 complains, the innocent animals *are* included in God's revenge; and contrast also, as noted above, Ghazali's adducing the suffering of innocents as evidence for the aggressive doctrine of theistic subjectivism.

THE THAMUD STORY

The legend of the prophet Salih, which, along with those of other ancient prophets such as Noah, Hud, Lot, Shu'ayb, and Moses, is repeated several times in the Qur'an, is as follows.

> *To the Thamud people*
> *(We sent) Salih, one*
> *Of their own brethren:*

He said: "O my people!
Worship Allah; ye have
No other god but Him.
Now hath come unto you
A clear (Sign) from your Lord!
This she-camel of Allah
Is a Sign unto you:
So leave her to graze
In Allah's earth, and let her
Come to no harm,
Or ye shall be seized
With a grievous punishment. 7:73

The leaders of the arrogant
Party . . . said
To those who were reckoned
Powerless—those among them
Who believed: "Know ye
Indeed that Salih is
A messenger from his Lord?"
They said: "We do indeed
Believe in the revelation
Which hath been sent
Through him." 7:75

The arrogant party said:
"For our part, we reject
What ye believe in." 7:76

Then they hamstrung
The she-camel . . .
. . .
Saying: "O Salih! bring about
Thy threats, if thou art
A messenger (of Allah)!" 7:77

So the earthquake took them
Unawares . . . 7:78

The background to these verses is that the she-camel

> was a Sign or Symbol, . . . used for a warning to the haughty oppressors of the
> poor; (2) there was scarcity of water, and the . . . privileged classes tried to
> prevent the access of the poor or their cattle to the springs, while Salih inter-
> vened on their behalf (26:155, 54:28); . . . (4) this particular she-camel was
> made a test case (54:27).[47]

The animal is a test not only of the specific response of the private land-
holders to her introduction into their pasture, but also of their level of morality, in that to meet the "lower" creature's needs would require greater
compassion. Masri has recognized its significance, writing, "This historic
incident sets forth the essence of the Qur'an's teaching on 'animal rights.'
Cruelty to animals is so offensive to God that it is declared as a serious
sin."[48]

The test is, additionally, one of true belief, as Ali explains, referring to the
prophet Salih, discussed in verse 7:75:

> The godless chiefs . . . put a personal question, as much as to say, "Is he not a
> liar?" The Believers took back the issue to a higher plane, as much as to say,
> "We know he is a man of Allah, but look at the justice for which he is making a
> stand: to resist it is to resist Allah."[49]

SOME SUFI IMAGERY AND PRECEPTS

The Rose-Garden provides many examples of Sufism's animal-related symbolism and injunctions to kindness. Sa'di applies the good shepherd image to
monarchy:

> *Kings are but guardians, who the poor should keep;*
>   *Though this world's goods wait on their diadem.*
> *Not for the shepherd's welfare are the sheep:*
>   *The shepherd rather is for pasturing them.*[50]

The last two lines are evasive of human-animal relations, since the sheep, in
reality, are for human welfare, although not for that of the individual shepherd.

In the renunciation legend of Ibrahim b. Adham, prince of Balkh, which "has often been compared with the story of Gautama the Buddha,"[51] hunting is a symbol of wealth and worldliness, rather than cruelty, and the latter is not mentioned; hence the tale is evasive as regards animals. Nevertheless Foltz sees the story, which was told by al-Qushayri, as an example of Sufi sympathy for them.

> One day, as he was pursuing an antelope, he heard a voice asking him, "O Ibrahim, is it for this that We have created you?" Immediately he got down from his horse, gave his fine clothes to a shepherd in exchange for a wool tunic, and assumed the life of a wandering dervish.[52]

Sa'di includes animals in a story supporting compassion in general: "Shew kindness even to thy foes; / The dog's mouth with a morsel close."[53] Consideration for camels is expressed in a context illustrating the link between ethical and ascetic nonexploitativeness. A darwesh joins a caravan, saying,

> "I ride not on a camel, but am free from load and trammel;
>
> . . .
>
> One who rode on a camel said to him, ". . . turn back, or thou wilt perish. . . ." He did not listen, but entered the desert. . . . fate overtook the rich man and he died. The darwesh . . . said, "I have survived these hardships, and thou hast perished on the back of thy dromedary."[54]

Sympathy is brought out more in the version quoted by Shah: "Neither do I burden a camel / Nor do I carry a camel's burden."[55] Such working animals are often objects of concern: "O thou! who rid'st a mettled courser, see / How toils, mid mire, the poor thorn-loaded ass!"[56] The animal symbolizes a human being in poverty: the "mettled courser," although perhaps equally burdened, does not inspire concern, being identified with a wealthy rider. But, in each case, the explicit description of the animals' suffering makes it clear that they are more than symbols.

We can see the "superior virtue of the oppressed" in Sa'di's praise of kept animals for their patience and lowliness:

> Go, tell for me the pilgrims who offend
>   Their brother men, and cruel would them flay,
> To them none can the pilgrim's name extend;

> *The patient camel earns it more than they,*
> *Who feeds on thorns, nor does his task gainsay.*[57]

The thought of spiritual rewards for animals whose usage was at a high level of necessity must have brought some relief from the human being's sense of conflict.

Besides showing sympathy for beasts of burden, Sa'di describes a drought during which

> *Nor beast, nor bird, nor fish, nor ant was there,*
> *But to the sky arose its cry of pain.*
> *Strange that the smoke-wreaths of the people's prayer*
> *Became not clouds, their streaming tear-drops rain.*[58]

Except for the general acceptance of meat eating in this author, one might read a vegetarian tendency into the following verse, which serves as a concluding metaphor in an "out of the frying pan into the fire" story:

> *I've heard that once a man of high degree*
> *From a wolf's teeth and claws a lamb set free.*
> *That night its throat he severed with a knife.*
> *When thus complained the lamb's departing life,*
> *"Thou from the wolf didst save me then, but now,*
> *Too plainly I perceive the wolf art thou."*[59]

MASRI'S CAUTION

The late imam's reluctance to condemn meat eating outright is curious, especially in view of his own vegetarianism. Masri finds authoritative support for prestunning of animals as an acceptable procedure within halal slaughter,[60] which is evasive in offering kindness while tolerating the harmful act that it is meant to alleviate. The limits of his position on this issue perhaps derived from theological caution, in view of his official status within Sunni Islam, as Walters and Portmess comment:

> Although a vegetarian himself, who elsewhere insists "If only the average simple and God-fearing Muslim consumer of . . . food animals knew of the

gruesome details of [factory farming], they would become vegetarians rather than eat such sacrilegious meat," Masri recognizes that his position runs counter to mainstream Islam, so he struggles to at least convince his fellow religionists to ameliorate obviously wasteful or unnecessary taking of animal life.[61]

ANIMAL TITLES IN THE QUR'AN

The Qur'an's six surahs with animal titles perhaps show, as suggested by az-Zaybaq,[62] the importance of animals in Islam. Of these chapters, only one, s. 105, The Elephant, mentions the animal in the first verse; it is unusual also in being actually a story about the named animal (whose role is, however, a hostile one). Here a sacrilegious power, with an elephant or elephants as part of its army, is defeated by birds sent by Allah. The importance of the story is seen in the fact that Muhammad's birth is dated to that year, 570, the Year of the Elephant.

But although the other five animal title names do not occur in the first verse of their surahs, and occupy a very small proportion of the total verses, the episodes concerning them are linked, with varying degrees of tenuousness, to the themes of the surahs. Bear in mind that, according to Cook, "some catchword appearing in the text" after which a surah is named does not "ha(ve) much to do with content."[63] But their use as literary devices suggests an attraction to the respective images.

DEFENSE

The Qur'an and Hadith prescribe defensive rules and rituals applying to sacrifice, slaughter, and hunting for food, which make clear that although these acts are regarded as necessary, they are likely to produce regret. Thus Ali comments on the verse "Take not life, which Allah / Hath made sacred, except / By way of justice and law" (6:151): "It is not only that human life is sacred but all life is sacred."[64]

SLAUGHTER FOR FOOD

In discussing a rule regarding the time of slaughter, ibn Rushd (Averroes, 1126–98), writes: "Yet, someone may claim that the initial rule for slaughter is (general) prohibition and its permissibility (during the daytime) has been established (as an exemption) through an evidence, in which case those who permitted it during the night have to come up with an evidence."[65] The legal maxim that "necessity justifies committing that which is prohibited"[66] is qualified by "what has been allowed by necessity should be measured by that necessity and nothing more"; thus "what is exceptionally allowed on the grounds of necessity will not be allowed if the necessity ceases to exist."[67] Izzi Dien applies these observations to conservation measures—including negative ones such as hunting an endangered species for "its long-term protection"—which depend strictly on necessity; but, inconsistently, he does not apply it to eating meat.

Because of the need for ritual to sanctify the act, the Qur'an says:

> *Eat not of (meats)*
> *On which Allah's name*
> *Hath not been pronounced:*
> *That would be impiety. (6:121)*

Forward and Alam give a more aggressive slant to this rule: "The man who slits its throat says: *bismillahi, allahu akbar,* 'in the name of God, God is most great.' . . . Killing an animal for food is a devotional act. Pronouncing God's name while killing the creature is a reminder of God's permission and ultimate control over all things."[68] By contrast, Ali describes the *tasmiyah* as "a rite . . . to call our attention to the fact that we do not take life thoughtlessly but solemnly for food, with the permission of Allah, to whom we render the life back."[69] There is some dispute as to whether the rite "is an absolute obligation" or "is an obligation when remembered, but is dropped in the case of forgetfulness" or "is an emphatic *sunna.*"[70] Its status as a principle is nevertheless clear.

When given meat by other people of the desert, "and we do not know whether they have mentioned Allah's name over it," Muhammad advised, "Mention the name of Allah over it (the meat) and then eat it."[71]

The rules of halal slaughter, evasive by virtue of those measures designed to spare the animal suffering, are also defensive because of their ritual application within a sacramental setting, which serves to legitimate a problematic act. Although the words may be pronounced routinely and unthinkingly, they have a sacred origin.

RULES OF SACRIFICE

In "the most sacred place," the Kaaba, "it is forbidden to kill any animal . . . in whatsoever circumstances, even killing (Halal) an animal to eat."[72] Ali clarifies that "actual sacrifice is not performed in the Ka'bah, but at Mina, five or six miles off, where the Pilgrims encamp."[73] Ibn Rushd is conclusive: "The jurists agreed that no one is permitted to slaughter inside the Ka'ba, nor in all-Masjid al-Haram."[74]

To exclude the act of killing from the most sacred places suggests the recognition that it is a negative act—even when undertaken for a sacred purpose! The conflict between sympathy and acts springing from (however irrationally) perceived necessity could not be more evident than in the linkage of doctrines that enjoin or recommend sacrifice to God, with those that try to distance it from him.

Ibn Rushd reports much hairsplitting over whether sacrifice on pilgrimage is obligatory or merely recommended.[75] In the canon,

> ritual sacrifice, such as that customarily performed by Muslims on the occasion of 'Id al-Adha, is not prescribed as a duty in the Qur'an, but a hadith is sometimes cited to provide the sense that it is an obligation:
> "He who can afford (sacrifice) but he does not offer it, he should not come near our places of worship. On the day of sacrifice no-one does a deed more pleasing to Allah than the shedding of blood of a sacrificed animal."[76]

The ritual during the hajj is surrounded with defensive practices.

> . . . then pronounce
> The name of Allah over them
> As they line up (for sacrifice): (22:36)

> Violate not the sanctity
> Of the Symbols of Allah,
> Nor of the Sacred Month,

Nor of the animals brought
For sacrifice, nor the garlands
That mark out such animals. (5:2)

It seems a further sign of defensiveness that "the Prophet ordered me to supervise (slaughtering) of *Budn* [sacrificial animals] and not to give anything of it to the butcher (as wages for slaughtering)" (bk. 26, ch. 66, no. 848).

HUNTING FOR FOOD

Ibn Rushd cites 5:95 of the Qur'an, "Kill no wild game while ye are on the pilgrimage."[77] Jurists "agreed that the person in a state of *ihram*"—a ceremonial condition in which certain prohibitions, not operative at other times, are imposed on the worshipper—"is not permitted to hunt nor to eat what he has hunted."[78] Nor is hunting allowed in the Sacred Precincts (5:1), which "are sanctuary both for man and beast."[79] But there is disagreement, yielding three different opinions, "about whether it is permitted to the *muhrim* to eat game when someone not in the state of *ihram* hunts it."[80] (The *muhrim* is someone on pilgrimage.)

When hunting in permissible circumstances, the name of Allah must be pronounced over the hound, and one must be sure that the game was killed by a hound so authorized; otherwise, according to the Hadith, "you should not eat of it because you have mentioned Allah's Name on (sending) your hound only, but you have not mentioned it on some other hound" (bk. 65, ch. 1, no. 1915).

POLITICAL DEFENSE

Defensiveness is noticeable in Forward and Alam's comments on Islamic attitudes to animals:

> Muslims are not mawkish about such matters. Islam began on the fringes of the desert, where staying alive was the pre-eminent concern of many people, and meat was regarded . . . as a necessity. . . . Most Muslims today live in relatively poor countries, where survival counts for more than middle-class values, which can seem excessively indulgent.[81]

This argument, despite its hostility, acknowledges that killing requires defense (other than theistic justifications, which the authors also use) by an appeal to economic necessity.

A more animal-friendly commentator, Masri, nevertheless feels impelled to defend the practice of sacrifice, here on similar social justice grounds, pointing out that

> Islam also carried on with this practice, but with a difference. It channeled the whole concept of animal sacrifice into an institution of charity. Instead of burning the meat . . . at the altar or letting it rot, Islam ordered it to be distributed either wholly or partly among the poor. Since then Muslims from all over the world sacrifice animals and distribute the meat among the poor in their neighborhoods.[82]

But see chapter 6 for social justice arguments *against* sacrifice and meat eating.

Islam draws upon the doctrine of divine voluntarism to support animal usage and to demand the abandonment of sympathy where necessary to that end. Here the Abraham story acquires an even more fundamental role than that of explaining the origin of animal sacrifice: it demands that the worshipper abandon all personal moral sense in favor of obedience to God. The need for such submission thus gives a particularly Islamic tone to otherwise familiar beliefs in human superiority and the right of dominion. Sufism, which supports animals in some respects, also contains a humanist mystique.

But the compassionate nature of Islam's God, emphasized in the Qur'an, leads to conflict between kindly and detrimental commands. Animals are presented as important in themselves, and their conditions are improved, although they can be used for meat, sacrifice, and work. As in the earlier Abrahamic religions, vegetable food imagery is prominent, and the Prophet is portrayed as caring for animals. In the Thamud narrative, cruelty to an animal stands as the emblem of wickedness and false belief.

Similar imagery and values may be found in Sufism. Recently, alongside writers echoing familiar Qur'anic themes, the more radical Masri is still evasive in advocating improved slaughter methods, but without promoting the vegetarianism that he practiced.

Divinely imposed Islamic rules and rituals express defensive regret over the killing of animals for food and sacrifice, although both are seen as necessary. Qur'anic translator and commentator Ali has been explicit about the sanctity of animal life in such contexts. And here, too, there is political defense.

In this chapter and the two previous, comparisons and contrasts have been noted among three religions with a common source. The subject of chapter 5, Buddhism, comes from a vastly different geographical and cultural background. Its more pro-animal outlook is shared with Hinduism, which it influenced, and Jainism, which influenced it, and is compatible with its non-theistic, predominantly mystical ideology. However, India has hardly been innocent of animal exploitation, so that the same conflict-resolving strategies have emerged in the religion of Gotama as in Judaism, Christianity, and Islam. These and the thinking behind them will be discussed next.

5. Buddhism

IN ITS VALUATION OF ANIMALS BUDDHISM STANDS midway between Hinduism and Jainism, to both of which it is connected by geography, history, and some of its central ideas. It is closer to Jainism, however, in that the two are considered "heterodox schools of Indian thought" because they "reject the authority of the Vedas,"[1] and neither "allow[s] for a creator god; the cycle of life has been present from beginningless time."[2]

The broader heterodoxy was to a great extent fueled by revulsion against the Vedic practice of animal sacrifice—observed by Joseph Campbell as late as 1954–55[3] and even by the late twentieth century still practiced illegally in parts of India.[4] According to Chapple, Hinduism, whose ancient roots and later forms alike otherwise show much of the same ambiguity as Buddhism toward other species, finally abandoned sacrifice in theory, largely under pressure from the other two religions.

> For years, Buddhists and Jainas lobbied against all animal sacrifice, using the argument that such activities violated the first and most important ethical principle: non-violence. They were successful in many respects. Within many later Hindu texts, non-violence is accorded the same respect it is given in Jainism.[5]

Vegetarianism was also gradually adopted "by the Brahman or priestly caste. In the *Rg Veda*, Brahmans and others eat meat; by the time of the classical period, vegetarianism becomes a hallmark or indicator of high-caste status."[6] But, to give credit, mainly Hindu India now has the world's highest rate of religiously inspired vegetarianism.[7] And in the discussion of the Laws of Manu later in this chapter, the reaction against meat eating will be seen to have emerged from within the proto-Hindu tradition as well, rather than being entirely a response to outside pressure.

Although I have characterized the teachings of Gotama[8] on animals as "centrist," they form the most animal-supportive worldview considered in this book. Buddhism, like Hinduism, was modified under pressure from the Jains, and it retains its aggressive side, expressed particularly by the idea of animal birth as the result of sin, or (in the Buddha's argument) lack of moral discrimination, and (following from that) the principle that generosity to animals incurs the least merit, compared with generosity to recipients higher up the karmic scale.[9] The jatakas—tales of the Buddha's earlier lives, which on the whole encourage identification with animals by depicting the future Awakened One as having taken animal form—nevertheless sometimes give approval to meat eating, exclude animals from enlightenment, or reflect the negative aspect of karma.

Evasive attitudes are found particularly with regard to work animals, whose exploitation is not recognized as wrong, perhaps because it seemed more necessary in the Buddha's culture than did meat eating. These animals' servitude is even likened to the rigors of monasticism. We can also see evasion in the second aspect of karma, which enjoins good behavior toward nonhumans by means of the hope that kindness to them, despite their lowly bourn (state of rebirth), will be rewarded: a qualified level of obligation. The jatakas also contain some examples of evasion.

Since Buddhism acknowledges, though it does not always meet, the claims of animals, its methods of dealing with the discrepancy are mostly defensive. The Buddhist defensive strategy's tactics are many, beginning with those ethical ideas that came, literally, from the wish to defend oneself against possible harm from animals: principles of noninjury and friendliness—values that affect relations among humans also.

Another source of defensiveness is the capacity to identify with animals. Because of such feelings, when killing is felt to be necessary, much effort is made to prioritize species so as to do the least harm. Meat eating is allowed on the basis of two state-of-mind defenses and a third, lack of intention, is stressed to excuse the killing of small creatures. Rituals of propitiation persist in modern Buddhist culture, whereas political defensiveness is found particularly vis-à-vis the Jains and other rival creeds, and in the Lankavatara Sutra's response to criticism of Buddhist ascetics who ate meat.

AGGRESSION

BAD KARMA

The most marked aggression is found in the unfavorable aspect of karma, an idea not confined to Buddhism. According to the Laws of Manu, which "codify the Hindu customary law,"[10] "transmigration means that 'people of darkness always become animals.'"[11] Even the Jains believe in "a hierarchy of states ranging from that of the gods (*devas*), humans (*manusya*), hell beings (*naraki*), to plants and animals (*tiryanca*)." [12] As in Buddhism, "the most important state to achieve is that of the human being, as this is the only state in which a living being (*jiva*) can be freed totally from the bondage of action (*karma*)."[13]

The Buddha specifically excludes beings *in an animal bourn* (that is, having been born as animals: my emphasis is meant to call attention to the absence of a fixed species identity) from entry into *nibbana* (Sanskrit *nirvana*: see note 9), since "there is no *dhamma*-faring there, no even-faring, no doing of what is skilled, no doing of what is good. Monks, there is devouring of one another there and feeding on the weak" (*M.iii.169*). So the lack of moral judgment in animals is the substance of his aggressive argument. But in most cases the scriptures give no empirical reasons when animals are placed on a lower level than humans.

The Buddha's wish to place some distance between himself and animals is shown by his consignment of the canine and bovine ascetics to "companionship with" those animals on rebirth, and if such asceticism is accompanied by spiritual pride, to companionship with animals or to Niraya Hell (*M.i.388*).

The five states of rebirth, as outlined in *M.s.12* (Majjhima Nikaya, sutta no. 12), are hell, where one experiences "feelings that are exclusively painful, sharp, severe"; animal birth: "feelings that are painful, sharp, severe"; the realm of the departed: "abundantly painful"; the human realm: "abundantly pleasant"; and heaven: "exclusively pleasant." In the Majjhima Nikaya animals can be reborn as humans, but it takes a depressingly long time. The Buddha uses the famous simile of the blind turtle "who came to the surface once in a hundred years" and might eventually "push his neck through the one hole in the yoke" thrown by a man into the sea, and blown about by the winds, to illustrate the chances of such a progression. Having achieved it, the person is still in a very low family, "ill-favoured . . . deformed or paralysed" or otherwise disadvantaged (*M.iii.169*), and thence may go slowly upwards.

Revealing the moral ambiguity of karma, jataka no. 18 tells of a sacrificial goat who warns the priest that he himself (the goat) was once a priest and, for sacrificing a goat, was condemned to be slaughtered through five hundred lives: now it will be the priest's turn. This seems to neutralize sympathy for the goat, whose slaughter, although wrong, is at the same time seen as a punishment for his earlier cruelty.

Past sins of animals are seldom mentioned in the Pali jatakas. However, in no. 159 we find that the Bodhisatta[14] himself has "[become] a peacock in consequence of some sin; however, golden I became because I had aforetime kept the commandments." (ii.37 (159,25)).[15] In no. 73, one of the many stories of mutual aid between human and animal, the snake and rat (neither of them the Bodhisatta) are said to have bad kamma, hence their form, but no further censure falls on them. In the Jatakamala, too, animal birth is identified with past sins.

HIERARCHY OF MERIT OF GIVING

While generosity is a key Buddhist virtue, the degree of merit attached to giving varies with the recipient according to a formula that contributes to the aggressive strategy by devaluing animals. When you give to an animal "the offering (yields) a hundredfold" (M.iii.255). For an "ordinary person of poor moral habit," the yield is a thousandfold; for an "ordinary person of moral habit," a hundred thousandfold; and so on up to the Tathagata (M.iii.255).[16]

MEAT EATING

Although meat eating is mostly treated defensively in the Pali scriptures, one jataka tale which positively legitimizes the practice is no. 241, in which Devadatta as a jackal king rouses lions to besiege Benares by frightening people with their roaring. The Bodhisatta outwits him, with the result that the elephants kill the jackal and the other animals fight and die.

> There was a heap of carcasses covering the ground. . . .
>
> The Bodhisatta caused proclamation to be made. . . . : ". . . they that desire meat, meat let them take!" The people all ate what meat they could fresh, and the rest they dried and preserved.
>
> It was at this time, according to tradition, that people first began to dry meat. (ii.245 (241,170))

In jataka no. 537, Angulimala, as a man-eating king exiled by his subjects out of fear, is converted by the Bodhisatta, plans to become an ascetic living on the vegan diet, which the jatakas formulaically attribute to ascetics, but is tempted back to his kingdom by the Bodhisatta with (among other things) the mention of the meat he will enjoy there. Afterwards he is "established . . . in the moral law" (xxi.509 (537,278)), but (unlike in some other reformed-king jatakas that refer to the treatment of animals) here only with regard to cannibalism. The same values are found in the Jatakamala version of the story.

EXCLUSION FROM ENLIGHTENMENT

Although karmic fluidity undermines hierarchy, even the more pro-animal jatakas contain the latter. The Bodhisatta as Naga-King (no. 506) wants to become enlightened and so leaves his lavish royal existence to enter the human world:

> *Comes control and cleansing when*
> *One is in the world of men,*
> > *Only there: once man I'll never*
> *See nor birth nor death again.*
>
> (xv.467 (506,289) and similar in stories 524 and 543)

The Pali jataka version of the Nalagiri story[17] is likewise inegalitarian: "The whole body of the elephant constantly thrilled with joy, and had he not been a mere quadruped, he would have entered on the fruition of the First Path" (xxi.336 (533,177)).

The Buddhist attitude toward animals in heaven—not the same as enlightenment, but representative of high spiritual attainment—is inconsistent. "As a rule, no being is born into Paradise in an animal body. But the Buddha does in fact *create* certain animals (notably birds) to dwell within Paradise forever."[18] Page makes the further point that where they are excluded "only animal *bodies* are excluded from this Paradise—not necessarily the animal *beings* (from former lives) themselves."[19] The Animal Judge would point out that, if the bodily form doesn't matter, there seems no reason why an enlightened or blessed mind shouldn't occupy an animal form.

EVASION

ELEPHANT AND MONK

The Buddha uses the domestication of a forest elephant as a simile for the process of monastic discipline, in that the elephant "has this longing . . . for the elephant forest," but human beings, with a combination of force and kindness, pursue the aim of "subduing his forest ways . . . memories and distress . . . by making him pleased with the villages and by accustoming him to human ways" (*M*.iii.132).

The analogy is, of course, false. The difference between elephant and monk is that the latter voluntarily seeks mental freedom through monastic routine, while "a king's elephant is one who endures blows of sword, axe, arrow, hatchet, and the resounding din of drum . . . he is . . . a royal possession" (*M*. iii.133)—neither his starting point nor his destination being one of choice and fulfillment.

The passage thus illustrates a difference in attitude toward kept animals and free animals, the latter being accorded considerable respect. The Buddha himself is symbolically identified with one of the most unambiguously free creatures: the lion, which, by contrast with the Christian lamb, is not domesticated for any economic purpose. We see here again the power of the daily habits of life, including the keeping of beasts such as cattle by ordinary people, plus the luxurious use of elephants and horses by Gotama's upper-class supporters and family, who prized these animals: the wheel-rolling king receives, among other worldly benefits, the Treasure of the Elephant and the Treasure of the Horse (*M*.iii.173–74).

KARMIC REWARD FOR KINDNESS

"The doctrine of non-injury was based on the belief that violence to any living being belonging to the wheel of rebirth had karmic consequences."[20] Even though the unfortunate being, reborn as an animal, has erred in a previous life, if you take advantage it might be your turn in the next life. But this type of motivation is more self-interested than the wholeheartedly empathic facet of karma, which encourages identification with the other being, and which is discussed further in chapter 6. Kindness from fear of retribution is further limited by awareness of karma's aggressive side, with kindness to former sinners being considered worthy but optional: it might be all right to hitch an animal to a treadmill as long as one does not starve or beat him also.

Evasion emphasizes kindness or welfare rather than equal moral status. Thus, although the Jains value noninjury more foundationally than Hinduism or Buddhism, it is "the Jaina community" that controls much of the pharmaceutical industry in India and is undoubtedly required to adhere to safety and testing regulations. The compromise solution . . . combines modern exigency with tradition. Animals are used for testing but then are "rehabilitated" through shelters and recuperation facilities maintained by the laboratories. For instance, one Jaina-controlled pharmaceutical company uses animals for the production of immunoglobulin but then releases them into the wild. This practice fits well with the ages-old Jaina tradition of constructing animal shelters for infirm animals, allowing them to survive until their natural demise.[21]

The Animal Judge finds this very dubious. "If the Jains accept their role on the ground that others would perform it less humanely, that is no different from British vivisectors—who are by no means as kind as the Jains—lamenting that protests will lead to the experiments being done abroad where standards are much lower. One can only ask whether the Jains would test on nonvolunteer humans, so long as the humans were treated well and released after the tests. It also seems unlikely, because of the nature of medical research, that all animals can be rehabilitated or spared extreme suffering."

Because of their usual extreme stringency, this departure by the Jains is surprising, whereas the participation in vivisection of individual Buddhists or Hindus, on various rationalizations, would not be.

EVASION IN THE JATAKAS

The jatakas contain some passages that are evasive by virtue of condemning some act or attitude related to animal abuse, but not the abuse itself. For example, in no. 423 a man goes into the forest to live by killing deer, because (this being the story's main moral criticism) he wishes to avoid work and family responsibility. In no. 30, in a lesson against envy and greed, an ox who envies a pig being fattened for slaughter is admonished:

> Then envy not poor Munika; 'tis death
> He eats. Contented munch your frugal chaff
> —The pledge and guarantee of length of days.
>
>   (i.197 (30,76))

DEFENSE

Since Buddhism rejected animal sacrifice, it lacks this means of sanctifying the consumption of meat. The Aryans, from whom the Brahmin priests came, "enjoyed the meat of sacrificial animals."[22] That such sacrifices played an at least partly defensive role is indicated by the fact that the Laws of Manu "indicate that vegetarianism is part of this concept" (*ahimsa*), while, at the same time, other sections of these laws "seem to sanction flesh-eating under certain circumstances, such as during religious ceremonies involving ritual animal sacrifices."[23] Specifically, the Laws of Manu "contain three separate recommendations: that only 'kosher' meat may be eaten; that only meat obtained through ritual sacrifice may be eaten; and that one should eat no meat."[24] Bryant suggests that Manu's simultaneous tolerance of sacrifice and intolerance of other meat eating is not just a pair of inconsistent, but equally endorsed, beliefs. Manu, he argues,

> is obliged to defer to the sanctity of Vedic injunctions, and thereby is forced to allow the performance of animal sacrifice and the eating of meat in ritualistic contexts. But ... his invectives against meat-eating for the purpose of satisfying the palate suggest that were it not for such scriptural constraints, Manu would have no tolerance for the slaughter of animals. Indeed, he ... undermine[s] normative sacrificial practices by authorizing a substitute ..., and declaring that abstinence from meat produces the same benefit as the ... prestigious horse sacrifice.[25]

If Vedic sacrifices began with "attitudes ... comparable to that in other sacrificial cultures ... that invoked scriptural authority for legitimacy in the matter of the slaughter and consumption of animals,"[26] they soon acquired a dogmatic authority of their own; but conflict such as found in Manu and throughout the literature, reflected in the growth of the *ahimsa* principle, turned around to produce what Bryant refers to as "subversion" both of sacrifice and meat eating. See chapter 6 for Gotama's denunciations of sacrifice.

Buddhism's defensive realm includes ethical doctrines to protect against feared revenge or attack; attempts, through selection of which species to eat, to reduce the harm done by killing for food; state-of-mind defenses that establish the conditions under which monks are allowed to eat meat; and, finally, political defense through accommodation to outside criticism.

LITERAL DEFENSE

Free animals inspire respect as well as fear, both of predators and (where hunting takes place) of revengeful prey. In the Buddha's time, when meat was apparently obtained mainly from kept animals, the fear of revenge could still exist in two ways: through seeing the free animals as in a position to avenge slaughtered kept animals; and through the legacy of *ahimsa*, which "appears to have started, in the Brahmana period, as a way of protecting oneself from the vengeance of injured animals (and plants) in the yonder world, and probably also from the vengeance of their congeners in this very life."[27] Thus, "at the earliest phase of Hindu culture, *ahimsa* is not emphasized. The *Rg Veda* mentions *ahimsa* only in supplication to Indra for protection from violent enemies."[28]

(Kropotkin advanced a similar idea, "that the sense of justice originated in a guilty feeling that animals would revenge harm done to their kin.")[29] Schmithausen identifies another Buddhist value, *metta*,[30] as having a "Vedic background of self-protection, though not so much from revenge than from spontaneous aggression."[31]

In these cases of literal defense, conflict is expressed through fear rather than remorse, a fact that can be explained by the greater respect felt for free animals and also by the greater likelihood of encountering predators in the forest. But fear also requires sufficient empathy to credit the animal with a motive for revenge and to believe in the possibility that one might forestall aggression by communicating friendliness and goodwill.

The retributive aspect of karma, namely, the fear that cruelty to an animal may result in rebirth as one, may be seen as a form of literal defense, with the animal's vengeance shifted to the next life.

HIERARCHY OF WRONGNESS OF KILLING

When choices apparently need to be made, whether in the context of blame attached to killing human beings or of which animals to kill for meat, different formulas have been used to protect the Buddhist against loss of merit.

It may be considered "worse to kill a large animal than a small one, for the former involves a more sustained effort (*Script.* pp. 700–3). . . . To harm a virtuous person, or a respect-worthy one . . . is worse than harming others. Similarly, it is worse to harm a more highly developed form of life."[32] Many conflicts and ambiguities result from this hierarchy. Considering "size, complexity, and sanctity"[33] as factors identified by Ling (as by Harvey), Keown finds only the last straightforward in the sense that "to kill a Buddha would be to destroy not only life, but also the other goods such as knowledge and friendship which he has fulfilled to perfection"[34]—but the later *tathagata-garbha* idea, namely, that potential Buddhahood resides in all beings, seems to undermine this.

Size and complexity are more difficult.

> In terms of size we begin with the mosquito and should logically end with the elephant: instead we find man at the top [in Ling's outline of views on abortion in Theravada Buddhist countries]. . . . And as regards complexity, does it make sense to say that an elephant is more "complex" than a dog?[35]

Since size and complexity do not go together, the variations in one, he points out, would have to exist as a subcategory within the other. Buddhaghosa "confines himself instead to the twin criteria of size and sanctity," further introducing the factors of the assailant's state of mind and degree of effort:

> Taking life in the case of [beings such as] animals and so forth which are without virtue . . . is a minor sin if they are small and a great sin if they are large. Why? Because of the greater effort required. In cases where the effort is identical, the offence may be worse due to greater size.[36]

After specifying the criterion of sanctity, Buddhaghosa distinguishes that "where both bodily size and virtue are the same, it is a minor sin if the wickedness (*kilesa*) involved and the assault itself are moderate, and a great sin if they are extreme."[37] Querying the importance of size in itself, Keown surmises that because of the extra effort required, size "here is only shorthand for the determination on the part of the assailants to do wrong."[38]

Another variation is that, in Northern Buddhist countries where the climate makes vegetarianism seem "impractical," but much distress is felt about killing animals, "in general, large animals are killed for food, in preference to killing many small ones for the same amount of meat."[39]

All these rather tortuous formulas show clearly the regret felt over killing animals and the attempt to console oneself with the thought that at least one has done one's best to limit the damage.

STATE-OF-MIND DEFENSES

IGNORANCE

Monks' responsibility for meat eating is denied by pretending not to know what they are doing, reinforced by the obligation to accept *dana*. Pointing out that monks' food "is of course received in alms," Ruegg summarizes the Vinaya rules:

> a monk must never knowingly eat the flesh of an animal killed for him. But provided that the monk has neither seen . . . nor heard . . . that the meat offered to him comes from an animal butchered for him in particular, and if he also has no reason to suppose that it was . . . the meat (if it is not of a prohibited kind) is considered to be pure in these three respects.[40]

As for the donor, he "may procure 'available' meat . . . without making himself guilty either of intentional . . . killing or of instigating others to kill"[41]—and this meat is all right for monks.

Mahayana[42] Buddhists have argued strongly for vegetarianism, particularly in the Lankavatara Sutra, yet the Mahayana Surangama Sutra—which condemns meat eating—also contains concessions like those in the Pali scriptures. For example, it refers to the "five kinds of pure flesh that may be eaten by a beginner who does not see, hear of, or doubt about the animal having been killed purposely for him to eat, but is certain that it either died naturally or that its flesh had been abandoned by birds of prey."[43]

Harvey, noting that "Buddhist countries lack the mass slaughter-houses of the West" and that meat is more likely to be personally commissioned (which would have been even more likely in the Buddha's time), remarks, "The position that meat is acceptable if someone else kills the animal is not necessarily an easy get-out clause."[44]

"But," argues the Animal Judge, "consider the equivocacy of 'knowing' as against 'not knowing' in this situation. The monk may not know that the animal whose flesh is offered was killed specifically for him, or may definitely know that it was not; and the donor may similarly avoid establishing any direct link between the monk and the act of slaughter. But both donor and monk know that the animal was killed and in the process was caused to suffer, as described in the following passage, which refers to the demerit acquired by the killer in the case of *unallowable* meat":

In that, when he speaks thus: "Go and fetch such and such a living creature," in this way he stores up much demerit. In that, while this living creature is being fetched it experiences pain and distress because of the affliction to its throat—in this second way he stores up much demerit. In that, when he speaks thus: "Go and kill that living creature"—in this third way he stores up much demerit. In that, while this living creature is being killed it experiences pain and distress, in this fourth way he stores up much demerit. In that, if he proffers to a Tathagata or a Tathagata's disciple what is not allowable, in this fifth way he stores up much demerit. (*M.i.371*)

As Kapleau has observed, "Aren't domestic animals slaughtered for whoever eats their meat? If no one ate their flesh, obviously they would not be killed, so how can there be a distinction between 'It was not killed specifically for me' and 'It was killed for me'?"[45] Indeed, procuring such a product specifically for a holy person would only incur additional demerit for the donor if the product were in some way wrong in itself. There is also (as in the hierarchy of merit for generosity) conflict with the doctrine of *anatta* (insubstantiality; the person as a temporary set of conditions) in this moral separation of one prospective recipient and another.

As far as *dana* is concerned, there is an easy way out of the problem: just let it be known to supporters that meat is not welcome. Some British Theravadins today do this by specifying vegetarian food in lists of requisites pinned up in monasteries, a measure that reflects their surrounding culture and personal background. That the earliest Buddhists, who evidently had close contact with laypeople, were not able to convey a simple prohibition on meat (at least as *dana* for monks), but were able to convey the devious terms of its permissibility, creates a suspicion that the monks were, for whatever reason, not willing to give it up, uneasy though they were about it.

The resulting hypocrisy was noted by Ethel Mannin, writing in 1961, "that the Hindu and Buddhist 'reverence for life' often manifests itself in a refusal to kill animals, but at the same time readily accepts the products of other people's killings."[46]

ATTITUDE

The Jivakasutta's allowability rule—the same as that quoted above by Ruegg from other scriptures—is followed by a dialogue describing the desirable attitude of the monk who has accepted meat from a lay supporter:

"He dwells having suffused the whole world with a mind of friendliness. . . . A householder . . . invites him to a meal. . . . It does not occur to him: 'Indeed it is good that a householder . . . waits on me with sumptuous almsfood . . . ' . . . . He makes use of that almsfood without being ensnared, entranced or enthralled by it, but seeing the peril in it, wise as to the escape. . . . Is that monk . . . striving for the hurt of self, or is he striving for the hurt of others or is he striving for the hurt of both?"

"Not this, revered sir."

"Is not that monk at that time, Jivaka, eating food that is blameless?" (*M.*i.369)

This implies that you can do something morally questionable as long as you have a pleasant attitude toward it. The same defense is echoed in a jataka tale, which even applies it to cannibalism:

"The wicked kills, and cooks, and gives to eat:
He is defiled with sin that takes such meat."
[263] On hearing this, the Bodhisatta recited the second stanza:
"The wicked may for gift slay wife or son,
    Yet, if the holy eat, no sin is done."
(ii.262–3 (246, 182))[47]

The villain in this particular story is Nathaputta the Jain, who as a wealthy man in a previous life deliberately serves the ascetic Bodhisatta fish and then denounces him as in the first stanza. You can surmise that omnivorous Buddhists were a bit sensitive to the Jains' disapproval.

While Buddhist vegetarianism has grown in the West, the "good attitude" argument is found among some meat-eating Western Buddhists today. "Kjolhede warns against vegetarianism as a kind of attachment";[48] "I am vegetarian most of the time. If I feel I need to eat fish or fowl (occasionally), I do so with great gratitude and mindfulness of the life that supports my own."[49]

To the dismay of many Buddhist vegetarians, the Dalai Lama did not stick to the practice, which he adopted in 1965 on being moved by the suffering of a chicken being slaughtered for his lunch. He abandoned vegetarianism "on medical advice," having "become severely jaundiced."[50] Although he still believes "that a meatless diet is one of the practical corollaries of Buddhism's pity for all sentient beings," he too has used the "good attitude" argument:

I am thinking here of some Tibetan butchers. Although they make their livelihood as butchers, at the same time they show kindness and love toward the
animals. Before the slaughter, they give the animal some pills, and after they
finish, they say a prayer. Although it is still killing, I think it is better with that
kind of feeling.[51]

In this emphasis on spiritual merit Buddhism is not so far from Hinduism. Even Gandhi, despite his own vegetarianism and ethical arguments,
wrote:

Though the question of diet is very important for a religious man, yet it is not
the be-all and end-all of religion or non-violence; nor is it the most vital factor. The observance of religion and non-violence has more to do with the
heart. He who does not feel the necessity of abstaining from meat for inner
purification need not abstain from it.[52]

NONINTENTION

Closely connected to ignorance, nonintention becomes a defense of killing
small creatures and may have been stressed by Buddhism to make life tena-
ble for people striving for perfection, the problem being where to draw the
line. For the Jains, "all . . . strict vegetarians,"[53] "nonintention" excuses a nar-
rower range of activities than it does for Buddhists.

"There might be a Jain here who is controlled by the control of the fourfold
watch: he is wholly restrained in regard to water; he is bent on warding off all
evil; he has shaken off all evil; he is permeated with the (warding off) of all
evil—but, while going out or returning he brings many small creatures to destruction. What result, householder, does Nataputta the Jain lay down for
him?"
". . . being unintentional, there is no great blame'" (*M.i.377*).

"It should be acknowledged" comments the Animal Judge "that the Jain's
good intentions in a case where he is causing harm are still consequentially
valuable; because his drawing the line of tolerable harms so close to the
limits of survival, thus requiring a much higher threshold of necessity to
excuse animal injury, means that he will endure more inconvenience and
do less harm than the Buddhist who draws the line further in from those
limits."

Sutta 56 of the *Majjhima Nikaya*, the attack on the Jains, is an argument about intention, in which Upali claims that "wrong of body" is worse than "wrong of mind," and the Buddha the reverse, his point being made with reference to unintentionally harming small creatures, as above. Nevertheless, consequences are important in Buddhism:

> If you . . . should find, "That deed which I am desirous of doing . . . would conduce to the harm of self and to the harm of others and to the harm of both; this deed of body is unskilled, its yield is anguish, its result is anguish"—a deed of body like this, Rahula, is certainly not to be done by you. [416] But if you . . . should find, "That deed . . . would conduce neither to the harm of self nor to the harm of others nor to the harm of both; this deed of body is skilled, its yield is happy, its result is happy"—a deed of body like this, Rahula, may be done by you. (*M.*i.415–16; and the same for deeds of speech and mind)

DEFENSIVE RITUALS

In Mahayana Tibet and Mongolia, where "the harsh, cold climate . . . has meant that most people . . . eat meat . . . those *Lamas* who eat meat . . . may perform a ceremony to help the dead animal gain a good rebirth."[54] The sincerity of such actions is seen by the fact that in Tibet "hunting for sport is considered immoral, and Tibetans who move to more fertile lands, such as America, may become vegetarian."[55] In modern Japan "animal experimenters will on occasion meet ceremonially to offer thanks to the animals they have sacrificed in pursuit of their biomedical goals."[56] In the same spirit,

> Buddhist monks sometimes carry out memorial rites for the whales killed by Japanese whalers. Kapleau reports one such in 1979 put on by a Zen temple, and with government officials and executives of a large whaling company in the audience. . . . Unfortunately, the service did not seem to contain any discouragement of whaling, but was more like a way to salve people's consciences. . . . The rite seems similar to the popular mizuko kuyo rites for aborted foetuses.[57]

"The different degrees of necessity facing the Tibetan meat eater and the Japanese whaler are obvious," observes the Animal Judge. "Still, there is hope in the fact that the whaling executives at least possessed consciences to salve."

POLITICAL DEFENSE

Criticism and the claims of rivals contributed to a policy of avoiding the de-struction of small animals. The Sangha's responsiveness to lay opinion is shown by the pro-*ahimsa* adoption of the rains retreat after

> people were annoyed and complained angrily: "How is it that these ascet-ics ... keep on travelling during the summer, winter and also in the rainy season? They tread on young plants and damage them, and destroy many small living creatures. *Those who belong to other schools* may not be very well-disciplined, but at least they withdraw somewhere to make a residence for the rainy season."[58]

Defensiveness is further reflected in the hostility shown in the Majjhima Nikaya toward Jainism, which "in the Buddhist texts ... comes out, with the Brahmins, as the chief rival to Buddhism."[59] If as Berry contends, "In all likeli-hood, the Buddha was himself a Jain, and his teachings were a stripped down version of Jainism designed for the export market,"[60] once he had formed his own system, a negative reaction set in. There is great antagonism, for example, in *M.* sutta 56. Here and in sutta 35, a Jain sets himself up for defeat by brag-ging about how he is going to refute Gotama. In sutta 56 Nataputta is made to speak angrily and coarsely to Upali, saying "You, householder, are out of your mind; you, householder, are idiotic" (*M.*i.383), and at the end is portrayed as a foiled villain: "But because Nataputta the Jain could not bear the eulogy of the Lord, then and there hot blood issued from his mouth." (*M.*i.387) Throughout *M.* sutta 101 the Buddha refers to the Jains' views as "contemptible."

In its rivalry with the Jains, Buddhism may have benefited from the for-mer's more stringent and demanding observance of the non-injury principle. Schmithausen notes

> the tendency of Buddhism to keep life *practicable*. This tendency is in tune with the principle of the Middle Way.... For Buddhist *monks*, non-injury is not as strict as for Jaina monks.... As for *lay* people, their life is kept practi-cable by confining non-injury, by and large, to *animals*, whereas plants may be utilized more or less freely.[61]

The response to censure continues in later Buddhism. Suzuki explains at the start of the Lankavatara Sutra's chapter on meat eating: "This chapter ...

is another later addition to the text. . . . It is quite likely that meat-eating was practised more or less among the earlier Buddhists, which was made a subject of severe criticism by their opponents . . . hence this addition in which an apologetic tone is noticeable."[62] Here the political reaction contributed to the effective-defensive policy of advocating vegetarianism. The following is one argument advanced by the Buddha in this chapter:

> There are some in the world who speak ill of the teaching of the Buddha [they would say,] "Why are those who are living the life of a Sramana or a Brahmin reject such food as was enjoyed by the ancient Rishis, and like the carnivorous animals . . . ? Why do they go wandering about in the world thoroughly terrifying living beings . . . ? . . . [248] let the Bodhisattva whose nature is full of pity and who is desirous of avoiding censure on the teachings of the Buddha refrain from eating meat.[63]

As a primarily mystical worldview (that is, an account that promotes the experiential dimension of religion and the oneness of reality), Buddhism is favorable to animals but also contains aggressive features: most importantly, the belief in animal birth as a result of past sins or, as expressed more empirically, as lacking in the capacity for moral discrimination. Because of this, good behavior toward animals is considered less meritorious than that toward human beings. Jataka tales, despite sometimes portraying the Buddha as an animal in a previous life, can echo these negative ideas and even give explicit approval to meat eating.

Buddhist evasion is found in the case of animals used for work, a usage that, unlike killing for food, was not regarded as wrong; one text draws an analogy between their subjugation and monastic discipline. The doctrine of karma contains, besides its aggressive and defensive potential, the warning that although animal birth attracts a lower level of obligation, to mistreat animals will bring bad karma on the offender. This principle still leaves many dubious options open to human beings. Some examples of indirect (as distinct from the more usual direct) disapproval of animal abuse are also found in the jatakas.

Buddhism has various defensive means for confronting its culture's violations of *ahimsa*. Noninjury itself, as well as the principle of *metta*, has been interpreted as emerging from a literal defense against possibly vengeful or predatory animals. Killing that is regarded as necessary is subject to a hierarchy of wrongness depending (varyingly and inconsistently) on size or complexity of species. Monks are provided with two excuses, related to their state of mind, for meat eating and are (more straightforwardly) absolved of guilt over the unintentional killing of small creatures. We also find rites of propitiation in present-day Buddhist societies and political defensiveness at both early and contemporary stages.

Having reviewed the means used by the four worldviews for dealing with conflict over animal exploitation, we can now turn to the forces both ancient and more especially modern that have impelled believers toward the more radical step of abandoning such exploitation. All these forces have emerged in various ways from the fact and principle of change, and I've called them in sum the effective-defensive strategy.

6. Change and the Effective-Defensive Strategy

THE PARAMOUNT CHANGE DISCUSSED HERE IS THE movement of all the traditions toward support for animal rights. Such support existed in ancient times in pre-Socratic Greece, in vegetarian Jewish groups, and in early Christianity, and has been theoretically present all along in Eastern religion. So the movement being traced is uneven and interrupted, but culminates in a worldwide trend that can be observed today.

Other aspects of change have contributed to the historical one. The right of reinterpretation of scripture, already present in Judaism, Christianity, and Islam, has been freshly invoked on behalf of animals, and Buddhist texts unfavorable to other species have been reread. I examine the types of argument and the religious principles offered on behalf of animal rights to combat adverse traditions or to reinforce existing favorable ones.

Even as conventionally understood, the texts contain dynamic accounts of reality. The responsive and active God encountered in Judaism and Christianity, Sufi relativism plus mainstream Islam's acknowledgment of historical change, and Buddhism's doctrine of impermanence have, in different ways, upheld a growing identification with animals by undermining the notion of eternal difference or inevitable relationships.

When considering worldly events rather than metaphysics, vegetarians have argued that because of changed conditions (e.g., factory farming, environmental degradation, and the readier availability of vegetable foods), the God of the ancient scriptures would not permit today what he (only reluctantly, it is claimed) permitted then. In another move, the East-West interchange resulting from progress in communications and transport, different cultures have appealed to one another's values to support consideration for animals.

So, over time, the effective-defensive strategy has emerged in the different faiths, its tactics consisting both of broad ethical doctrines and of direct arguments for the practical measures advocated.

CHANGE

REINTERPRETATION

"The fact that religious beliefs do not lend themselves to any kind of clear and final comprehension allows their learning, teaching, exegesis, and circumstantial application to go on forever."[1] Atran's investigations revealed how different members of conservative Christian groups would interpret the most basic religious phrases in such varying ways as to render them unrecognizable.[2]

This observation is well illustrated by the spirit of the Talmud, which

> is open-ended and invites you to join in its discussion. The main trait of the Talmud is its argumentative character, its argument, back and forth. Once you have not only a proposition but the reason for it, then you may evaluate the reason, criticize it, or produce a contrary proposition based on a better reason and argument.[3]

Of the midrashim, or interpretations of practical and philosophical issues within Judaism, Cohen explains: "The Hebrew verb . . . for 'to seek,' *darash*, [means] 'to deduce, interpret' the ideas which profound study of the text could elucidate. . . . By its aid a Scriptural passage yielded far more than could be discerned on the surface."[4]

Within Islam, Ahmed offers an argument that leaves the interpretive door wide open:

> There is a Hadith to the following effect:
> If during the process of living your life on this earth, you come across a situation whereby your action gives/produces a doubt in you i.e. you find something of contradiction as a Muslim . . . you are implored to follow the course which is better and beneficial to everybody concerned.[5]

Daniel links independent judgment to theism, appealing to "our God-given sense of reason."[6]

Traditional Islamic law provides leeway through the principle of *ijtihad*, or "rational interpretation" as applied "to the divine revelation in order to meet the needs and conditions of the present age."[7] But, when addressing animal rights, "Islamic jurists . . . typically do little more than rehearse the positions of their ancient predecessors."[8] Masri is an exception, as will be discussed later in this chapter.

At the same time, alongside scripture-bound readings, Izzi Dien notes cautiously: "there seems to be an inclination among contemporary Muslims towards experiential interpretation, which represents a new tendency distinct from the previous traditional dependency on the text. . . . It is only the future that will determine whether . . . these new developments will be of value or will lead to cultural and social upheaval."[9]

TYPES OF REINTERPRETATION

Akers has analyzed ways of "evad[ing] the literal meaning of the Old Testament." He lists "making an unwelcome text an allegory," "putting the unwelcome commands lower in priority," "explain[ing] unpleasant commandments as divine concessions to human weakness," and "denounc[ing] the text as . . . a false text, not properly part of the scripture at all."[10]

Another frequently used method is challenging the translation of the scriptural language. Jewish and Christian animal supporters have examined the Bible's translations for egalitarian implications or, alternately, for humanist bias. Regenstein finds evidence of a belief in the souls of animals:

> In most modern versions of the Bible "nephesh," the Hebrew word for the "soul," has been mistranslated and its meaning changed. The Hebrew words for "soul" (nephesh) and "living soul" (nephesh chayah) are mentioned on several occasions in Genesis, and when they refer to humans, they are translated properly. . . .
>
> But in nine other passages in Genesis, where the identical Hebrew words are used in reference to animals, the word "soul" is *not* used as the translation in many Bibles.[11]

(See chapter 2, however, for more aggressive readings of the various related Hebrew words in the Bible.) Regenstein's claim is the equivalent of Masri's, that the Qur'an has been mistranslated so as to deny souls to animals:

> The Arabic word for "breathing beings" is "Nafs." Until recently it used to be taken as meaning "human beings" only. All the Arabic dictionaries give the meaning of "Nafs" as "Ruh" (soul), and since they are breathing creatures,

there seems to be no reason why the Qur'anic verses No. 6:151, 152 and others should not comprehend all "breathing beings", i.e. all species of animals.[12]

Masri points out that the Prophet used the word *Nafs* in the verse "And kill not a 'Nafs,' which Allah has made sacrosanct— / except for a justifiable reason" (6:151; 17:33).[13]

In Indian religion, as far back as the post-Vedic period, with the emergence of nonviolent values, "many orthodox Brahmanas . . . devise[d] strategies of subversion or reinterpretation of the ancient sacrificial injunctions, despite being constrained by the very nature of orthodoxy to stop short of explicitly rejecting Vedic authority altogether."[14] In the Mahabharata's picture of a nonslaughtering golden age from which human morality declined, "we see the beginning of a rewriting of the old Vedic script concerning the legitimacy of sacrifice," in which the Vedic rules "are not ostensibly rejected, but . . . demoted to a later, more degraded period of human history."[15]

These moves pointed to the total rejection of sacrifice by the Jains and Buddhists. But the continued acceptance of meat eating in Buddhism has led to reinterpretation of its "allowability of meat" texts, through challenging either their words or their provenance. Page uses the passage quoted in chapter 5, describing the benevolent state of mind of a meat-eating monk, to support the claim—based on a different possible translation of the "allowability" rules—that in fact the *intentional* consumption of meat must *not have been* allowed:

> Surely the idea is merely that meat is not to be eaten if it is seen, heard from others or suspected by oneself *to be meat*! If, however, one accidentally were to eat a meal which—without one's knowing it—contained meat, no unwholesome . . . deed would have been committed. After all, there are certain plants which look like meat . . . and food-preparations which disguise the appearance of actual meat.[16]

Kapleau accepts the conventional translation of the allowability passage, but claims that "monks and scribes still attached to meat eating put them [the words about the animal being killed especially for a recipient monk] there."[17] In support, he alludes to the doubtful authenticity of the Buddhist canon, which, "Mr and Mrs Rhys Davids assure us, is no different from any of the other ancient religious literatures of the world in that it developed gradually to become 'a mosaic of earlier and later material'" (40), and recalls Conze's observation "that the Buddha spoke not Pali but a dialect called Magadhi, and that all his sayings, like those of Jesus, are lost in their original form" (41). We cannot know what he said, but can ask, "Was the Buddha so obtuse that he failed to understand" that the meat eater is "contributing to the violent deaths of harmless animals?" (31).

DYNAMIC ONTOLOGIES

CAN GOD CHANGE?

The Jewish-Christian-Islamic narrative embodies change: from a lost Golden Age, through human history and the appearance of prophets, toward the hope and varied means of achieving eventual perfection. It might seem that the God in charge of all this, in order to change, destroy and replace created things, *must* change in the course of accompanying them through time, as implied in the rabbinical assertion that "the processes of Nature represent the unceasing functioning of the divine creative power (Mech. to xviii. 12; 59*a*)."[18]

This is the "endless-duration" interpretation of timelessness, to which Brian Davies, in the course of criticizing process theology, objects: "whether it makes any sense to suppose that God could have eternity in this sense is another matter."[19] Process thinking actually portrays God as "dependent on the world just as the world is dependent on God. In fact, God develops through experiencing the world, sharing in our achievements as well as our sufferings."[20]

Such views are echoed by the familiar animal-supportive account of a God who at one point enjoins vegetarianism, then makes concessions to human sinfulness, but (as is predicted) withdraws them at a future date.

The "temporary-concession" view was advanced as early as Clement, whose third-century *Recognitions* suggest "that we could accept the texts about animal sacrifice but deny that God wants us to sacrifice animals *now*."[21] Isaiah 11 shows that, in early Hebrew belief, "the world would one day be restored according to God's original will for all creation."[22] Such a view can be reconciled with the Christian theme of redemption, upon the universal achievement of which "there will be no more death or mourning or crying or pain, for the old order of things has passed away" (Rev. 21:4).

Modern theists who are inclined to support animals and/or the environment are thus modifying the concept of God to suit their moral preferences. This is not as cynical a claim as it seems, for the question can be asked: why does this happen?

DUCK OR RABBIT?

In (1) the projectionist view (the duck version), human beings construct God, then change their values and reconstruct God accordingly. In (2) the believer's view (the rabbit version), either (a) God changes (in nature or in policy) or (b) God causes humans to change both themselves and their understanding of God.

I have employed the first approach. But the second view—namely, that what changes is not our idea of God, but actually God or our own values as a result of God's actions—could just as well accommodate the cultural-ideological facts.

View (2a), God changing, is expressed by Linzey in the aspect of suffering: "if it is possible for God in Christ to enter into the suffering of the world, and yet transform that suffering into joy, why should this capacity be limited in time and space to one event only? . . . what is seen in Christ is one instance of the perpetual transformation of suffering happening throughout time";[23] and in the aspect of God's changing policies: "Under the dispensation of the Old Covenant it was clear that God allowed humans rights to use creation. . . . But it is not at all clear, as defined under the New Covenant, that humans have these same rights."[24]

In the (2b) view, it is purely a case of God changing human beings:

> God alone remains in absolute repose; and His perfect unmovability places him outside space and time. If one attributes movement to Him in His rela-
> tionship to created being, it is meant that He produces in creatures the love
> which makes them tend toward Himself, that He draws them to Him.[25]

The skeptic would say that God will survive the most fundamental changes as long as believers want to continue using, and redefining, the word; the believer could counter that this will happen as long as God (by any definition that allows a purposeful consciousness) wants it to.

EVOLVING ISLAM

The conservative view of Islam is of an unchanging creed, because "fundamental human nature remains unchanged,"[26] a view modified by the statement "Neither is everything permanent, nor is everything changeable. The fundamental principles . . . do not invite change. It is the outward forms which change." In Sufism, also, the teachings "belong to their own time. The

Sufi message in written form is regarded as being of limited effectiveness . . . because 'that which is introduced into the domain of Time will fall victim to the ravages of Time.'"[27]

Rafeeque Ahmed describes Islam as "a dynamic and not static way of life,"[28] although his values are still derived from the Qur'an. The Islamic tradition of kindness co-opted by new developments, including the existence of the animal rights movement, is exemplified by Bina Ahmed, an American lawyer for PETA, who explained at a demonstration against live exports that "she has begun receiving phone calls from Muslim men and women 'who are introspective and looking at their place in the world. . . . Muslims are advocating for their own rights, and so that calls into question Muslims being compassionate toward other living things as well, advocating for others as well as self.'"[29]

Far removed from PETA, the venerable Al-Azhar Seminary, the opinions of whose jurists "come closest to constituting a normative voice for Sunni Muslims,"[30] has ruled that stunning animals before slaughter is acceptable and has "hosted an important conference on animal rights—apparently the first recognized Islamic institution in the world to do so."[31]

BUDDHISM'S THREE MARKS OF EXISTENCE

Of the three facts on which the Buddhist analysis and search for enlightenment are built, the second and third—suffering or unsatisfactoriness (*dukkha*), and nonsubstantiality (*anatta*)—emanate from the first, impermanence (*anicca*). This is because, as regards *dukkha*, all pleasant things pass away, as does life itself, and people consequently feel restlessness and anxiety even when things are going well: while, as regards *anicca*, if compounded things (such as a person) consist of perpetually changing bits and pieces, they can have no fixed identity. Skilton explains it thus:

> [The Buddha] taught that things neither exist permanently, nor have absolutely no existence. Like the leaf, where a red leaf arises in dependence upon a green leaf, neither entirely different from its cause, nor wholly the same, so all other conditioned things arise in dependence upon other factors, neither entirely different nor wholly the same.[32]

All these three core principles can be accepted more easily by persons who do not feel impelled to separate themselves from animals, since the acknowledgment of impermanence threatens the fixed human state. The importance of suffering reflects identification with sentient rather than solely with intellectual beings. And the lack of essential identity, again, undermines human supremacy. Keown notes that *anatta* implies a rejection of "personhood," which concept is seen as a "narrowing of the moral universe," leading to "the exclusion of not just some human beings but the animal kingdom as well."[33]

The doctrine of no-*fixed*-self (often misunderstood as no-self-at-all) acquires a narrative dimension in the myth of karmic rebirth, with its varied implications for animals.

Jainism expresses its reverence for life through a similar doctrine of impermanent identity; Hinduism believes in cross-species rebirth, though of a fixed soul. Nevertheless, alongside these dynamic accounts there are in Buddhism, Hinduism, and Jainism alike various ultimate goals (nirvana, freedom from karma and from rebirth) and unchanging substrata (the uncompounded or Brahman in Hinduism). A further complexity is offered by the Mahayana view "that *samsara* is none other than *nirvana*."[34]

ARGUMENTS FROM CHANGED CONDITIONS

The authors of these accounts first try to explain why God permitted harmful acts in the past, without intending them to continue forever; and then insist that in the light of current conditions God would now certainly proscribe such acts. Here the "concession to human weakness" argument is prominent. R. Abraham I. Kook (1865–1935), one of the most frequently cited animal supporters of the modern era,

> believes that the permission to eat meat was only a temporary concession; he feels that a God who is merciful to his creatures would not institute an everlasting law permitting the killing of animals for food. He states:
> "It is inconceivable that the Creator who had planned a world of harmony and a perfect way for man to live should, many thousands of years later, find that this plan was wrong."[35]

For some theorists, the destruction of the Temple, and the resulting abandonment of blood sacrifice, legitimized vegetarianism (however fortuitously). At Passover, "The eating of the Paschal lamb is no longer required now that the Temple has been destroyed. One is required to commemorate this act, not to participate in it."[36]

As with meat eating, some thinkers have sought to deny even the original validity of animal sacrifice, seeing that practice also as a temporary compromise. R. Isaac Abarbanel (1437–1509)

> cites a *Midrash* that indicated that the Jews had become accustomed to sacrifices in Egypt. To wean them from these idolatrous practices, God tolerated the sacrifices but commanded that they be offered in one central sanctuary. . . .
>
> Rabbi J. H. Hertz states that had Moses not instituted sacrifices, which were the universal expression of religious homage, his mission would have failed, and Judaism would have disappeared. With the destruction of the Temple, the rabbis state that prayer and good deeds took the place of sacrifice.[37]

Maimonides took a similar view, which "was bitterly criticized for seeming to relegate the whole sacrificial system, the sphere of the holy in ancient Judaism, to the mundane level of an educational policy."[38]

The chief justification for animal sacrifice, the story of Abraham, is queried by Ahmed, who claims that the patriarch "misunderstood" God's command. "God never asked Abraham to sacrifice his son. What he asked for was the dearest thing to him. The question arises is why Abraham chose his son instead of his own life?"[39] He sees the solution in God's wish to abolish the custom of sacrificing first-born children. Abraham "did the original service to humankind by abolishing the human sacrifice to God. But God's Creation does not stop there, evolving further."[40]

The cruelty of factory farming has provided one of the strongest present-day arguments for vegetarianism in all the worldviews. By itself, it is an evasive argument since it sidesteps the question of killing animals, but because it is used to challenge all meat eating it counts as "effective defense." The evasion is clear in Schwartz's attempt to reconcile vegetarianism with an otherwise nonsupportive rabbinical pronouncement:

> The pre-eminent 18th-century rabbinic authority, R. Ezekiel Landau asserted that the mere killing of an animal for food does not violate the prohibition against *tsa'ar ba'alei chayim*; this prohibition is only applicable "if he causes (the animal) pain while alive." In view of the horrible conditions under which animals are raised today, it would be difficult to argue that this biblical prohibition is not being severely violated.[41]

Christian vegetarians argue from these same evils, which "demand Jeremiah-level condemnation."[42]

For Ahmed, also, lack of necessity plus the cruelty of present-day meat production mean that God would not permit now what he permitted in the seventh century.[43] The argument for consistency with Islamic values joins the evolutionary case in Tappan's observation: "In contrast with the Qur'anic approval of animal and flesh use, we have also seen powerful Islamic admonitions to kindness for animals. Activists should ask Muslims how the two strands reconcile in today's world of meat production and consumption."[44]

But the view that what was formerly acceptable to God is not acceptable now, because of factory farming and lack of need, raises a distinct problem of evil. If God had always intended to abolish meat eating, one could hardly hypothesize that he (I use "he" to conform to scriptural usage) introduced the cruel modern practices to provide a case for vegetarianism—although he might have ended the need for meat eating in order to do so. But why did he permit the consumption of animal flesh, and even cause it to be sometimes necessary, in the first place? Why did he permit predation by any species against any other?

Implicit in the "temporary-concession" picture offered by theistic vegetarians is the traditional answer of free will, with God having allowed both the ancient and modern practices, or moral evil, because people were and are not yet capable of abandoning them.

As regards geographical need (i.e., natural evil), which affected humans in the past and still affects predatory animals, and cannot be explained in terms of free will, the problem remains. Young, who also endorses the temporary-concession view,[45] reflects, "We do not understand why God has made or allowed the world to be as it is, with its predation, suffering, and death. . . . However, in the end we must let God be God and not impose our conceptions and agendas upon the God of creation."[46]

But this "mysterious-ways" response avoids the problem, except insofar as it offers the authoritarian view that whatever God does is by definition right: unsatisfactory from an ethical standpoint.

Apart from "free-will" or "mysterious ways" explanations, some solutions to the problem of evil rely upon the concept of the "greater good," of which Swinburne's theory is an example. According to Swinburne,[47] the all-benevolent, omnipotent God allows both types of evil—in the present context, the human capacity to kill and eat animals (natural evil), as well as the decision to do so, plus factory farming (moral evil)—when they are outweighed by certain goods that they entail and there is no other way to secure those goods.

For example,

> a particular natural evil such as pain makes possible felt compassion—one's sorrow, concern, and desire to help the sufferer. . . . But of course, the objector will say, even if pain is better for the response of compassion, better still that there be no pain at all. . . . But I suggest that a world with some pain and some compassion is at least as good as a world with no pain. (161)

Moreover, animals gain knowledge, and the opportunity to display courage, from the painful experience of other animals. "If deer are to learn how to help prevent their offspring from being caught in fires, some fawns have to be caught in fires for the deer to see what happens." Without such catastrophes, "animals will be deprived of the possibility of serious and heroic actions" (190).

As regards moral evil, he writes of the slave trade:

> But God allowing this to occur made possible innumerable opportunities for very large numbers of people to contribute or not to contribute to the development of this culture; for slavers to choose to enslave or not; for plantation-owners to choose to buy slaves or not and to treat them well or ill; for ordinary white people and politicians to campaign for its abolition or not to bother, . . . and so on. (245)

As an analogy, we might consider that awareness of the horrors of factory farming promotes, and in many cases actually leads to, the choice of vegetarianism.

In evaluating this picture, we could try the utilitarian exercise of weighing the number of animals saved in future (N1) as a result of people gradually becoming vegetarian, against the number of animals killed in the past (N2). The number saved from death in future must be positively weighted by the suffering they would also be spared, but negatively weighted by the fact that most would not be born anyway as they would not be bred for meat. The number killed in the past must be positively weighted by the suffering caused by factory farming as well as by traditional animal farming and slaughter.

But even if N1 should outweigh N2, the objection to this theodicy is that it has God sacrificing some beings for the sake of others, an unjust procedure where the sacrifice, unlike that of Jesus, is involuntary. The same objection applies to the argument that natural evil leads to compassion and to knowl-edge on the part of those who have not suffered the evil themselves.

But, says Swinburne, the sufferers can gain the benefits of patience (170) and of being useful: "Puny humans and even punier animals are given a role to play in [God's] plans by the all-good source of all things. Being of use is indeed a privilege" (236); so that "some animal suffering may be justified by the good of being of use, even if the use is not freely chosen" (241). Besides showing God as sacrificing some beings for the benefit of others, this argument lacks compassion, which Swinburne regards as a virtue. If you consider the exis-tence of battery chickens, you cannot imagine a benevolent God inflicting it in order to confer on them the supposed benefit of being useful to the humans who will eventually eat them or to the producer who profits from them.

And the logical flaw of these claims can be shown more clearly by replacing the supposedly compensatory moral benefits with material benefits: thus, without cold weather there would be no anoraks; without wounds there would be no bandages. Just as in a world without cold weather one would not need anoraks, in a world without suffering one would not need compassion (though one could still feel love), heroism, or patience. Human and animal nature would take different forms that we can hardly imagine from our own vantage point.

So far, then, these "greater-good" arguments undermine God's benevo-lence, in that he seems to have created or allowed suffering and death without good cause. What about his omnipotence? The other side of Swinburne's "greater good" claim is the "lesser evil." But a God who must choose a lesser evil is not omnipotent.

It would seem to be more acceptable for vegetarian theists, or for other humanitarian theists, to accept that God is not all-powerful—an element of process theology, Swinburne observes (30–31)—than to believe that he is not all-benevolent. People offering the "temporary concession which God would not allow now" argument are trying to justify their God's past tolerance of evil, while interpreting his benevolent nature as supporting their current policies. But they do not seem to have come to grips with the "omnipotence" problem. I suggest that "mysterious ways" avoids it and that "free will" is ac-ceptable regarding moral evil, but that regarding natural evil they must ac-knowledge that God, if he exists and is all-benevolent (thus *not* willingly tol-erating or creating harm for a greater good), is not all-powerful.

BROAD PRINCIPLES USED TO SUPPORT
THE EFFECTIVE DEFENSE

IN JUDAISM

GOD'S MERCY
is emphasized in all the Abrahamic religions.

> "The attribute of grace," it was taught, "exceeds that of punishment (i.e. jus-
> tice) by five-hundredfold." . . . "Even in the time of His anger He remembers
> mercy," declares the Talmud (Pes. 87b); and He is actually depicted as praying
> to Himself that His compassion should overcome His wrath.[48]

Psalm 145.9, "His mercies are over all his works," is quoted in the Judah the
Prince story as told in Bava Metzia 85a.[49]

THE DIET OF EDEN
Schwartz points to the commentator Rashi (1040–1105), who observed that
"God did not permit Adam and his wife to kill a creature and to eat its flesh.
Only every green herb shall they all eat together."[50] He lists other writers
from the eleventh to the twentieth centuries who note this fact—but whether
they interpreted Genesis 1.29–30 as a contemporary moral imperative or as
a golden-age ideal is unclear. Certainly R. Joseph Albo gave the theme a
moral inflection: "In the killing of animals there is cruelty, rage, and the accustoming of oneself to the bad habit of shedding innocent blood."[51]

HUMAN AND ENVIRONMENTAL CONCERNS
Besides compassion for animals, Schwartz offers indirect arguments that
biblical and Talmudic principles of sharing, environmental protection, and
peace "point to vegetarianism as the diet most consistent with Jewish values,"[52] inasmuch as world hunger and environmental damage are increased
by meat production, and hunger can lead to war.

Kalechofsky, in the same way, offers "five important Jewish mandates
which are rooted in Torah and which were expanded by Talmudic and rabbinic commentary."[53] In addition to the directly animal-relevant *tsa'ar
ba'alei chaim* (avoid causing pain to any living creature), they are: "*pikuach
nefesh* (the commandment to guard your health and life); . . . *bal tashchit*

(the commandment not to waste or destroy anything of value); *tzedakkah* (to help the needy and work for a more just society); and *klal Israel* (to work for the welfare of the Jewish people)."[54]

STEWARDSHIP HIERARCHICAL AND HUMBLE

The replacement of "dominion" by the concept of stewardship is found in Judaism, Christianity, and Islam. It is true that, in applying the "image-of-God" idea, rabbinic thought can combine speciesism with stewardship. For Solomon, "the hierarchical model" suggested by the "image-of-God"

> has two practical consequences. First . . . is that of responsibility of the higher for the lower. . . . The second is that, in a competitive situation, the higher has priority over the lower. . . . so that, for instance, it is wrong for a man to risk his life to save that of a dog, though right . . . to save that of another human.[55]

But he is less aggressive when reviewing the writing of Joseph Albo, who "articulates the attitude of humble stewardship towards creation which characterises rabbinic Judaism,"[56] in "commending the reading" of the animal-centered *Pereq Shirah.*[57]

The implication of abusing power over animals is spelled out by R. Arthur Hertzberg: "The way that we exercise our power over the rest of God's creatures . . . must be the way of love and compassion. If it is not, then we ourselves have made the choice that the strong can do what they like to other living beings."[58]

INDEPENDENT JUDGMENT IN FOLLOWING TORAH

Although the Abraham story encourages blind obedience, which acts against the interests of animals, as noted in chapter 1, the rabbis modified "divine voluntarism" by asserting, rather oddly, that we should not imitate God's bad qualities. To be sure, "what the Torah commands and prohibits is the sure guidance, and morality consists in compliance with its precepts."[59] Yet we also read that "in the Bible qualities are attributed to God which should not be copied by man, such as jealousy and anger; and they [the rabbis] offer a reason why in such matters the doctrine of Imitation does not apply."[60] Reflecting a judgment based on independent human ideas of right and wrong rather than on mere obedience, this rabbinical doctrine offers scope for a range of normative principles any one of which might be identified as part of the good aspect of God.

Thus, besides rejecting anger and jealousy, we should seek reasons when trying to comply with God's wishes. Maimonides, denying God's arbitrariness, "would argue that [the Mishna on silencing prayer which appeals to God's compassion for a bird] reflects a minority opinion."[61] In the same context (the rule in Deuteronomy 22:6–7), Kalechofsky observes that arbitrariness "is an unJewish attribute of God, for one cannot assert that God is merciful, just, providential, *and* arbitrary."[62]

IN CHRISTIANITY: *CREATEDNESS*

> As the disastrous consequences of this exploitation . . . Christians have reread the creation story. . . . Before and apart from the creation of human beings, God sees that the animals are good. When humanity is added creation as a whole is very good. . . .
> Human sin disrupts this integral creation.[63]

But is it good because it was created by God or is God good because of having created it? On the one hand, "practically every mention of natural phenomena is associated with their divine originator. . . . Nature exists not in its own right but as a created entity."[64] On the other, "The belief that God's creation of nature is a cause of worship . . . is already found in the Jewish scriptures, and furnished Christianity with a fundamentally important view of the universe."[65]

If the latter, the argument brings us—again—to the problem of evil: "we can also think of this creativity as an actual power surging through all things. But then it becomes highly problematic why it should unfailingly produce the good. How can this be, especially if on Whitehead's showing creativity can produce the greatest evils as well as the greatest goods?"[66] It might be done by denying God's omnipotence, as I suggested earlier, and attributing the bad things to some other source. In that case the real ground for animal support would be not createdness but goodness.

Nevertheless, twentieth-century theologians have appealed to createdness in urging concern for other species. Cardinal Francis Bourne told children in 1931: "This kindness is obligatory upon us because God made the animals, and is therefore their creator, and, in a measure, His Fatherhood extends to them."[67] In 1966 the Very Rev. Agius "wrote of the two basic rights animals have: '*ratione Creatoris*,' meaning animals cannot be maltreated without infringing on the rights of their Creator; and '*ratione ordinis creatae*,' disturbing

God's natural order."[68] Linzey's "theos-rights" are similar: "The notion of 'theos-rights' then for animals means that God rejoices in the lives of those differentiated beings in creation enlived by the Spirit. In short: If God is for them, we cannot be against them."[69]

THE INCARNATION

The doctrine of the incarnation contains reasons why people should draw pro-animal conclusions from it.

> 1. It gives primacy to sentience. The cosmos (God) is embodied in a suffering being, symbolized by the cross. That Jesus was in human form is no reason for excluding animals from this symbolism: such an "understanding of the incarnation . . . excludes not only animals, but also women; not only women but all Gentile, uncircumcised men."[70]
>
> 2. It stands for the lowest common denominator. Jesus is shown as born in a manger, the significance of which (as more than a sign of human poverty and humility) has been overlooked by theologians, though not by the popular imagination, as noted in chapter 3. He associates with the lowest human beings; in death he shares the depth of experience.
>
> 3. Christ represents the sacrifice downward that Linzey presents as a model for human behavior toward animals (see the discussion of Christian ethics later in this chapter.)

THE FALL

For Shelley, "an animal diet is the 'original and universal sin.'"[71] Bradley gives the Fall a more broadly ecological meaning—"Humans are directly responsible for shattering the primeval harmony of the world of nature"[72]—as well as a closely animal one:

> The accounts of the fall and the flood in Genesis seem to reflect some of the most important transitions in the evolution of the human species—the shift from vegetarianism to meat-eating, the change from . . . gathering . . . to the hard physical effort of tilling the soil to grow crops, the increasing differentiation between humans and animals as the latter became reared for food.[73]

Of course, given the obscure meaning of the "eating from the tree of knowledge" story, people are free to seize on anything they disapprove of and label it the real original sin. What matters is that present-day Christians are starting to select this interpretation of the Fall and can find support for it in such evidence as exists that people were once vegetarian.

A weaker version of meat eating in connection with the Fall, rather than that it was the original sin, is the observation that it *followed* the Fall and was accordingly seen by the biblical writers—themselves "neither pacifists nor vegetarian"[74]—as, along with the killing of humans, "simply inevitable" since human "corruption and wickedness had made a mess of God's highest hopes for creation."[75]

CHRISTIAN ETHICS

Linzey's "moral priority of the weak" rejects claims of species equality, substituting something that would sound very like Russell's "superior virtue of the oppressed" were it not given the status of an active imperative: "The pattern of obligation is always and everywhere on the 'higher' to sacrifice for the 'lower'; for the strong, powerful and rich to give to those who are vulnerable, poor or powerless. This is not some by-theme of the moral example of Jesus, it is rather central to the demands of the kingdom."[76]

We can also extend to animals the principle of charity to humans, as did St. John Chrysostom, who believed that "saints should extend their gentleness even to unreasoning creatures," while Basil the Great "composed a prayer for animals in which he indicated that God saves human beings *and* beasts."[77]

Indeed, the strongest Christian support for animal rights is found in extrapolation from such fundamental values, rather than in directly animal-related passages of scripture or the saints. D. Davies writes, "There is no strictly theological or biblical basis for vegetarianism"—an exaggeration whose truth depends on what he means by "strictly"—"or for this attitude in Christianity, but it can be seen as an extension of the ideal of love. The growth of animal rights follows on from an immense increase in awareness of human rights."[78]

To these principles can be added that of stewardship, endorsed by Linzey, Bradley, and the Church and Society Consultation.

IN ISLAM

COMPASSION

"In the name of Allah, Most Gracious, Most Merciful," are the words prefixed to all except surah 9 of the 114 surahs of the Qur'an.

Compassion underlies the rules about halal meat, which are intended to ensure that the animal to be eaten suffers as little as possible. This evasive policy creates a problem for Muslim animal rights campaigners who wish to appeal to coreligionists, since in working to reform conditions in which animals are raised, transported, and slaughtered, so as to meet halal standards, the campaigners seem to endorse meat eating. So Maya Linden, a PETA activist, says, "We're urging the Australian government to enforce these humane slaughter laws [in Australian-certified halal slaughterhouses]," while Bina Ahmed, participating in the same protest, points out that there are now Muslim men who are vegetarian.[79]

There is no real inconsistency here, since vegetarianism and veganism are halal by virtue of avoiding meat altogether, but a political difficulty could arise when campaigners address Muslims who are sympathetic to the reformist argument but reject or even disapprove of vegetarianism.

An example of compassion as a motive can be seen in the challenge by Khaled Abou El-Fadl, "one of the most rigorously critical living legal thinkers in the Islamic world today,"[80] to Islam's long-standing prejudice against dogs. Although his argument proceeds through painstaking examination of Hadiths and legal sources, the comments opening and closing the discussion portrayed seem to provide the real impetus for change. The fatwa against dogs "seems awfully cruel!" says one student. The student who speaks last says, "the author of the fatwa did not attempt to find a merciful solution and he did not at all consider the well-being of the dog . . . Negligently contributing to the death or to harming an innocent animal that we are in a position to help . . . is a significant violation and sin."[81]

RESPECT FOR LIFE

The positive value that Islam places on life is found in the Hadith that helping any living creature confers merit; another "teaches that those who provide food for anymals, including birds, have 'given a charitable gift' that will yield great rewards from above."[82] The lines of Qur'an 6:151—"Take not life, which Allah / Hath made sacred, except / By way of justice and law"—constitute a prima facie ban on killing, found also in the prohibition on sport hunting, as explained by az-Zaybaq:

> The sanctity of life prohibits the killing of animals for amusement . . . making them shooting targets, and other similar cruelties. "Abdullah bin 'Amr narrated, 'Allah's Messenger said, "Any person who kills a small bird or larger animal without a legitimate cause will be questioned about it by Allah." When asked "O Allah's Messenger, what is a legitimate cause?" he said, "Slaughter it

to eat it; do not cut off its head and then throw it away." In other words, the animal must be killed for food.[83]

Foltz notes "a subtle, if rarely explored, undertone in Islamic law that killing in general is essentially a bad thing. . . . The underlying principle seems to be that Muslims should kill animals only to satisfy their hunger or to protect themselves from danger."[84]

CREATEDNESS

When the Qur'an extols creation, it is in order to celebrate Allah's power and goodness and to urge people to believe in him.

> *Do not the Unbelievers see*
> *That the heavens and the earth*
> *Were joined together (as one*
> *Unit of Creation), before*
> *We clove them asunder?*
> *We made from water*
> *Every living thing. Will they*
> *Not then believe? (21:30)*

Yet in the listing of natural phenomena as signs, we can see a love of nature—including plants, animals, and the inorganic—for its own sake. As with this same theme in Christianity, we wonder whether we are to worship nature because God created it or to worship God because he created nature. The latter interpretation, which would be unorthodox within Islam, is nevertheless plausible if you ask what there would be to worship in the absence of anything good in nature. Would you worship the creator of a hellish world, simply because of his power?

But as with Christianity, Islamic animal supporters have sometimes argued from "createdness": "Creation has 'intrinsic value' through Allah"; "Creation points back to Allah, but is itself due 'watchfulness, gratefulness, and respect.'"[85]

ANIMALS AS SIGNS

It was suggested by Nursi (d. 1960), a Turkish Sufi, "that Creation is the original form of revelation, upon which the revealed Qur'an is merely a commentary."[86] Hence the frequent Qur'anic declaration that every phenomenon is a sign from God. (See chapter 7 for discussion of logomysticism.) The ethical problem is the same as that found in createdness and in ecologism, namely, that inanimate things are included along with the sentient.

> *Behold! In the creation*
> *Of the heavens and the earth;*
> *In the alternation*
> *Of the Night and the Day;*
> *In the sailing of the ships*
> *Through the Ocean*
> *For the profit of mankind;*
> *In the rain which Allah*
> *Sends down from the skies,*
> *And the life which He gives therewith*
> *To an earth that is dead;*
> *In the beasts of all kinds*
> *That He scatters*
> *Through the earth;*
> *In the change of the winds,*
> *And the clouds which they*
> *Trail like their slaves*
> *Between the sky and the earth—*
> *(Here) indeed are Signs*
> *For a people that are wise. (2:164)*

Within the animal kingdom and within nature as a whole, are we to consider every sign of God equal to every other? If not, it might seem, according to our usual hierarchical thinking, that God becomes less when signified by an insect than by a horse, and even less when signified by a mountain.

This problem only arises, however, if we read the concept of signs pantheistically, as the Sufis tend to; whereas the orthodox view is that each sign exists to remind us not of God's presence in each being but of his creative power as a whole. In any case, the fact that "the Islamic tradition . . . has much to say about the need to respect all parts of God's creation, even insects"[87] suggests that, on the pantheistic view itself, God might not be diminished by any particular manifestation. In addition, one could maintain egalitarianism while still distinguishing between sentient and nonsentient in terms of their needs and corresponding human obligations, rather than in terms of how we value them.

Creatures may sometimes be considered negative signs, at least from a human utilitarian view, like that of al-Jahiz, who suggested that dangerous or annoying creatures may have been created "precisely to test the endurance and patience of humans."[88] Although al-Jahiz urges us to praise God for creating these beings, the reasons given do not imply any obligation to spare them. By contrast, Nursi, who believed "that the signs of nature . . . are to be read like the signs of written language,"[89] found partly anthropocentric grounds for *valuing* flies, mosquitoes, and fleas. He saw them as environmental agents, not just tests of endurance and "opposed any killing of animals, even flies."[90]

COMMUNITY

An explicit expression of kinship occurs in the Qur'an's "communities" verse (6:38), which is prominent in current animal rights argument:

> *There is not an animal*
> *(That lives) on the earth,*
> *Nor a being that flies*
> *On its wings, but (forms*
> *Part of) communities like you.*
> *Nothing have We omitted*
> *From the Book, and they (all)*
> *Shall be gathered to their Lord*
> *In the end.*

SOCIAL JUSTICE AND HELPING THE POOR

The Thamud story directly links social justice with kindness to animals. The need to water the animals, primarily for human benefit but for their own sake as well, sets the narrative in motion, but it is sympathy for the camel that arouses moral indignation against the wealthy.

Because of conditions of great inequality at the time of the Prophet, "social justice is one of the major themes of the Qur'an."[91] Foltz therefore regrets that mainstream Islamic commentators do not acknowledge the role of meat production in contributing to world hunger. Bina Ahmed, however, does: "It takes 5,000 gallons of water to produce one pound of beef, but only 25 gallons of water to produce one pound of grain. In the Middle East, farmable land and water is scarce, so it's absurd that we're wasting these resources raising animals for slaughter rather than growing food directly to feed people."[92] The principle of helping the poor has been used to oppose animal sacrifice. The imam of the Paris mosque, when there was a European foot-and-mouth outbreak in 2001, "issued a *fatwa* . . . that animal sacrifice on 'Id al-Adha is not required" and suggested instead "giving a third of the price of a sheep in cash to the poor." That particular ceremonial slaughter was banned during the 1990s by King Hassan of Morocco "for economic reasons, citing the well-being of poorer Muslims for whom paying for a sacrificial animal posed financial hardship."[93]

ENVIRONMENTALISM AND STEWARDSHIP

Commitment to the environment does not necessarily lead to support for animals, but it is helpful in moving away from human centeredness and dominionism.

Izzi Dien (environmentalist but antivegetarian) explains the Islamic commitment to "stewardship":

> The Arabic root that denotes trusteeship which is sometimes translated as "viceregency"[94] is khalafa. From it is derived the word istikhlaf which is also used by the Qur'an to indicate appointment as a trustee. . . . When the Qur'an used these words, it always employed them as a given privilege and never as an assumed right.[95]

Naseef observes that "the three central concepts of Islam are also the pillars of the environmental ethics of Islam." Besides *khalifah* (the word for the steward or viceregent), these are *tawhid* and *akhirah*. *Tawhid* means unity: "Allah is Unity and His Unity is also reflected in the unity of mankind, and the unity of man and nature." *Akhirah* mean the Hereafter and the Day of Reckoning, when the *khalifah* "will have to render an account of how he treated the trust of Allah."[96]

Besides *tawhid* and *khilafah* (a different transliteration of *khalafah*), Khalid adds the principles of *fitrah,* "the natural pattern of creation,"[97] and *mizan,* or balance.[98]

A particularly Islamic feature of environmentalism is the prohibition on *riba,* or usury, which facilitates planet-destroying growth through the generation of artificial money. "Cartesian rationalism licensed the human community to plunder the earth. The new usurocracy provided the means with which to do it," writes Khalid.[99] Dutton explains how exploitation of the earth can be undertaken not even to meet immediate needs, but simply to make the most of existing facilities in which borrowed money has been invested, and to "keep [money] on the move and maximise the flow to keep up with . . . interest rates."[100]

All these animal-supportive principles come from God, whose supremacy and responsibility for everything are constantly attested in the Qur'an. Just as, according to Islam's pantheistic implications denied by the mainstream but found in Sufism, God is present in everything, so Islamic principles may be seen as emanations from God.

IN BUDDHISM

IDENTIFICATION

"Animals are ourselves in different rebirths; they experience pain and we should show them compassion. There are no absolute borders between species."[101] Because of this identification, the key Buddhist value of compassion does "not seem to derive from . . . self-protection" but "is usually an attitude primarily directed towards *feeble*, suffering creatures, not so much towards strong and dangerous ones."[102] *Metta*, also, has the aspect of identification. Schmithausen cites "*VisM* [Visuddhimagga] 9.10 . . . where friendliness or loving kindness towards all sentient beings is based on the 'Golden Rule,' i.e., on the awareness that like oneself other sentient beings, too, seek happiness but dislike pain, want to live but are afraid of death."[103]

Comparable values are found in Hinduism, the *Padmapurana* stating that "one who views every other living being as oneself, one who views others' wealth as a clod of earth, one who looks upon others' wives as mothers, he sees verily."[104] And for the Jains, "To do harm to others is to do harm to oneself. 'Thou art he whom thou intendest to kill!'"[105]

EGALITARIANISM

Such values depend upon a degree of species egalitarianism. The classification of beings into "spontaneous birth . . . birth from a womb, an egg, or moisture"[106] blurs the distinction between human and animal, as does their karmic interchangeability, which is the third and most favorable aspect of karma. Although it is very difficult for animals to be reborn as humans and thus achieve enlightenment, and the interchangeability of humans and animals takes place between higher and lower bourns, signifying unequal degrees of merit, nevertheless the concept of species having no fixed identity is egalitarian. The idea's pro-animal implications are more emphasized by the Mahayana, but the fifth-century Theravadist commentator Buddhaghosa also "advis[es] the meditator to consider, for the sake of arousing loving kindness, the fact that in the beginningless *samsara* all beings have already been one's father, mother, etc."[107]

There is certainly an egalitarian core to the Tibetan myth that Avalokitesvara and Tara (male and female Bodhisattvas of compassion) "procreated monkeys who transformed themselves over generations into the Tibetan people. (No emotional problems here over the theory of evolution!)"[108]

Moreover, the Buddhist definition of death does not attach it to the loss of higher cognition; a definition that does so "can apply only to human beings. . . . What is required by Buddhism is a definition of death which will apply to all karmic life."[109]

NONINJURY

The full formula corresponding to the first precept is "He being thus one who has gone forth . . . abandoning onslaught on creatures, is one who abstains from onslaught on creatures; the stick laid aside, the knife laid aside, he lives kindly, scrupulous, friendly and compassionate towards all breathing things and creatures" (*M.i.*179 and many other places). Summarized sometimes as "I undertake the rule of training to abstain from harming living beings"[110] or as "*panatipata*—to refrain from intentionally taking the life of any living creature,"[111] but sometimes without clear animal reference as, e.g., "I undertake to abstain from taking life,"[112] this is the first of the precepts that in predominantly Buddhist cultures "become expected norms for people to seek to live by."[113] Translating it so as to include animals unambiguously is essential if it is not to be associated in Western minds with the purely human centered prohibition on killing.

So important did the principle become that a story found both in the Pali jatakas and in the Jatakamala uses it to support the Buddha's metaphysical arguments—analogously to the treatment of the camel as a test of true belief in the Qur'an's Thamud tale.

The historical Gotama had five prominent philosophical rivals whose earlier incarnations sometimes appear as villains, known as the five heretics, in the jatakas. In the story in question, the Bodhisattva refutes the five heretics while wearing a monkey's skin.

Having left the kingdom because of plots against him, the Bodhisattva, Mahabodhi, returns to prevent the king being victimized by the heretics' intrigues and wicked views. He takes a monkey skin with him, the procuring of which differs in the two versions. In the original jataka story (xviii.235–6 (528,121)) the Bodhisatta "entered a frontier village and after eating the flesh of a monkey given to him by the inhabitants [236] he begged for its skin which he . . . made . . . into an inner and outer robe." But in the Jatakamala, he "conjured up a large monkey. As soon as the monkey appeared . . . , he caused all but its hide to disappear, and this he used as a cloak. Clothed in this cloak . . . he presented himself at the entrance to the king's palace."[114]

On the Bodhisattva's arrival at the palace, the king enquires about the monkey skin and Mahabodhi replies that he has himself killed the monkey. This incurs silent disapproval from the king (in the Jatakamala) and ridicule from the heretics (in both versions), whereupon the Bodhisattva refutes the five wrong views in turn, by showing in each case how conformance to that view would justify the act that his opponents all, by Indian tradition, condemn.

Space permits only one example, the refutation concerning karma. In Buddhism, as we have seen, animal birth is identified with past misdeeds. But the aggressive use of this doctrine to absolve people of guilt toward animals is rejected on grounds that it would justify the killing of the monkey. In the Pali jataka the Bodhisatta argues,

> *If such the creed thou holdst and this be doctrine true,*
> *Then was my action right when I that monkey slew.*
>
> (xviii.239 (528, 123))

The case made in the Jatakamala is more intricate:

> If everything is due to preceding karma, why should you blame me for killing this monkey? . . . On the other hand, if you say I committed a bad action in killing the monkey, then I must be the cause of his death, not the monkey's immediately preceding action. And if, as you assert, karma always produces more karma, there can never be final emancipation.
>
> If, however, misery could change into happiness [and vice versa] . . . we could infer that good and evil fortune depend exclusively on immediately preceding karma. But if misery and happiness cannot become each other, preceding actions cannot be the only cause of events. If one can never generate new, fresh karma, then how could one ever have had the "old" karma . . . ? If,

nonetheless, you persist in this way of thinking, how can you judge that I killed the monkey?[115]

At the end of the story, in the Pali account, the Bodhisatta never disabuses his audience of their belief that he has killed the monkey. (Indeed, it is not made explicit that the monkey was dead when given to him, although we may assume it from the traditional rules of permissibility of meat eating.) This lack of clarification may have been merely a narrative oversight.

In any case, the Jatakamala, by contrast, has the Bodhisattva inform his hearers: "In truth, Your Majesty, I have never killed even a single living creature. This skin I wear comes from a monkey I created [i.e., "conjured up," not created in the flesh] solely for the purpose of this conversation."[116] So pure must the Wise One be that the animal whose skin he wears cannot have been killed by any human being, let alone by himself.

It is true that, in telling this tale, the Buddha is asserting that right views must lead to right behavior, thus giving primacy to theory rather than ethics. But his underlying argument gives noninjury a determinant role. The argument runs, "If your views were correct, it would be right to kill the monkey. But it is not right to kill the monkey. Therefore your views are not correct." The ethical principle is a premise of the argument. Treated as axiomatic, the prevailing value of *ahimsa* stands unchallenged, with the various philosophical views circling round it and assessed by their consistency with it.

RIGHT LIVELIHOOD

Right livelihood is a stage of the Eightfold Noble Path that people are advised to follow in order to escape from suffering. Examples of wrong livelihood occur at *M.i.343*: "the person who is a tormentor of others . . . is a cattle-butcher, or pig-killer, fowler, deer-stalker, hunter, fisherman, thief, executioner, jailer, or (one of) those others who follow a bloody calling." (Buddhism disapproved of hunting not only as an occupation, but as a sport; the Buddha being "strongly critical of . . . the hunting enjoyed by the royalty.")[117]

Even now, "in Buddhist societies, butchers are usually non-Buddhists, for example Muslims, and are seen as depraved or as outcastes. . . . Indeed raising livestock for slaughter is generally seen as a breach of 'right livelihood.'"[118] Since food is the primary sector of any economy (more visibly so in nonindustrial societies), and a large proportion of workers are involved in animal abuse, we may surmise that concern for animals was an important motive for introducing this principle into the Noble Eightfold Path.

While meat eating by laypeople, and in some circumstances by monks, was condoned, those practicing it could defend themselves against guilt by blaming the butcher who actually did the killing. In that sense the ban on "wrong livelihood" was evasive, but insofar as the immediate act of killing was condemned, it was a form of effective defense.

Although the "right livelihood" principle is found in Hinduism, it is compromised by the caste system, combined with theistic authoritarianism. On the one hand, "He who permits the slaughter of an animal, he who cuts it up, he who kills it, he who buys or sells meat, he who cooks it, he who serves it up, and he who eats it, must all be considered as the slayers of the animal."[119]

Yet on the other, Krishna declares, "the four-caste system did I generate,"[120] so that "however evil a man's livelihood may be, let him but worship Me with love and serve no other, then shall he be reckoned among the good indeed, for his resolve is right."[121]

There were guilds "for butchers, trappers, hunters, fishermen, leather-workers, and ivory-workers" in towns in India "as early as two and a half millennia ago,"[122] which compromises Buddhism as well.

THE BODHISATTVA IDEAL

In the jatakas and in Mahayana Buddhism, the Bodhisattva ideal, which depends on the belief in karmic interchangeability, promotes concern for sentient beings of all species, as is shown by the Bodhisatt(v)a's sometimes taking animal birth, and by mutual aid between species, reaching its culmination in the Mahayana story of the hungry tiger. Through such inclusiveness the consequentialism that comes to the fore in the Bodhisattva ideal has indirect links to animals.

The Animal Bodhisattva

In the Pali jatakas the Bodhisatta is often (in 104 out of 547 stories) incarnated as an animal or (in 6 stories) as a mythical part-human Naga (serpent) or Garuda/Garula: a "mythical bird . . . able to assume human form. Morris . . . concludes that the *supanna*, here translated *Garula*, was a 'winged man.'"[123] In the Mahayana selection of jatakas, the Jatakamala of Aryasura, the Bodhisattva has animal form in 11 out of 34 tales. This brief collection sheds the folkloric diversity of the original, its aim being to promote the Bodhisattva ideal.

Karmic fluidity is emphasized by the expression sometimes found in the *paccuppannavatthu* or introduction to each jataka tale, "even when he was born in an animal form" (e.g., xxi.337 (533,178), here with reference to Ananda) or "even when born from the womb of animals" (xi.90 (455,58)). The animal is a temporary form, not a fixed being occupying a place in a rigid hierarchy.

Cross-species rebirth, including the god/prophet as animal, is found in Hinduism and Jainism also, reflecting the egalitarian strand in the former and the egalitarian basis of the latter. Vishnu "takes several births into animal forms before taking human ones" in the *Dasavatara* legend.[124] And the foremost Jain teacher, Mahavira, "[in] a prior birth as a lion . . . is said to have been so moved by a sermon on the importance of *ahimsa* that he refrained from all food normally consumed by a lion, resulting in his death and subsequent human birth wherein he achieved enlightenment."[125]

The Hungry Tiger

In the Pali jatakas, the many tales of self-sacrifice include examples of humans or animals willing to give their lives for members of their own kind; of great kindness between species; of humans willing to risk their lives to help or to avoid hurting animals; and of an animal Bodhisatta (the "hare in the moon," no. 316) suicidally offering his flesh to a brahmin.

But the "hungry tiger" jataka in which the human Bodhisattva does the equivalent of the last-named act for an animal is found not here but in the Mahayana *Suvarnaprabhasa*[126] and in the Jatakamala. Chapple cites other such tales, but does not say where they come from except for one Chinese (Mahayana) precept.[127] The choice of species in the story might have come from the experience of forest ascetics. Tiyavanich reports: "The tiger occupies a conspicuous place in the monks' accounts of their life in the forest. The monks regarded this animal with a mixture of fear and respect. Fear of tigers and the vivid imagining of oneself being devoured by tigers often drove the mind to one-pointed *samadhi* (concentration)."[128] The animal significance of the hungry tiger story is overlooked by Govinda (quoted with approval by Sangharakshita) when he offers apologies for it:

> To the modern man such a story may appear unreasonable. . . . The preservation—or rather prolongation—of the life of some wild beasts does not seem to be worth the sacrifice of a human life. [But] it is not the factual . . . reality that matters but the motive . . .
>
> That the lives of the tigress and her cubs are saved, is not of such fundamental importance as that the Bodhisattva experiences . . . their suffering . . . , and that . . . there is no more difference for him between his own suffering and the suffering of others.[129]

The argument resembles that surrounding the Rebecca story in the Bible: in both cases, the spiritual state of a person being kind to an animal is held to be the only important thing, while the benefit to the animal doesn't matter. "But if the animals' suffering is less important, why is this feeling of the Bodhisattva's valuable?" asks the Animal Judge, echoing Kalechofsky.

Consequentialism

By contrast with Govinda's view, the Lankavatara Sutra's promotion of vegetarianism entails an increased emphasis on the consequences of actions rather than on the state of mind prompting them. Here the terms of allowability of meat—which depends on the eater's unawareness, or nonsuspicion, of its provenance—are denounced as "sophistic arguments."[130] In addition, the sutra links such criteria to violation of the *anatta* doctrine: "They may talk about various discriminations which they make in their moral discipline, being addicted to the view of a personal soul."[131] At a much later date, antivivisectionist Helena Blavatsky's famous lines "Can there be bliss when all that lives must suffer? Shalt thou be saved and hear the whole world cry?"[132] convey the principle that the Bodhisattva's own spiritual purity is less important than the results of her acts for other beings.

Of course, consequentialism is not restricted to the Mahayana. The twentieth-/twenty-first century Theravadin Ajahn Sumedho rejects the notion that a spiritually sound state of mind is compatible with and excuses bad behavior: "Anyhow, that's how we would like it, isn't it? Just be mindful, whatever you are doing: drinking your whisky, smoking your marijuana cigarette, picking a safe open, mugging someone . . . as long as it's done mindfully it's all right."[133]

ADVOCACY OF SPECIFIC MEASURES

THE MIXED ROLE OF ASCETICISM IN PROMOTING VEGETARIANISM

Before looking at policies of individual worldviews, it seems useful to consider the partly supportive but largely harmful role of asceticism as a basis for vegetarianism in many cultures.

In the past, self-denial often provided the main or only motive for abstention from meat. Chapple finds similarities to Jainism in the Gnostics, Manichaeans, Bogomils, and Cathars, "especially in their emphasis on the purgation of

evil through asceticism and their practice of vegetarianism."[134] For the Cathars, who emerged in the 1140s and had been violently suppressed by the early
fifteenth century, "the purpose of human life was to purify the soul through
chastity and vegetarianism, thereby avoiding reincarnation and attaining release. The killing of animals was forbidden because animals were said to possess a soul; meat, eggs, and milk were all forbidden because they arose from the
sinful act of sexual intercourse."[135]

Yet asceticism not only seems to deemphasize or ignore vegetarian morality, but has actually worked against it. In Judaism the rabbis repudiated vegetarianism partly as a reaction against the ascetic movements that existed
before and especially after the destruction of the Temple:

> The Talmud documents how the rabbis debated . . . over whether to prohibit
> the eating of meat and the drinking of wine as a perpetual sign of mourning
> for the destruction of the Temple. Finally, the rabbis decided to reject the as-
> cetic argument. Judaism, after all, was a religion of life, and "the rabbis [con-
> sidered] asceticism and privation as a sin against the will of God, [and be-
> lieved] that people should enjoy the gift of life."[136]

Early Christian practice, too, had the drawback that it "grounded vegetarianism in self-denial (implying that meat was a luxury, something good but
not necessary), which overshadowed the message of compassion for animals.
By making abstention from meat rare and heroic, asceticism thereby con-
firmed the value of what it avoided and denied."[137] We have seen how the antiworld views of his Manichaean former copersuasionists helped to turn St.
Augustine against vegetarianism.

But asceticism is not totally antagonistic to ethics. In tales of the desert
fathers "friendship with animals is a special sign of holiness,"[138] while the
ascetic Manichees "believed that humans had no right to kill animals for human consumption."[139] In Eastern religion, particularly in Jainism, valuation
of abstinence is accompanied by core beliefs in noninjury and compassion.

In nineteenth-century America, where speciesist attitudes and meat eating
were well established, those branches of Protestantism that promoted vegetarianism emphasized abstinence and a rigorous health program. Nevertheless, the founder of the rather ascetic and health-oriented Seventh-Day Ad-
ventists, Ellen G. White, "taught love for animals and a vegetarian diet."[140]

Besides being accompanied by altruistic ethics, ascetic vegetarianism may
contain a moral truth of its own. Linzey finds in its Christian form the ethical

implication "that humans should live gently on the earth and avoid luxury food," finding such meaning in "the rule of life penned by St Benedict for his religious community," which "included the injunction 'Except the sick who are very weak, let all abstain entirely from the flesh of four-footed animals.'"[141] For, as noted in chapter 1, regarding negative biblical images of meat eating, the exploitation of animals is more costly than vegetable production, so that in earlier times meat was a relative luxury. Indeed, for Akers, the "simple living" associated with vegetarianism in early Christianity "is *not* ascetic. It is outward-looking, emphasizing the rewards and satisfactions of righteousness and positive involvement with the world. Jesus advised his followers not to be anxious about food or clothing, because these would be provided."[142]

At present, in any case, asceticism has been totally abandoned, as vegetarian campaigners regale the public with elaborate, expensive recipes and celebrity endorsements. There is even (as of 2008) an annual competition for the "Sexiest Vegetarian Celebrity."[143] Between hairshirts and hedonism, where is the animal?

Here are some of the more relevant moves by individual worldviews on vegetarianism and other issues.

IN JUDAISM

As early as the fifteenth century, ethical vegetarianism could be found in Jewish writings. As noted by Solomon, who, despite taking a conservative humanist line, recognizes the frequently adduced "temporary concession" view of divinely sanctioned meat eating,

> Joseph Albo (1380–1435) wrote that the first people [i.e., Adam and Eve] were forbidden to eat meat because of the cruelty involved in killing animals (*Sefer Ha-Iqqarim* 3:15). Isaac Abravanel (1437–1508) endorsed this in his commentary on Isaiah, Ch. 11 and also taught in his commentary on Genesis, Ch. 2, that when the Messiah comes we would return to the ideal, vegetarian state.[144]

In the nineteenth century Aaron Frankel wrote *Thou Shalt Not Kill or the Torah of Vegetarianism*, which according to Berry was "the first book written by a Jewish author urging vegetarianism." Lewis Gompertz (1779–1865), a vegetarian and "non-practicing Jew . . . was one of the first modern spokesmen for the cause of animals rights"[145] and a founder member of the Society for the Prevention of Cruelty to Animals.

"Today," Solomon observes, "the popular trend to vegetarianism has won many Jewish adherents though little official backing from religious leaders."[146] Vegetarianism is indeed vigorously promoted by modern Jews. The international Jewish Vegetarian Society began publishing a quarterly periodical in 1966;[147] an affiliate is the Jewish Vegetarians of North America.[148] Jews for Animal Rights has demonstrated for animals and produced much literature through the Micah Press, founded by its leader Roberta Kalechofsky.[149] Recently Israel has been described as "the country second only to India in vegetarians for religious reasons per capita," and its largest milk producer has begun to market soy milk.[150]

At the very least, factory farming is increasingly condemned: "In 1988, the late Rabbi Moses Feinstein issued an authoritative 'responsa' stating categorically that Jewish law forbids the raising of animals under inhumane conditions to produce white veal."[151]

More radically, Mordecai Ben Porat tried unsuccessfully to get the Israeli parliament to outlaw meat eating: "he argued that the state's fragile economy was being damaged by the cost of fighting diseases associated with eating meat."[152] Here the human centeredness of the health argument is outweighed by the comprehensiveness of the demand.

While the Talmud accepts meat eating, so that vegetarianism remains controversial, blood sports are a different matter. The rabbis derived from the seventh Noachide law a condemnation of "any sport which involved the mutilation of an animal while alive. . . . For that reason the arenas were shunned by the pious. 'One who attends the stadium sits in "the seat of the scornful" (Ps. i. 1)' (A.Z. 18b)." [153]

Cohen adds in a footnote that "the loathing of Jews for cruel sports of this nature has the testimony of Josephus."[154] R. Ezekiel Landau (1713–93), after referring to the Torah's implied disapproval of hunting in that "it is imputed only to fierce characters like Nimrod and Esau," goes on to say "I cannot comprehend how a Jew could even dream of killing animals merely for the pleasure of hunting. . . . It is downright cruelty."[155] In the 1970s the deputy attorney general of Israel gave eight reasons derived from Jewish law, including ethical ones, for objecting to sport hunting.[156]

In keeping with most secular or religious arguments against animal experimentation, the Jewish ethical case tends to be compromised by challenges to the practice's scientific validity, as is shown by the articles on the subject in *Judaism and Animal Rights*.[157] After devoting most of her paper to empirical considerations, Cramer writes somewhat more strongly, though still tempered by pragmatism:

> It is impossible to live in harmony with God's world and cause suffering to parts of it.... We could do a lot worse than return to the wisdom of our religious tradition ... and ask ourselves ... what we have gained from animal experimentation, how much we can expect to gain in the future, what is the cost in public revenues and, more importantly, can we as Jews live with the possibility that we are turning our backs on our religious tradition.[158]

As noted in chapter 2, Schwartz also has attempted to reconcile disapproval of vivisection with traditional Jewish humanism. He argues for preventive healthcare including vegetarianism, questions the usefulness of experiments (e.g., the justifiability of experiments for cosmetics), and urges the use of available alternatives.[159]

Andre Menache, a well-known medical opponent of vivisection, uses science to bolster a "gut feeling [that] told me that animal experimentation was basically wrong."[160] Noting that an international medical antivivisection conference took place in Tel Aviv in 1990, he expresses the hope that in this area "Israel will continue to strive to be a 'light unto other nations.'"[161] The tone more than the content of Robert Mendelsohn's article (which still argues on scientific grounds), makes it a strongly moral statement: "This wild blood-lust, starting with animal vivisection and proceeding to human mutilation, stamps Modern Medicine as the most primitive religion ever known to mankind."[162] In the same vein, activist Henry Spira declares, "We cannot be selective about permitting the more powerful to dominate, experiment upon, confine or butcher for dinner those who are less able to defend themselves"; but he still refers to "useless" experiments.[163]

Looking back in Jewish history, we encounter the significant move of abandoning animal sacrifice. Of course, it was conclusively ended because of the destruction of the Temple, although much prophetic disapproval had preceded and encouraged the development. The need to replace Temple sacrifices was largely met by the "Synagogue Ritual of the Day of Atonement [which] became in the popular mind the supreme path to purification from sin."[164] But "even when the sacrificial system was in operation, the rabbis assert, contrition was essential before an offering could prove acceptable to God,"[165] and prayer was held to exceed in importance both sacrifice and even good deeds.[166]

Because of the "don't be holier than Jesus" argument, there have been efforts to show that Jesus was vegetarian, although other animal supporters, such as Linzey and Young, have denied the all-determining significance of the question. Akers finds evidence from the Sufi al-Ghazali, who "is not himself a vegetarian and clearly has no axe to grind one way or the other." The medieval philosopher described a Jesus who "lives in extreme poverty, disdains violence, loves animals, and is vegetarian. It is clear that al-Ghazali is drawing on a tradition rather than creating a tradition, because some of the same stories . . . are also related by others both before and after him. . . . Thus, these stories came from a pre-existing tradition that described Jesus as a vegetarian."[167] Akers uses both the allegorical meaning and later-insertions methods of denial that Jesus, as portrayed in the New Testament, served or ate fish (129).

That the earliest Christians were vegetarians is demonstrated, according to the same author, not only by the sympathetic and pro-vegetarian third-century writings of Clement but also by the "hostile hence reliable *Panarion* of Epiphanius" a century later (21).

Even beyond the claim that Jesus made the (relatively inactive) choice of vegetarianism, Akers declares that "'cleansing the temple' was an act of animal liberation" (117). Emphasizing the animal sacrifice purpose of the vendors and moneychangers, he denies the common belief that Jesus's main target was commercialism. For, according to Epiphanius, "The gospel which they [the Jewish Christians] recognize contains the provision that 'I came to abolish sacrifices, and unless you cease from sacrificing, my anger will not cease from you' (30.16.5)" (233).

Thus, Akers argues, the "crucible of Jesus's ministry, for Jewish Christianity, was the opposition to animal sacrifice and Jesus' confrontation in the temple" (111), and it was this that most provoked the priests, whose chief source of status was being attacked. On historical or interpretive evidence, he explains away "scattered references to Jesus approving of sacrifices, approving of meat-eating, or telling parables involving meat" (129–30).

Webb is more cautious, finding it "very difficult to determine on historical grounds what attitude Jesus had toward the practice of Temple sacrifice," since the "evidence . . . is not clear or consistent."[168] He does say, however, that while "readers and interpreters of the struggle in the Temple rarely if ever think of Jesus as acting out of compassion for the animals," nevertheless "such an interpretation . . . is at least as plausible as others. Sanders points out that the animals are the focus of the Temple cult, which makes it at least plausible that Jesus' action was not unrelated to the animals themselves."[169]

It is known, without need for reinterpretation, that many early Christians were vegetarian. The grazing monks of the early Byzantine era, who "wander in the desert as if they were wild animals: like birds they fly about the hills; they forage like goats.... They feed on roots, the natural products of the earth,"[170] were not merely ascetic. The desert fathers in general "were returning to the conditions of the Garden of Eden, in harmony with both the natural world and its Creator. This is particularly true of the grazers, who like Adam ate without planting and were supposed to have command over the wild animals."[171] Command, yes—but without killing.

Linzey calls attention to

> the wide variety of saints who have expressed a particular regard for animals and opposed their destruction. "Poor innocent little creatures", exclaimed St Richard of Chichester when confronted with animals bound for slaughter. "If you were reasoning beings and could speak you would curse us. For we are the cause of your death, and what have you done to deserve it?"[172]

Alongside its predominant humanism, Christianity has influenced the modern turn against meat eating. In the eighteenth century, William Paley, archdeacon of Carlisle, "believed that killing animals for food could not be justified."[173] "Inspired by the original command in Genesis 1, an Anglican priest, William Cowherd, founded the Bible Christian Church in 1809 and made vegetarianism compulsory amongst its members."[174] The founder of the Salvation Army, the Methodist preacher William Booth, was a vegetarian.[175] In 1907 Rev. J. Todd Ferrier started the vegetarian Order of the Cross and "wrote many books aimed at recovering the theme of animal compassion in Christianity."[176]

Unfortunately, "by the end of the nineteenth century, the voice of biblically based vegetarianism had lost its power, and vegetarianism increasingly was just one of the many crazy health and diet fads that proliferated during that time."[177] We must leap ahead to the present day to find vegetarians, such as some of those quoted in this book, whose arguments, although often compounded with health or environmental concerns, are also unapologetically animal-oriented and who, more importantly, form a religious sector within a recognized political movement.

On other issues, Catholic precursors of modern active zoophiles include Pius V, who in 1567 forbade bullfights, and the English cardinals Manning and Newman who promoted the first antivivisection society. Newman declared that "cruelty to animals is as if a man did not love God."[178] The pope in 1982 implicitly criticized Mediterranean blood sports by saying at a St. Francis birthday celebration, "It is necessary and urgent that, following the example of the poor little man of Assisi, it be decided to abandon ill-considered forms of a dominating custody of all creatures."[179]

The Catholic Church has always been under pressure from pro-bullfight interests, leading to the modification by Gregory XIII of the 1567 ban by lifting the threat of excommunication for attendance. The penalty was reinstated in 1583 by Pope Sixtus V, but more pressure, especially from King Philip II of Spain, who "argued that such an amusement was necessary in order to train and prepare the knights for war," caused Pope Clement VIII to remove "most of the former prohibitions and punishments, banning only friars and monks from attending bullfights."[180] Regenstein comments that "despite these enormous pressures" the Church "never renounced its original opposition. . . . But neither has it taken sufficient action to end" bullfights.

Bruce Friedrich, a practicing Catholic, is a prominent figure in one of today's most influential—and ideologically uncompromising—animal rights organizations, People for the Ethical Treatment of Animals. In support of PETA's exposé of battery-egg production at a Trappist monastery, Colman McCarthy, now a vegan, described his former moral blindness when he was a Trappist lay brother working with cows:

> I was oblivious to the cruelty endured by the animals. . . . These were the most heinously sinful years of my life. . . . All the while, I thought I was leading a holy life of prayer and penance at a seemingly sacred place, on the moral high ground, not the immoral low ground that it really was when the violence done to animals is weighed. . . . The priests and brothers at Holy Spirit were among the kindest and most devout people I have ever known. It never occurred to them, as it didn't to me, that we were torturers and exploiters of animals.[181]

His experience, and the fact that all three letters responding to his article were supportive, shows how the consciousness of a religious group can change.

Many reforms, impressive for their time and culture, were introduced by the Moghul emperor Akbar (r. 1556–1605), under the influence of the Jain teacher Hiravijaya Suri. Having asked the Jain how best to repay him, Akbar was requested to "use his influence to spread the teaching of non-violence. . . . Many prisoners were released and animal slaughter was prohibited every year during Jaina festival days in regions where Jainas lived. Personally, Akbar . . . very nearly gave up eating meat and hunting." Besides legal protection for certain animals,[182] there were laws calling for the voluntary practice of *ahimsa* in the first lunar month and the avoidance of leather in the sixth month.

In a substitutive argument against the persistent Muslim tradition of animal sacrifice, Daniel refers to the Qur'an, 22:37, "It is not their meat / Nor their blood, that reaches / Allah: it is your piety,"[183] a verse appealed to also by Fadali and Masri,[184] and suggests that while fourteen hundred years ago "animals were the primary form of property owned by most people, and their primary form of . . . survival itself," so that animal sacrifice was "an act of extreme devotion," today "a more comparable method . . . would be giving up our car." Sister Hermana, also quoting 22:37, suggests "pledg[ing] . . . money or free volunteer service to some Da'wah organization or an Islamic charity."[185] According to Masri, "A learned Muslim scholar, Sheikh Farid Wagdi, says . . . that there might come a day when Muslims shall have to substitute the rite of animal sacrifice with other methods of giving alms";[186] nevertheless, "for the most part his call has been ignored."[187] As Foltz observes, "a number of religious traditions, including Judaism, Vedism, and others, historically evolved metaphorical substitutions for blood sacrifice; it is therefore not inconceivable that such a development could occur in the future within Islam."[188]

In such suggestions, similar to the development described in early Buddhism, we see a decline in the perception of need for a certain *form* of sacrifice, which was inconsistent with the value of compassion, but the survival of a feeling that sacrifice itself is still necessary. On the other hand, the two Syrian Muslim cosmonauts who offered a sacrificial sheep to the Virgin Mary to express gratitude for their safe return from outer space[189] provide grounds for doubt about the prospect of rapid change.

Despite his reluctance to condemn meat eating outright, Masri does argue strongly against the claim that vegetarianism is forbidden:

Meat-eating is neither encouraged nor even recommended by Islam: "Say {O Muhammad!} I find not in what has been revealed to me any food {meat} forbidden to those who wish to eat it, unless it be dead meat, or blood that pours forth, or the flesh of swine—for it is unclean {rijs}—or the sacriligious {fisq} meat which has been slaughtered in anybody's name other than that of Allah." It is significant to note that these laws have been laid down for those "who wish to eat it" (Ta'imin yat'amohu). Eating meat is not required.[190]

In practice, Bina Ahmed, as noted earlier, tells us: "I know Muslim men who are vegetarian and even vegan. Men are looking at how they treat animals in both a religious and humane issue."[191]

Muslim vegetarians have sometimes found support in Sufi traditions. In one well-known story the Sufi saint Rabia (d. 801) "was sitting in the midst of a number of animals. As soon as Hasan approached, they ran away." When asked why, Rabia answered: "You have been eating meat. All I had to eat was dry bread."[192] Although ascetic vegetarianism is regularly praised by the Sufis, Rabia's answer is animal-oriented as well. There is today in Istanbul a region "called 'Etyemecz' (noneater of meat) because of a mystic Sufi sect,"[193] but we are not told how their practice is motivated.

The illustrious Sufi poet Rumi (1207–73), who founded the Order of Whirling Dervishes,[194] composed an unambiguously ethical attack on meat eating in "The men who ate the elephant." Taking a cautionary approach reminiscent of the Buddhist literal defense—nonviolence as protection against animals' revenge—he told of a group of hungry travelers who were warned by a sage not to eat some nearby young elephants. Their mother "would wander a hundred leagues seeking her offspring with many a moan and many a sigh. Fire and smoke issue from her trunk: beware that you harm not her fondly cherished little ones!"[195] All but one of the travelers rejected his advice. While the meat eaters were all asleep, the mother elephant ran toward the group and tested the one, still watchful, abstainer by sniffing his mouth:

But no unwholesome odor came from it. . . . that huge queen-elephant harmed him not at all. Next she smelt the lips of every man that lay sleeping; the smell of her young one's flesh came to her from them each . . . , for each had eaten of the roast-flesh of her offspring. The mother-elephant swiftly rent and slew them one by one.[196]

It might be queried whether the lesson here is indeed wholly ethical, in that it advises refraining from evil out of fear of punishment, compassion for the mother elephant seeming to provide only a secondary motive. But such fear, felt in everyday life even when no immediate threat of revenge exists, reflects the awareness, through identification with a prospective victim, that a contemplated act *is* evil. Accordingly, the storyteller provides a threat to symbolize that awareness. The message to the ordinary meat eater is to remember that what you are doing is cruel and, even though no vengeful animal is likely to attack you for it, that you may suffer in other ways, if only in your conscience and from the fear of ill-luck that a bad conscience can produce.

Yahya Monastra names (besides Rabi'a of Basrah) as "an early Muslim vegetarian . . . the famous poet Abu al-'Ala' al-Ma'arri"[197] and Bawa Muhaiyaddeen. The latter has written: "You love flesh and enjoy murder. If you had any conscience or any sense of justice, if you were born as a true human being, you would think about this."[198] We learn from Foltz that "among the Sufis of North Africa and the Ottoman world saints were often believed to take animal form, and vegetarian anecdotes were widely told. An early female Sufi, Zaynab, is said to have been persecuted for her refusal to eat meat."[199]

The Sufis also invoke Kabir (1398–1448), a Muslim who was interested in Hinduism and influenced the founder of Sikhism: he attacked the hypocrisy of religious practitioners who kill and eat animals—"Here prayers, there blood— / Does this please God?"[200]

Conclusively, on this issue, Yahya Monastra declares,

> Some Muslims will tell you that in Islamic law you are not allowed to refuse to eat meat. This is mere opinion unsupported by any evidence from the sources of the Shari'ah. Suppose they establish the "Islamic State," then how will they enforce this ruling? Hold me down, force my mouth open, and shove kebabs down my throat?[201]

Next to meat eating, the practice that affects the most animals, namely, vivisection, is banned in traditional Islam. Muhammad is said to have "cursed the one who did *Muthla* to an animal (i.e., cut its limbs or some other part of its body while it is still alive),"[202] in a Hadith evidently addressing the same Middle Eastern practice as was forbidden by the seventh Noachide law (see chapter 2). Forward and Alam and Masri[203] cite this hadith as forbidding vivisection; Ahmed uses both number 1923 and number 1927 for the purpose.[204]

The term *vivisection* is nowadays applied to a variety of injurious laboratory procedures, not all of them involving cutting or mutilation, but the anti-vivisection tradition has been extended by analogy.

The interpretive potential of *ijtihad* is shown in Masri's appeal, when attacking vivisection, to Islamic ethical formulations having no reference to animals. For example,

> "One's interest or need does not annul other's right."
>
> Needs are classified in three categories: necessities . . . without which life could not be sustained; needs required for comfort and easement from pain or . . . distress, or for improving the quality of life . . . ; and luxuries . . . desirable for enjoyment or self-indulgence.
>
> Some rules that can be applied to these needs to determine whether experiments on animals would be allowed: "What allures to the forbidden, is itself forbidden. . . ." This rule implies that material gains, including food, obtained by wrongful acts, such as unnecessary experiments on animals, become unlawful (haram).
>
> "No damage can be put right by a similar or a greater damage."[205]

The first and last of these principles could be squared with an absolute prohibition on vivisection; the intervening argument is compromised by the word *unnecessary*. There is much ambiguity in the following points from Masri:

> Some research on animals may yet be justified, given the Traditions of Islam, only if the laboratory animals are not caused pain or disfigurement, and only if human beings or other animals would benefit. . . . The most important of all considerations is to decide whether the experiment is really necessary and that there is no alternative for it. . . . The basic point . . . is that the same moral, ethical and legal codes should apply to the treatment of animals as are being applied to humans.[206]

The earlier-stated conditions reluctantly justify vivisection, but the last one, calling for equal treatment, would wipe out the other justifications, since humans would not be used without their consent, however great the prospective benefit, whereas animals cannot give their consent to being imprisoned, experimented on, and killed and would presumably withhold it.

As previously discussed, faithfulness to the requirement of necessity is found in several Hadiths "forbidding blood sports and the use of animals as targets."[207] To reinforce this principle, the Prophet declared that the meat of animals used originally "as targets or in blood sport" was unlawful.[208] This was to make sure that people did not try to legitimize a cruel practice, undertaken frivolously, simply by eating the meat afterward.

IN BUDDHISM

There is strong feeling in Gotama's description of the process of sacrifice, and the inclusion of oppressed humans and of trees shows the value placed on all life forms:

> The person who is both a self-tormentor ... and also a tormentor of others ... is a noble anointed king or a very rich brahman. ... [344] ... He speaks thus: "Let so many bulls be slain for sacrifice, let so many steers ... heifers ... goats ... let so many rams be slain for the sacrifice, let so many trees be felled. ... Those who are called his slaves or messengers or workpeople, they, scared of the stick, scared of danger, with tearful faces and crying, set about their preparations." (*M*.i.343–4)

The reasons for abandonment of animal sacrifice are partly, like the Christian ones, substitutive. "Union with the god Brahma after death," according to the Buddha, "could be attained by meditative development of deep lovingkindness and compassion rather than by bloody Vedic sacrifices."[209] It seems that, as with Judaism, Christianity, and Islam, a need was still felt to find other means of retaining a traditional ritual theme. Yet belief in the superiority of the alternative methods is accompanied by a consciously and explicitly ethical revulsion (the Buddha's condemnation of "tormentors" of self, others, or both) against the original practice.

Another antisacrifice sermon, containing allusions to brahminic literature and practice, is, according to Gombrich, an example of how the "Buddha's message is to be understood in opposition to the other articulated ideologies of his day. The most important of these was the brahminical."[210] Here Gotama reworked the sacrificial procedures in terms of Buddhist moral psychology, identifying the sacrificial knives with wrong application of the organs of ethical choice, namely, body, speech, and mind: "Even before the sacrifice takes place one is setting up three knives which are morally wrong,"[211] and identifying the sacrificial fires with the "fires of passion, hate and delusion."[212]

The Bhagavad Gita lists different forms of sacrifice resembling the Buddhist substitutes,[213] but contains no ethical attacks on the existing practice.

Generosity, the positive form of Buddhism's second precept (abstention from *adinnadana*: taking what is not given), is expressed by the fact that "Buddhism understands by such *dana* [alms; charity] the service not of human beings alone but also of animals. Asoka established hospitals for man and beast; and institutions for the care of sick or infirm . . . four-footed creatures are still found in Buddhist lands."[214]

The humanitarian emperor Asoka (third century BCE) called for medicinal herbs, roots, and fruits "suitable for men and suitable for animals" to be planted where they were not already found; wells to be dug and trees planted "for the use of animals and men."[215] Like those of Akbar, some measures promulgated in Asoka's inscriptions constituted "only a partial assertion of animal rights," but "nonetheless reveal a highly unusual compassion on the part of a temporal ruler."[216] These included the protection of many species as "inviolable," together with "those she-goats, ewes and sows (which) are either with young or are giving milk (to their young)" and "those (of their) young ones which are less than six months old." In addition,

> Husks containing living beings (i.e. insects) are not to be burnt.
> . . .
> One animal is not to be fed with another animal . . . on every fast-day, fish are inviolable and are not to be sold . . . [on specific days] he-goats, rams, boars, and other animals that are usually castrated are not to be castrated . . . [and] the branding of horses and bullocks is not to be done.[217]

Under Asoka, "in time, the large royal household became completely vegetarian."[218]

On vegetarianism, Buddhism is somewhat closer to Hinduism than to Jainism. Hinduism shows a mixed pattern regarding food:

> The upanisadic concept of all living creatures being part and parcel of *Brahman* emphasizes the sacredness of all forms of life, and thus the killing of animals is unjustifiable. During the developing period of Buddhism and Jainism . . . this moral issue gained ground. . . . [but] not all Hindus are vegetarians, e.g., Bengalis are non-vegetarians.[219]

Where vegetarianism is advocated, the texts are emphatic. "'The meat of other animals is like the flesh of one's son. That foolish person . . . who eats meat, is regarded as the vilest of human beings.' *Mahabharata* XIII:114:11." [220] According to the Laws of Manu, "meat can never be obtained without injury to living creatures, and injury to sentient beings is detrimental to the attainment of heavenly bliss; let him therefore shun the use of meat."[221] It will be recalled from chapter 5 that these strictures were intended by Manu to subvert the practice of animal sacrifice, which, however, he formally sanctioned for the sake of tradition.

Jainism is unequivocal from the beginning. From the Akaranga Sutra:

> The first great vow, Sir, runs thus:
> "I renounce all killing of living beings, whether subtle or gross, whether movable or immovable. Nor shall I myself kill living beings nor cause others to do it, nor consent to it." [222]

As for Buddhism, despite the equivocal doctrines on meat eating discussed in chapter 5,

> that the idea of vegetarianism was however at least partially thematised in Buddhist thought from an early period is shown by the references in the Vinaya to abstention from meat-eating in certain conditions and also . . . by the mention of it as one of the ascetic practices that the Buddha's cousin-antagonist Devadatta insisted upon. [223]

These five ascetic practices were not rejected by the Buddha: "he even authorised their observance by his monks, but only as optional rules."[224]

Among canonical works, proscription of meat eating is found "only in certain Mahayana texts."[225] One of them is the Lankavatara Sutra. Containing "perhaps the strongest advocacy of vegetarianism in the Buddhist tradition," which "helped shape strict adherence to this practice in the Chinese monastic tradition,"[226] it uses the more positive side of karma to argue against meat eating: "in this long course of transmigration here, there is not one living being that, having assumed the form of a living being, has not been your mother, or father, or brother, or sister, or son, or daughter, or the one or the other, in various degrees of kinship; and when acquiring another form of life may live as a beast."[227] The influence of such scriptures has been particularly important in

China, where cruelty to animals is severe because of the speciesist Confucian tradition. Yet "with the development of the Mahayana school of Buddhism and the rise of compassion as the primary virtue, vegetarianism increased in popularity, to the extent that all Buddhist food in China is vegetarian."[228]

Apart from the Lankavatara Sutra, there are Mahayana sutras "teaching the theory of the *tathagatagarbha* and the Buddha-Nature" which "condemn [meat eating] outright." This theory "states that all incarnate sentient beings . . . have the capacity of certainly attaining Buddhahood sooner or later."[229]

In practice, "when certain Mahayanist groups came to accept their own code of discipline, represented by the Mahayanist *Brahmajalasutra*, a prohibition against meat-eating was included in it as one of forty-eight secondary injunctions."[230] But see chapter 5 for defensive exceptions to vegetarianism in the Mahayana Surangama Sutra.

Buddhism, Judaism, Islam, Hinduism, Christianity, and Jainism were represented at the first British Interfaith Service in celebration of animals, June 13, 2004, hosted by Golders Green Unitarians.[231] The Society of Ethical and Religious Vegetarians[232] promotes pro-animal policies generally and within the churches through relevant news, articles, and suggested actions.

THE EAST-WEST INTERCHANGE

> Even if Oriental and Aboriginal attitudes are . . . less admirable than they are customarily portrayed . . . the positive attitudes represented in the belief systems of others offer us stimulating ways to imagine what kinds of relationships to nature might be preferable to those currently prevailing in the West. They can become useful metaphors for action within our own cultural context.[233]

Then they can be transmitted back to the original culture to refresh its commitment. Thus the Western trend to vegetarianism, which has attracted animal lovers to Buddhism and other Eastern religions, has encouraged Buddhism to live up to its sometimes exaggerated reputation:

> In the West, vegetarianism among Buddhists is more common than in many parts of Buddhist Asia. This is due to Western expectations of what "non-harming" Buddhists should do, a general increase in vegetarianism in the

West, along with ease of obtaining good vegetarian food, and the influence of the East Asian Buddhist model, particularly via America. In Britain, when food is offered to Western monks trained in the Thai tradition, Thais often give meat dishes, but Westerners give vegetarian ones. This is gradually having the effect of the Thais offering more vegetarian ones.[234]

The trend is the less surprising in view of the fact that "there are now more Buddhists in America than there are in India."[235]

Gandhi, who was influenced by Tolstoy, Edward Carpenter, G. K. Chesterton, and Ruskin,[236] admired vegetarian Trappist monks, was shocked by meat-eating nuns, and only became "vegetarian by choice" rather than by religion and vow "after reading Henry Salt's *A Plea for Vegetarianism*."[237]

Increasing Islamic support for animals has been influenced by the West, a "disproportionate number of Muslim animal rights activists appear[ing] to be Western converts to Islam."[238] Islamic vegetarians have turned to Christian figures for support. Besides quoting many pro-animal Qur'anic verses and the Hadith, Fadali reminds readers of St. Francis[239]—who himself, as well as Richard of Wyche, was influenced by the persecuted vegetarian Cathars; they in turn "probably descended from the Thari," an ancient Indian vegetarian culture.[240]

In addition, Fadali has praised the reverence for life found in Krishnamurti and even in the nontheistic religions of Buddhism and Jainism.[241] Compare his appreciation of Eastern traditions with Salam's attack on "the unbeliever who prohibits the slaughtering of an animal," which may, according to Izzi Dien, have referred to those faiths.

ACTIVISM VERSUS QUIETISM

Jewish and Christian activism has been taken up by modern Buddhists such as Page. The influence was needed, since "while there is much beauty, wisdom, and compassion in Oriental thought, there is also disengagement."[242] Preece, however, exempts the Jains from "the Oriental quietist tradition.... Their activism has not only succeeded in changing the face of Eastern philosophy but it has also vastly improved the animal reality of the Orient,"[243] by seeking, "with some success, to influence the adoption of vegetarianism and the elimination of animal sacrifice."[244]

The Talmud supports activism. Defending the effort to convert people to vegetarianism, Schwartz quotes Shabbat 54*b*: "Whoever is able to protest against the transgressions of the entire world and does not do so is punished for the transgressions of the entire world"[245]—a rabbinical version of "If you're not part of the solution, you're part of the problem."

Such Western attitudes have affected Buddhism. There are Buddhist animal rights groups in Britain and the U.S.[246] But political engagement remains controversial within Buddhism: "People have confronted me . . . saying: 'What are you monks doing sitting there? What are you doing to help humanity? . . . You're running away from the real world.' . . . But that world is a condition of mind. Meditation is actually confronting the real world."[247] Mahayanist Page, by contrast, arguing that "inaction in the face of animal suffering is not an option,"[248] quotes the Brahmajala Sutra: "Disciples of the Buddha, you should willingly and with compassion carry out the work of setting sentient creatures free. . . . Should you see a worldly person intent on killing an animal, attempt by appropriate means to rescue or protect it."[249]—and makes clear that illegality should be no obstacle: "the lion, Subuddhi, . . . set free animals who had been 'lawfully' trapped by a hunter. Subuddhi's compassionate act was not denounced or condemned by the Buddha. Rather, it was praised."[250]

However, the ritual animal liberation events to which such precepts led have their unfortunate side. On the one hand, "in the sixth century, the monk Chi-I reportedly convinced more than 1000 fishermen to give up their work. He also purchased 300 miles of land as a protected area where animals could be released."[251] On the other hand,

> today in Bangkok, Thailand, one may see as many as half a dozen birds crammed into a small cage and being offered for sale near the shrine of the four-faced Buddha. Devotees purchase and release the caged birds to declare their affinity with nature. But, of course, that means other Buddhists capture and cage the birds . . . just for the worshippers to release.[252]

However, such examples illustrate false application of the activist policy, rather than any flaw inherent in it.

Altogether, as Gary Snyder summarized the activist versus quietist situation: "The mercy of the West has been social revolution; the mercy of the East has been individual insight into the basic self/void. We need both."[253] Although activism has more support from Buddhist tradition, particularly through the Bodhisattva ideal, than this statement implies, it may be as a result of Western influence that followers of Gotama increasingly call upon such traditions.

A DRAWBACK

There is a disquieting aspect to Western influence, as meat-eating habits, declining in the West, emigrate eastward, along with support for vivisection, which is definitely not declining in the West. A growth of vegetarianism in the West (the estimated UK figure in 2006 being 5 to 6 percent), with even veganism becoming a recognized practice,[254] has been accompanied by a drop in vegetarianism in India, "where more than half . . . professed to vegetarianism just 20 years ago," but "barely a third are vegetarian today."[255] And in Nepal, where monkeys are "worshipped by the Hindu population," they are now "undergo[ing] tests to benefit biomedical research in the U.S.A." [256]

Organizations such as Asia for Animals and Animal Nepal are working hard to make the Eastern contribution to the interchange an entirely benign one.

All the four worldviews have changed by becoming more favorable toward animals, either through endorsing animal rights views new to the tradition or (in the case of Buddhism) through strengthening an existing doctrinal commitment. But change has informed this ideological progression in other ways. The right to reread canonical texts has been used by Judaism, Christianity, Islam, and Buddhism.

In addition, the worldviews contain ontologies of dynamism and progress toward perfection. The Jewish and Christian God is held to change through accompanying ordained events or responding to the suffering of beings; conservative Islam's static view of the world has been balanced by Sufi relativism and replaced by today's more progressive views; Buddhist wisdom and ethics alike rest upon the fact of impermanence.

Altered conditions have been prominent in modern religious support for animals. Ancient abuses such as sacrifice are held to have been tolerated by the deity only in reluctant and temporary concession to humanity's misuse of free will. Meat eating—another concession possibly justified by earlier necessity—has been judged irreligious in the era of readily available vegetable foods, combined with worse farming practices, and of rising concern with environmental damage.

The effective defense of urging the abandonment of animal exploitation has rested on prevailing ethical doctrines with which animal abuse is seen to conflict. All the Abrahamic religions emphasize God's compassionate nature.

Vegetarianism is held to serve Jewish ideals not only of empathy and respect for animals but also of generosity and peace among humans. Christians have appealed to the createdness of animals and less problematically to the incarnation and the Fall. But, more strongly, Christian ideals of charity and love, originally applied only to humans, have been given animal implications. Islamic vegetarians, like Jews and Christians, redefine "dominion" as "stewardship." Egalitarianism in Buddhism exists not only in nature but in karmic interchangeability and embodies compassion in the ideal of the Bodhisattva who is sometimes reborn as an animal. The consequentialist values of this ideal have received more approval from Buddhists in modern times.

In addition, there has been an interchange of values between East and West, as persons in one culture have found certain doctrines of another useful to their case and then sometimes transmitted these doctrines back to receive greater attention in its original home. Eastern doctrines of the moral considerability of animals have permeated the West, while activism has been urged against the traditional passivity of the East. But there is concern over the adoption in Asia of Western habits of meat eating and vivisection.

In the peaceable world toward which humanity may, according to the evidence given here, be progressing, animals will be accorded equal moral status. For it seems that the ancient conflict faced by humans, which was painful even when it was needed for survival, is now beginning to be seen as avoidable, thus capable of being resolved in the right direction. So another type of evolution emerges, namely, the moral evolution of our species, as will be discussed in chapter 9, after chapters 7 and 8 consider some philosophical issues.

7. Seeing as a Whole
The Animal Perspective

THE GLORIFICATION OF HUMAN LANGUAGE AND REASON has been used to justify control of and moral priority over animals, while systems of classification place them low in the hierarchy. For this reason, antiverbal accounts of reality, particularly in mysticism, lend themselves to the arguments of animal supporters, although the original theorists might not recognize that potential. Animals themselves, with their lack of language and—a perhaps exaggerated assumption, as current research suggests—of discriminatory concepts, have often been described, both in myth and in direct commentary, as offering truer visions.

Yet the obliteration of distinctions can get rid of "right and wrong" as well as of aggressive dualisms like "soul and body." This is part of the problem of Oneness, explored in chapter 8. In chapter 7 I want to examine those tendencies that work, in all the worldviews, against logocentrism and rationalism and raise the status of animal experience.

LOGOMYSTICISM AND ANTIRATIONALISM

Logomysticism confers mystical status or a supernatural role upon words, rather than seeing them as the tools of rational analysis. The attitude emerges from people's struggles to refer to a God (or, in Buddhism, a reality) that reflection tells them must be unnameable. Discussing the changing rules on uttering or not uttering the tetragrammaton, Cohen explains that "to the Oriental, a name is not merely a label as with us. It was thought of as indicating the nature of the person or object by whom it was borne."[1] As a result, language may be sanctified, attaining an emotional force exceeding its literal meaning.

Levinas defends the importance of names, in that "to refuse substances the dignity of the Name . . . is to exclude from the paths which lead to God the ascent to the Unconditional." Moreover, he writes, "Whatever our mistrust towards the letter and our thirst for the Spirit may be, monotheistic humanity is a humanity of the Book . . . [and] recognizes in the Written the trace of a past that precedes all historical past capable of being remembered."[2] At first glance the statement gives primacy to words. But it goes on to acknowledge the non-verbal reality to which words must refer, especially the beginning or the *arche*. For "absolute God . . . is beyond all thematization and all essence."[3]

Redeeming rather than demoting language, in the kabbalistic school of Abraham Abulafia "every different combination of letters and vowels could be seen in the radiance of that intellectual light which appears under certain circumstances in the meditations of the mystic."[4] A more clearly antiwords tendency appears in R. Hayyim Volozhiner's statement (1749–1821), "'The essence of *En-Sof* is hidden away more than any secret, and no name must name it, not even the Tetragrammaton, not even the end of the smallest letter.'" Moreover, "'even if the *Zohar* designates this essence by the name of *En-Sof* (Infinite), this is not a name. For this concerns only the way in which we reach it from out of the forces that have emanated from It, when It desires to associate itself with the worlds.'"[5]

For Linzey, Christ is "as Logos the decisive fact of being for all creatures."[6] See chapter 3, under "Logocentrism, Dualism, and Rationalism" for discussion of the Gospel of John in this context. In the light of this mystical Logos, "the foolishness of God is wiser than man's wisdom" (1 Cor. 1:25).

Although Dombrowski[7] shares Hartshorne's acceptance of human cognition as a form of superiority, he also quotes with approval the latter's comparison of "the merely pragmatic or emotional sanity of the other animals" with the human "metaphysical blundering"[8] promoted by language. Since God's vision is of the whole, Dombrowski suggests, then God sees "in a way more like the other animals than like us. . . . Human beings pay a price for their microscopic analyticity."[9]

Here there might be an objection: although God sees "the whole" in the sense of seeing everything at once, animals, like humans, can only see their own bit of reality. What Dombrowski might have in mind when applying "the whole" to the animal perspective is the idea that whatever they experience is experienced all of a piece, without concepts beyond those needed for meeting their needs. This slide in meaning of "the whole" reflects a longing for simplicity, made to seem attainable by the move away from rationalism.

In Islam's doctrine of the signs one can see an equivalence of each manifestation with the God it represents, although Izzi Dien interprets this in a more authoritarian manner: "Islam does not perceive the environment as a god, but rather as ontological symbols upon which people's minds can be focused to understand the Creator."[10] Either way, nature as sign expresses the idea that meaning need not depend upon human language.

We are also told of "the unlettered Prophet, / Who believeth in Allah / And His Words" (7:158), which Ali explains—beyond the reference to Muhammad's illiteracy—as follows: "human knowledge tends . . . to acquire a partial bias . . . of some 'school' of thought. The highest teacher had to be free from any such taint."[11]

The antilogocentric strand in Sufism is one side of "the irreducible antagonism between the spiritual Islam of Sufism and legalitarian Islam"[12]—as, for example, in the saying of Kitab-Ilahi (which recalls Wittgenstein's dictum):[13]

> When you speak the 99 names of God, you are . . . playing with a hollow nutshell. How can God be understood through names?
>
> Since you cannot speak in words about the essence of God, best of all speak about nobody at all.[14]

We also have Rumi's "Intelligence is the shadow of objective Truth. / How can the shadow vie with sunshine?"[15]

In Buddhism, the dharma (a word with several meanings: in the present sense, the teachings; the truth) is "self-realised, it is timeless, it is a come-and-see thing" (M.i.37 and elsewhere) rather than verbal. As expressed by a modern Theravadin,

> While it's natural that we learn and understand through language, and express our understanding through language, many of us have become prisoners of language. With meditation we have the opportunity now to bring about a profound change in our Western civilization. We are trying to understand on a "non-conceptual" level. In meditation we are realizing the nature of experience directly.[16]

In the meditative jhanic progression, "initial and discursive thought" are the first mental states to be dropped (M.i.347). The Buddha declared, "For this, Pessa, is a tangle, that is to say human beings. But this, Pessa, is an open clearing, that is to say animals" (M.i.341).

The ideal is modified by the disciple Sariputta's statement that intuitive wisdom and discriminating consciousness "are associated, not dissociated. . . . Whatever one comprehends, your reverence, that one discriminates; whatever one discriminates that one comprehends" (M.i.292). His thought might be clarified by reference to Moore's statement "we cannot even raise the question how what we do understand by it is to be analysed, unless we do understand it."[17]

The image of human beings as a "tangle" is echoed in the Jatakamala: "Birds and beasts express their true feeling in their calls; men are the only animals who produce sounds with meaning contrary to their intentions."[18]

Though the paradoxes of the Heart Sutra and other mystical writings may be explained in words, they also point to the inadequacy of words. In the Lankavatara Sutra, the antiwords theme is dramatically illustrated by the declaration "It is said by the Blessed One that from the night of the Enlightenment till the night of the Parinirvana, the Tathagata [143] in the meantime has not uttered even a word, nor will he ever utter; for not-speaking is the Buddha's speaking."[19] Realizing that the claim is symbolic, Mahamati asks its meaning and is told, among other things, that "the realm of self-realisation is free from words and discriminations, having nothing to do with dualistic terminology."[20]

Such valuation of direct experience may reflect an influence of shamanism, via earlier yogic practices. Shamanism has animal implications in that it expresses the conflicting wishes, on the one hand, to be effective in the hunt through gaining access to the animal's intentions and, on the other, to assuage the hunter's guilt. Thus the "special people who had strong visions and dreams would also have affinity with some animal kind,"[21] a tendency surviving into Buddhist culture. Indeed, the Buddha's enlightenment suggests a shamanic journey into past lives and the lives of others, and the accomplished monk

> experiences the various forms of psychic power; . . . manifest or invisible he goes unhindered through a wall, a rampart or a mountain as if through air; he plunges into the ground and shoots up again as if in water; he walks upon the water without parting it as if on the ground; [12] sitting cross-legged he travels through the air like a bird on the wing. (*M*.iii.11–12)

Abu Yazid, like a real shaman, "becomes" a bird during his spiritual journey—illustrating the need to escape from human limitations to find enlightenment.

> I saw that my spirit was borne to the heavens. It looked at nothing and gave no heed, though Paradise and Hell were displayed to it, for it was freed of phenomena and veils. Then I became a bird, whose body was of Oneness and

whose wings were of Everlastingness, and I continued to fly in the air of the Absolute, until I passed into the sphere of Purification, and gazed upon the field of Eternity and beheld there the tree of Oneness.[22]

THE ANIMAL PERSPECTIVE

A novelist describes a human being's sudden insight, when watching animals, into the relativity of "reality":

> To these creatures, he thought, the world looked quite different—different colours, different smells, different texture, different shape. This meant that the things humans took for granted—a world of green trees and blue skies—have no objective qualities at all. . . . Time and space were only aspects of human perception. These and other things men took for granted were part of the map of reality, not part of the territory itself.[23]

Accounts that endow animals with spiritual capacities, or portray them as guides and messengers, attest to people's wish to enter this unknown world of experience.

SPIRITUAL ATTAINMENT OF ANIMALS

THE SOUL

Whether animals, or humans for that matter, "have a soul" is not provable or disprovable. Such a condition is not easy to define, although theorists frequently associate it with immortality, another nondeterminable state of affairs. Often the reason people argue about it is to promote their views on how animals should be treated—the lack of an immortal soul sometimes working against them, the possession of one for them. But the argument does not necessarily go that way:

> Robert Bellarmine (1542–1621), the Italian prelate, cardinal, and archbishop who was beatified in 1924, was said to leave the fleas in his beard undisturbed, allowing them to bite him, because "we shall have heaven to reward us for our sufferings, but these poor creatures have nothing but the enjoyment of this present life."[24]

On the other hand, antivivisectionist Frances Power Cobbe argued that

> it is absolutely necessary to postulate a future life for the tortured dog or cat
> or horse or monkey, if we would escape the unbearable conclusion that a sen-
> tient creature . . . incapable of giving offence, has been given by the Creator an
> existence which, on the whole, has been a curse. That conclusion would be
> blasphemy.[25]

On which Preece comments, "A burning desire for justice, not a theological
interpretation or even a conviction that it will be so, appears to lead to her
conclusion."[26] We can see from the statements of Bellarmine and Cobbe how
similar ethical impulses can dictate contrasting intellectual theories.

Here are some other arguments concerning the animal soul. As noted in
chapter 6, Genesis uses the same words (*nefesh chaya*, "living soul") for Adam
and animals, although they have been translated differently depending on
whether humans or animals are referred to. One kabbalist, Robert Flood (or
Fludd; 1574–1637), "proclaimed souls to inhabit animals, plants, and minerals, as well as humans."[27] Hirsch offers a conventional mixed view that "since
the soul animates, all sentient beings must have souls. . . . But the human
soul is of a higher quality, inasmuch as man was destined for a dominating
position in the world."[28] Note here how the quality is inferred from the dominance, rather than vice versa.

The Talmud contains varied notions:

> Animals also die by the hand of the angel [ref. Baba Mez. 36b]. According to 2
> Enoch lviii, 6, the souls of animals survive death, and on the day of judgment
> will make accusation against those who ill-treated them. The Rabbis believed
> that souls of animals, being of earthly origin, were mortal. Demons are ani-
> mal souls without bodies [ref. Gen. R. 7]. They resemble angels in some re-
> spects and human beings in others. Like human beings, they are subject to
> death [ref. Hag. 16a].[29]

A recent papal pronouncement about animals having the "breath of life"
was seen by Catholics

> as affirmation that animals possess souls. Professor of Theology at Urbino
> University Carlo Molari says the statement "demonstrates the Church's desire
> and deep concern to clarify the present confused thinking and attitudes to-

wards the animal kingdom. . . . The Pontiff [John Paul II] . . . wanted to say that also these creatures as well as man are possessed of the divine spark of life and that living quality that is the soul. And are therefore not inferior beings or . . . purely material."[30]

In a story from Dix Harwood, "a grieving little girl [was] comforted by Luther, who assured her 'that her pet dog that had died would surely go to heaven.' Luther is said to have told her that in the 'new heavens and new earth . . . all creatures will not only be harmless, but lovely and joyful. . . . Why, then, should there not be little dogs in the new earth?' "[31] John Wesley (1703–91), who founded the Methodist Church, not only "alluded to animals having souls, saying, 'Something better remains after death for these poor creatures also,'"[32] but—with a curious similarity to the Buddhist view that animals could, with great difficulty, attain human form—argued that in the next life they would be "granted the additional benefit of human intelligence so that they can partake of the glories of God."[33] Bishop Joseph Butler, in like vein, asserted an immortal animal soul and in 1736 "hypothesized that 'in the natural immortality of brutes,' animals could 'become rational and moral agents.'"[34] A century later Rev. John George Wood "expressed the view that most people were unkind to animals because they were unaware that the creatures had souls and would enjoy eternal life."[35] In *The Immortality of Animals* (1903) Elijah D. Buckner claimed that God "gave to man and lower animals alike a living soul, which of course means an immortal soul."[36]

Masri, who has no doubt about the animal soul, deduces (1) the immortality of animals and (2) their inclusion in judgment as follows: "If . . . the souls of animals are also the Spirit of God, then they too are immortal—because the Spirit of God never dies"; the gathering together referred to in the Qur'an (42:29) must refer to souls since "God certainly does not collect the rotting bones and flesh of dead creatures."[37]

PRAYER
Webb[38] reminds us of Psalm 148, whose relevant lines my Bible translates as

> *Praise the Lord from the earth,*
>   *you great sea creatures and all ocean depths,*
>
> . . .
>
> *wild animals and all cattle,*

small creatures and flying birds

—but the psalm also addresses inanimate objects and humans. In the *Pereq Shirah* or "Chapter of Song," of uncertain authorship, "though it may have originated among the *hekhalot* mystics of the fourth or fifth centuries,"[39] animals as well as nonsentient things praise God. Verses from scripture

> are listed for each of God's creatures who "sing" His praises by their very being. For instance, the song of the birds is: "Even the sparrow hath found a house, and the swallow a nest for herself, where she may lay her young" (Psalms 84:4). Dogs sing: "O come, let us bow down and bend the knee; let us kneel before the Lord our Maker!" (Psalms 95:6).[40]

The work became popular in the Middle Ages.[41]

In his poem "The Oxen" and in *Tess of the d'Urbervilles*,[42] Hardy commemorated the Victorian tradition that farm animals knelt in their stalls on Christmas Eve. According to D. Davies, "the historian Keith Thomas has shown how popular religion in Britain often regarded animals as capable of having some sort of religion."[43]

Islam explicitly attributes a religious sense to animals.

> Muhammad once saw some people just sitting on their animal mounts. He told them to either ride on them or to leave them alone but not to use them as chairs to sit on while they watched the streets and markets. He added that some of these animals were better than those who rode on them, for they remembered God more.[44]

The Qur'an's declaration that animals can pray—

> *Seest thou not that it is*
> *Allah Whose praise all beings*
> *In the heavens and on earth*
> *Do celebrate, and the birds*
> *(Of the air) with wings*
> *Outspread? Each one knows*
> *His own (mode of) prayer*
> *And praise. (24:41)*

—is repeated in the Sufi writings. According to Sa'di:

> *All things thou seest still declare His praise;*
> *The attentive heart can hear their secret lays.*
> *Hymns to the rose the nightingale His name;*
> *Each thorn's a tongue His marvels to proclaim.*[45]

Even worms are included:

> *If there is a worm in a rock*
> *He knows its body. . . .*
> *The sound of its praise, and its hidden perception,*
> *He knows by His divine knowledge.*[46]

Waliullah depicts animals "stand[ing] before their Lord pleading . . . for their appearance in the world of mortals. . . .

> At times the causes unite for giving a punishment which is to completely destroy the species . . . , but there the Patterns plead in the language expressed by their condition and not in the language of their tongue for the preservation of their images on the earth. It is the reason why the prophet Noah was ordered to carry in the boat a pair from every species. . . . The Holy Prophet had once ordered the killing of dogs, but then he disliked that, and said "They are also one of the communities." This was so because the Patterns stood before their Lord pleading for the existence of the form of their image on the earth.[47]

Waliullah does not even require animals to have their own mode of communication: their very "condition" pleads for realization, just as the creatures in the *Pereq Shirah* praise God "by their very being."

By contrast with this view of existence as a form of devotion, modern commentators have used examples of animal prayer to challenge the claim that other species lack cognition. Masri, citing 24:41 quoted above, interprets it as evidence that animals "have the intellect to perform the act of prayer with a conscious mind." He sees the Qur'an as consistent with "modern science" which "has proved that animals, birds and even insects do convey their ideas and information to each other . . . at least in distinguishable and intelligible sounds."[48] Fadali comments that "according to the Koran, animals' consciousness transcends mere instinct and intuition. Animals have a cognizance of the creator and pay their obeisance to Him through worship and adoration."[49]

The idea is drawn to a vegetarian conclusion by Ahmed:

> The Qur'an specifically mentions that all the creation of Allah is engaged in following His way (i.e., praying to Him—if not all the time, then certainly when they are in trouble—suffering). . . . So when an animal is slaughtered, even for eating, won't it pray/beg/implore cry to Allah, in his own way, to save it from harm . . . ? And won't Allah listen/grant its prayers/pleadings? Allah does hear its prayers by . . . making the devourer sick.[50]

Although Buddhist doctrine precludes a being in animal form from attaining enlightenment, the Mahaparinirvana Sutra describes the arising of the will to enlightenment in birds: "The Buddha speaks of the animals thus: 'All flying birds and all those on water and land aspired to the unsurpassed Bodhi [Enlightenment] and having aspired abandoned their bodies.' . . . The birds were inspired by the Buddha's teachings to resolve there and then to strive for full Buddhahood themselves. It also seems that . . . they then 'died' to their animal forms and entered a higher realm of being."[51]

ANIMALS AS GUIDES AND MESSENGERS

The impulse to share in the animals' perspective by seeing the world as they do is reflected in the countless stories, found in all traditions, of animals as guides and messengers. Besides this human emotional need, there are practical reasons for attending to animal behavior:

> There is a relationship . . . between the height bees build their hives from the ground and the amount of snow the winter is going to bring. . . . It seems that animals know things we don't know. . . . Little wonder, then, that our ancestors revered the animals as teachers and guides to a world of mystery, thinking of them as creatures of power.[52]

Hinduism acknowledges "animals' knowledge of the medicinal properties of herbs."[53]

A transformation of affect from pragmatic to sacred occurs in Genesis 8:8–11:

He sent out a dove to see if the water had receded from the surface of the ground. [9] But the dove could find no place to set its feet because there was water over all the surface of the earth; so it returned to Noah in the ark. He reached out his hand and . . . brought it back to himself in the ark. [10] He waited seven more days and again sent out the dove from the ark. [11] When the dove returned to him in the evening, there in its beak was a freshly plucked olive leaf! Then Noah knew that the water had receded from the earth.

Some of the guide-and-messenger stories offered here may have a similarly natural basis. There are subtle differences in the meanings conveyed by the accounts. I have ranged them, broadly speaking, from the superficial to the more significant.

MIRACLE STORIES AND SUPERSTITIONS

For some of the rabbis, dreaming of an animal was significant, with the appearance of different species predicting different things.[54] In addition, "People practise divination by means of the weasel, birds and fishes (Sanh. 66a)."[55] Cohen relates a story about R. Ilish, who

was enslaved, and once he was sitting by a man who understood the language of birds. A raven came and croaked. The Rabbi asked, "What did he say?" He answered, "Ilish escape! Ilish escape!" He said, "The raven is a liar and I place no trust in it." After a while a dove came and cooed. He asked, "What did he say?" The other replied, "Ilish escape! Ilish escape!" He exclaimed, "The dove is likened to Israel; hence a miracle is going to happen to me" (Git. 45a).[56]

In the Eastern Orthodox tradition a wild ass responded to St. Sabas's prayers for water during a drought, by "charging down the valley as if sent by the Angel Gabriel himself. Then it stopped, looked around and began digging deep into the gravel. It dug for twenty minutes, then it bent down and began to drink."[57] Thus was St. Sabas's spring found.

Two Islamic stories concern camels who halt at important places. In one, when the Prophet's she-camel al-Qaswa stopped, the "Muslims thought that the she-camel was exhausted; but the Prophet explained that it was stopped by the same power which stopped the elephant from entering Makkah. . . . He then called upon the Muslims to encamp." It turned out that there was

water there.[58] Muhammad's mosque and living quarters in Madinah were
selected by a camel whom he allowed to run free

> until it stopped at a yard belonging to two orphans of Banu al Najjar. There,
> the camel lay down and the Prophet dismounted. . . . he learned from Muadh
> ibn Afra that it belonged to Sahl and Suhayl, sons of Amr, of whom he was the
> guardian. He asked the Prophet to build a mosque there and made a promise
> to satisfy the two orphans. Muhammad accepted the request by building his
> mosque as well as his living quarters there.[59]

According to Mernissi this event, which time has given legendary status, has
a worldly origin: letting the camel choose the site was Muhammad's way of
tactfully deciding among the offers made by rival followers.[60]

In all such tales and beliefs, the animal may be regarded as a messenger
from God.

ANIMAL SYMBOLISM

The "strange creatures of Ezekiel and Revelation" may represent "the fulness
and variety of God's creation,"[61] but since they form one creature they also
indicate the search for a total vision, unlimited by human capacities:

> In appearance their form was that of a man, [6] but each of them had four
> faces and four wings. [7] Their legs were straight; their feet were like those of
> a calf. . . . [8] Under their wings on their four sides they had the hands of a
> man. . . . [9] . . . Each one went straight ahead; they did not turn as they
> moved. (Ezek. 1:5-9; see also Rev. 4:6-8)

The four faces are those of a man, a lion, an ox and an eagle. Such composite
beings recall those of Assyrian and Egyptian art, which portrays animal or
part-animal gods.

While the notion of the soul as a bird is not much implied in the Bible or the
Talmud, still "in mediaeval Jewish literature, especially in the Zohar, human
souls were not infrequently described as winged birds."[62] In the New Testament, a directly religious role is played by the dove as symbol of the holy
spirit—"I saw the Spirit come down from heaven as a dove and remain on him"
(John 1:32)—a text that may have inspired the opinion within Catholicism that
Gregorian chants "were taught to men by birds sent from heaven."[63] Free animals are associated with the mystical side of Jesus: "At once the Spirit sent him

out into the desert, [13] and he was in the desert for forty days, being tempted by Satan. He was with the wild animals, and angels attended him" (Mk. 1:12–13).

The decision of the Islamic philosopher Muhyiddin Ibn 'Arabi (1165–1240) to go from Andalusia to the Eastern Islamic world was inspired by a vision in which

> [a] bird whose marvelous beauty surpassed the beauty of all other celestial birds was circling round the Throne [of God]. It was the bird who communicated . . . the order to set out for the Orient: he himself would be his companion and celestial guide. . . . In this bird . . . it is not difficult to recognize a figuration of the Holy Spirit, that is, of the Angel Gabriel, Angel of Knowledge and Revelation.[64]

THE ANIMAL PERSPECTIVE THROUGH SPEECH

In folklore and myth it is taken for granted that animals speak freely and are understood by human beings. But when a text calls attention to the ability, it is saying that only wise humans can understand the animals' speech.

The Qur'an, 27:16, mentions Solomon's knowledge of the speech of birds, 27:18–19, his knowledge of the speech of ants, and in this same surah a hoopoe brings a message about the Queen of Sheba (27:22ff). These features of the Solomon story are not found in the Bible.

Anis Ahmed ibn El-Alawi tells us that "Moses knew the language of animals."[65] Sa'di relates, "A foolish man was raving at a donkey. It took no notice. A wiser man . . . said 'Idiot! The donkey will never learn your language—better that you should observe silence and instead master the tongue of the donkey.'"[66] This story might be intended to illustrate the principle, important to Sufism, of adapting the teaching to its audience.

TEACHERS OF WISDOM

Job (12:7–9) says,

> But ask the animals, and they will teach you,
>   or the birds of the air, and they will tell you;
> [8] or speak to the earth, and it will teach you,
>   or let the fish of the sea inform you.
> [9] Which of all these does not know that the hand of the Lord
>   has done this?

In the Hadith, the idea that everything is as God wanted it is conveyed by a cow: "The prophet said, 'While a man was riding a cow, it turned towards him and said, "I have not been created for this purpose, I have been created for ploughing."'"[67] More complex ideas are suggested in the continuation of the same Hadith: "The Prophet further said, 'A wolf caught a sheep, and when the shepherd chased it the wolf said, "Who will be its guard on the day of wild beasts, when there will be no shepherd for it except I?"'"[68] In another version, the wolf says, "Be afraid of Allah, you have taken the provision from me which Allah gave me,"[69] and goes on to tell the shepherd that Allah's Messenger is preaching in Al-Madina. Is this meant to justify predation as something dispensed by God (with implications of theistic subjectivism)?

The editor's note continues, "Allah's Messenger said: '. . . the Day of Resurrection will not be established till beasts of prey speak to the human beings'" and until things and body parts speak to people.[70] An echo, this time, of the peaceable kingdom? Three different ideas emerge from the same narrative core: (1) the free animal as symbol of apocalyptic collapse, (2) justification of predation as coming from Allah, presenting the problem of evil, (3) a future transcending both (1) and (2).

Shibli tells of a dog who, because of fear of his own reflection in the water, refrains from drinking.

> Finally, such was his necessity, he cast away fear and leapt into the water; at which the "other dog" vanished.
> . . . the obstacle, which was himself, the barrier between him and what he sought, melted away.
> In this same way my own obstacle vanished, when I knew that it was what I took to be my own self. And my Way was first shown to me by the behaviour of—a dog.[71]

In this case, the pointed observation that the author has learned from a dog is more significant than the animal's contribution to the lesson. We should bear in mind that, because of the dislike of dogs in Muslim culture—a pre-Islamic Middle Eastern attitude reflected in various antidog Hadiths, "frequent positive references to dogs in Sufi literature may be largely a kind of shock-value device."[72] Or, when uttered by Sufi saints, moralistic stories such as those quoted later in this chapter enable the saints to demonstrate their "virtuous humility by associating with, caring for, or learning from dogs, 'the lowest of the low' in all creation."[73]

Another example of how animals are aligned with the path to wisdom is found in the derivation of the name of the foremost Mahayana philosopher, Nagarjuna, "from *arjuna*, a kind of tree, and *naga*, a serpent or 'dragon' as the Chinese translations more expressively have it." The name

> refers to the "legend" (according to modern scholarship) that the sage was born beneath an Arjuna tree and that he visited the submarine kingdom of the Nagas, where the Naga kings transmitted to him the large *Prajna-paramita Sutra*, which had been entrusted to their care by the Lord Buddha. . . . As in almost all traditions, the Naga or serpent stands for Wisdom.[74]

But teachers of wisdom are not always appreciated. The complex problem of innocence, free will, and authority is forced upon human beings in Genesis 3 by "that ancient serpent called the devil, or Satan, who leads the whole world astray" (Rev. 12:9) or as Green puts it, "that subtle hermeneut of suspicion" who deprives humanity of its animal-like innocence through the "earliest recorded misinterpretation of a religious text."[75]

PURVEYORS OF MYSTICAL EXPERIENCE

Saul finds Samuel while searching for lost donkeys (1 Sam. 9). Similarly, an animal acts as indirect guide in Bell's account of the garden of Irem. Built to rival Eden, it was thus destroyed by heaven but preserved invisible "unless very rarely, when God permits it to be seen, a favour one Colabah pretended to have received" when "as he was seeking a camel he had lost, he found himself on a sudden at the gates of this city."[76] In both stories the invisibility of the animals, suggesting that of God, and their lostness, suggesting spiritual loss followed by recovery, takes the events out of the realm of the adventitious and into that of the mystical.

The Qur'an's narrative of the cave (surah 18) includes animals in the total cosmology. The chapter retells a Christian Rip van Winkle story (the Seven Sleepers of Ephesus) that was popular in the Roman Empire. In the cave where the companions have hidden from persecution, there is also a dog:

> *And We turned them*
> *On their right and on*
> *Their left sides: their dog*
> *Stretching forth his two forelegs*
> *On the threshold: if thou*

Hadst come up on to them,
Thou wouldst have certainly
Turned back from them in flight. (18:18)

This may have been because the dog served as a guard; or because "perhaps their eyes were open, even though their senses were sealed in sleep."[77] The dog is important enough to have a traditional name, Qitmir,[78] although some scholars think it may have been Raqim.[79] This fact seems to take the story out of the category of "shock-value" or "*even* a lowly dog" messages, especially if the animal was a guard, an acceptable role for dogs in Islam.

The honored place of Qitmir/Raqim in Islamic lore is acknowledged twice in Saʿdi's *Rose-Garden*: "And the cave-sleepers' dog sometime remained / With good men and the rank of men attained"[80] (but see chapter 4, under "Perfectionism," for Saʿdi's own speciesist refutation of the claim); and in a description of a miser who "would not have given a loaf to save a life, nor would have indulged the cat of Abu Hurairah with a scrap, nor have cast a bone to the dog of the Companions of the Cave."[81]

A puzzling, because rather trivial, feature of the story is the doubt it expresses as to how many humans were present in addition to the dog:

(Some) say they were three,
The dog being the fourth
Among them; (others) say
They were five, the dog
Being the sixth . . . (18:22)

—an ambiguity "some commentators have interpreted . . . to mean that the dog became one of the faithful, indistinguishable in virtue from his human companions."[82]

In any case, the animal is a conscious participant in an account whose "lessons are: (1) the relativity of Time, (2) the unreality of the position of oppressor and oppressed . . . on this earth (3) the truth of the final Resurrection, when true values will be restored, and (4) the potency of Faith and Prayer to lead to the Right."[83]

TEACHERS OF MORALITY

Balaam's donkey conveys an ethical message in the course of delivering an instruction from God:

Then the Lord opened the donkey's mouth, and she said to Balaam, "What have I done to you to make you beat me these three times?"

[29] Balaam answered . . . "You have made a fool of me! If I had a sword . . . I would kill you. . . ."

[30] The donkey said . . . , "Am I not your own donkey, which you have always ridden . . . ? Have I been in the habit of doing this to you?" (Nu. 22:28–30)

The angel of God explains, "I have come here to oppose you because your path is a reckless one before me. The donkey saw me and turned away from me these three times" (Nu. 22:32). In the background may lie a natural explanation: "people familiar with horses, asses, and burros insist that these equines have an uncanny sense of danger [such as the presence of a hidden rattlesnake], and often cannot be made to go in a direction where they feel imperiled."[84] The donkey taught not only Balaam but Jews of the future as well, since, as noted in chapter 2, the rabbinical law against causing pain to an animal was said by Maimonides and R. Judah ha-Hasid to derive from the story.

Elsewhere in the Talmud, we find that

Praise is bestowed upon certain creatures for their habits which are said to be models for human beings to imitate. "Had the Torah not been given to us for our guidance, we could have learnt modesty from the cat, honesty from the ant, chastity from the dove, and good manners from the cock (Erub. 100*b*)."[85]

There may be a moral lesson in the legend that the Greek Orthodox convent of Seidnaya near Damascus was founded by the Emperor Justinian when he was out hunting. He

chased a stag up a rocky eminence. Just as he was about to draw his bow, the stag changed into the Virgin Mary. The Virgin commanded him to build a convent on the site, which, she said, had previously been hallowed by Noah himself, who planted a vine there soon after the Flood.[86]

Dalrymple suggests an etymological origin to the story, in that "in Aramaic Seidnaya means both 'our lady' and 'a hunting place.'"[87] Yet the identification of the persecuted beast with the innocent Virgin is compelling.

The two stories below illustrate how Sufis used the lowly status of the dog to praise humility. Maulana Dervish, when called a dog, said

> "dog" is indeed a good word. I am a dog who obeys his master, showing the sheep by signs the interpretation of our Master's desires. . . .
>
> Just as barking and wagging and love are attributes of the dog, we exercise them; for our master has us and does not do his own barking and wagging.[88]

But in the following story we find an ethic beyond humility:

> Bayazid encountered a dog and started to pull his robe away . . . so that it should not defile him.
>
> The dog, in a human voice, said;
>
> "If I had been dry, there would have been no purpose in avoiding me. If I had been wet, you could have washed your robe. But the hate which you have towards me can never be cleansed."
>
> Bayazid said:
>
> "O enlightened dog, come and stay with me for a while."
>
> The dog answered:
>
> "That is impossible, because the world uses me as an epithet, and you are regarded by the world as a paragon."
>
> Bayazid exclaimed:
>
> "Alas! I am not fit to live with one whom the whole world regards as inferior: how can I therefore approach the Truth which all regard as the Highest of all?"[89]

Not merely pride, but also hate, is condemned here; and the dog, according to the text, is not *actually* inferior, or the embodiment of an epithet, but is regarded as such by the world, whose distorted vision the mystic is expected to surpass.

But the most radical Islamic guide-and-messenger story is found in *The Case of the Animals Versus Man before the King of the Jinn*, in which the animals put humanity on trial. It was produced by the tenth-century Ikhwan al-safa' ("Pure Brethren"), whose ideas were only accepted by the heterodox Isma'ilis.

> We were fully occupied in caring for our broods and rearing our young with all the good food and water God had allotted us, secure and unmolested in our own lands. Night and day we praised and sanctified God. . . .

... God created Adam ... and made him his viceregent on earth. His offspring ... encroached on our ancestral lands. They captured sheep, cows,
horses, mules, and asses ... and enslaved them. ... They forced us to these
things under duress, with ... torture and chastisement our whole lives long.
Some of us fled to deserts, wastelands, or mountaintops, but the Adamites
pressed after us. ... Whoever fell into their hands was yoked, haltered, and
fettered. They slaughtered and flayed him, ... and put him onto the fire to be
cooked. ... Despite these cruelties, these sons of Adam are not through with
us but must claim that this is their inviolable right, that they are our masters
and we are their slaves, ... —all with no proof or explanation beyond main
force.[90]

By imagining themselves in the animals' place, these thinkers saw how aggressive doctrines such as "inviolable right" can be merely the legitimizations
of "main force."

The humans then present in support of their own hegemony some arguments familiar to modern secular discourse, and some based on religion, but
the animals refute them all. In the end, though, "the King of the Jinn decides
in favor if the humans," solely on the "capricious, unproven, and contested
premise that humans alone can have eternal life." Foltz continues:

This ... unsatisfying conclusion leaves one wondering just what point the
Brethren were trying to make. Is their treatise intended to awaken the reader
to a non-anthropocentric reality? If so, the ending is clearly unacceptable. But
if the intention is to re-assert ... human uniqueness, why so convincingly
make the case on the animals' behalf? Or is the reader's frustration meant to
be turned against God, for having established the hierarchy of creation on the
basis of such unfair and arbitrary principles? The question is not easily resolved.[91]

While it is true that the final judgment refers to the eternal human soul, a
more plausible motive appears earlier in the case, when the "King of the Jinn
takes counsel with his fellow jinn. What is to be done if the case is adjudi-
cated in favor of the animals? Who will purchase their freedom? And how
will humans, who rely so heavily on the labor and products of the animals,
continue to subsist?"[92]

The necessity argument, offering a comparatively understandable excuse
though it does, still conceals the speciesist assumption that human vital

interests must override the equally vital interests of nonhumans, with power, rather than merit or need itself, deciding the issue. There is no attempt to figure out how human life might be sustained without exploitation, although at one point the humans do agree to "show more kindness" to the animals.[93] The aggressive "eternal soul" argument provides a high-minded justification for self-interest.

Or could the heterodox and eclectic, but still Muslim, Ikhwan al safa' have been afraid of persecution? Could their intellectual and moral conviction have crumbled under the weight of tradition? Or perhaps, after all, they looked at their own personal use of animals—certainly for work, and possibly for food—and concluded that human needs must prevail.

But up to and despite the unfortunate ending, in this text the Ikhwan, using animals as advocates, "may have more to teach us in the twenty-first century than they did to Muslims of their own era."[94]

In the jatakas, the animal as moral teacher is more than a symbol of otherness, since the supreme teacher, the Bodhisatta, is believed to have occupied myriad human and animal forms during his previous lives. So the didactic or exemplary animal frequently appears in these tales. In numbers 159, 482, and 491 a queen dreams of an animal preaching and asks the king to find and bring back the animal. The stories have various structures, but in all of them the Bodhisatta (as goose, deer, and peacock respectively) preaches to a human being, the human (king, king, and hunter respectively) is reformed, and in 482 and 491 the reform has specific reference to animals. The animals may also set an example of self-sacrifice. "The king . . . lay down thinking, 'This animal, not reckoning his own life, has caused the safety of his troop.' . . . He thought, 'It is not right to destroy this king of the monkeys: I will bring him down by some means and take care of him' (vii.372 (407,226–27))." The king is later "established in the Bodhisatta's teaching" (vii.375 (407,227)).[95]

Christian theology, following the later Greeks, extended biblical appreciation of language to a rationalism used most damagingly against animals, but Jewish and Christian thinkers alike acknowledge the difficulty of applying to God or Christ words that convey the unified nature of the divine. In Islam and in mystical strains of Judaism, the phenomenon of logomysticism, or assigning less divisive meanings to language, is apparent.

A positive downgrading of language can be found in Sufism and in Buddhism, in keeping with the imperative of knowing God or reality directly.

Sometimes, therefore, the wordlessness of animals has seemed to contain the potential for spiritual advantage. Their perspective has also been valued for its otherness and the doors of possibility that difference seems to open. In conventional religious terms animals have been credited with an immortal soul and the capacity for prayer. Tales of animals as guides and messengers reflect these beliefs or hopes.

The impulse the stories show toward connection with the world beyond humanity has found its way into unitary philosophical theories such as monism, holism, pantheism, and panentheism. Since the relation to animals and to ethical thought generally is similar in these various approaches, I address them under the collective heading of Oneness. Attractive though such an outlook can be, it has its problematic side, and this, along with its positive features and, as I argue, its frequently ethical motivation, is the subject of the next chapter.

8. The Problem of Oneness

ARE WE TO SEE THE WORLD as in a sense "one" or as many? Both are true. No one can deny the diversity of what we experience or that the totality is by definition "one." But competing forms of words, such as that this totality with its diverse contents is all common, interchangeable atomic stuff, or that it constitutes a single cosmic consciousness, or is a collection of different things separate from their mutual, unified creator, are simply analyses of the same reality; the choice of words will be influenced by the writer's or speaker's attitudes toward humanity, animals, and the rest of nature. This leads us to the problem outlined in the introduction, namely, that while the Oneness view may appeal to animal supporters by conferring equality on all species, it also confers equality on the good and the bad in the world, obliterating the need for ethical decisions.

First let us look at the problem in the context of monotheism, where it arises when considering the immanence or transcendence of God.

IMMANENCE OR TRANSCENDENCE

For believers in God, Oneness is often expressed by the idea that the deity resides in everything (pantheism) or that everything is in the deity (panentheism). The transcendence view, which separates God from creation, allows distinctions between sentient and nonsentient as well as right and wrong, whereas a God who inhabits or contains everything must also—logically—partake of natural and even human evil. Yet the transcendence view can have antianimal implications, suggesting hierarchy.

In the Talmud, hierarchy is quantifiable, God being "located in the seventh heaven":

> The thickness of each firmament is equal to a journey of five hundred years, and so are the spaces between the seven firmaments. Above them are the holy *Chayyoth*. Their feet measure a distance equal to all of these put together; their ankles are of similar dimension. . . . The King, the living and eternal God, high and exalted, abides above them (Chag. 13*a*).[1]

Alongside such complex structures in Kabbalism, more unitary inflections can be found. The late-thirteenth-century *Zohar* "had pantheistic overtones."[2] For the kabbalists, who may have encountered Sufi influence, God was "the Ein Sof, the endless, ineffable, somewhat like the Neoplatonic One; but from the Ein Sof there emanate ten powers or entities, referred to as the Sefirot" which are "supposed to have played a part in the creation of the world."[3] In this literature "the unity of God in His *Sefirot* and the appearance of plurality within the One are expressed through . . . images which continually recur. They are compared to a candle flickering in the midst of ten mirrors set one within the other, each of a different color."[4]

By apparent contrast, the Lurianic (Isaac Luria Ashkenazi, d. 1572) "doctrine of *tzimtzum*, the withdrawal of God into Himself," implied "a real division between the infinite God and the finite world."[5] But the doctrine can be differently interpreted: for Solomon, it "stresses the 'inferiority' and distance from God of material creation, but compensates by drawing attention to the divine element concealed in all things."[6] Scholem refers to Lurianic doctrines as "nourish[ing] panentheistic tendencies which subsequently came to the fore once more in a number of the classic texts of Hasidism."[7] On balance, "while not a single kabbalist school of thought ever claimed that God has no existence apart from created beings, the position most commonly held was that He was nevertheless to be found within them in variously definable ways."[8] We can see how either perspective can be adapted to suit the theorist.

In the case of Spinoza (who was said by Wachter in 1699 to have been influenced by the kabbalist Abraham Herrera),[9] there was the task not only of articulating his account of "God or Nature" but also of defending it against charges of atheism. Replying to a critical letter from Oldenburg, he wrote:

> I maintain that God is . . . the immanent, but not the transitive, cause of all things. That all things are in God and move in God, I affirm, I say, with Paul, and perhaps also with all the ancient philosophers, although in another way; and I would also dare to say, with all the ancient Hebrews. . . . Nevertheless, some people think the *Theological-Political Treatise* rests on the assumption that God is one and the same as Nature (by which they understand a certain mass, or corporeal matter). This is a complete mistake.[10]

Yet, "since Nature or God is one being, of which infinite attributes are said, and which contains in itself all essences of created things, it is necessary that of all this there is produced in thought an infinite idea, which contains in itself objectively the whole of Nature, as it is in itself"[11]—a more panentheistic idea and one that, in his philosophy, did not give rise to any affection for animals.

The problem of oneness in Jewish mysticism, whereby a unitary *Ein Sof* wars with the moral law of the Torah, is addressed by Levinas:

> The notion of *En-Sof* is thus the perfection of the Torah, freed from the worlds whose incatenation and hierarchy its legalism presupposes through the plain meaning of the text. Is everything pure for the person who has reached that far? . . . Must we lay stress on the elevation above the Law and ethics from out of the Law. . . . ? . . . The spiritualism beyond all difference that would come from creature means, for man, the indifference of nihilism. . . . All is divine. All is permitted.[12]

Offering Volozhiner's conclusion that "we must therefore make space for . . . the Law of the Torah, 'for the God associated with the worlds in their differences,'" Levinas goes on to attempt a reconciliation of "the Infinite and the Law together" through humanity as "a new image of the Absolute."[13]

There is a marked strain of Oneness in process Christianity. Indeed, "for Hartshorne . . . *deity itself* is a sort of superanimal. . . . God, or the World Soul, is . . . the society of individuals in the world brought together as a single individual."[14] Sprigge speaks of "God, to call the totality that for now,"[15] and prefaces his book with a quotation from Pope: "All are but parts of one stupendous whole, / Whose body Nature is, and God the Soul." Hartshorne "calls his synthesis 'panentheism'"[16] and "views Plato . . . as a panentheist, such that all is *in* God."[17]

But panentheism and pantheism alike still keep God partly separate, as the deity must be in order to contain or inhabit everything else. Indeed any relationship of "God" to "everything" (or, for example, to "reality") implies separateness; otherwise you would not need to use different words. Douglas Davies, summarizing the traditional view, places more emphasis on difference: "Christian theology has always maintained a sharp distinction between God and the created order. Some mystical trends . . . suggest that God is one with the universe, as . . . Spinoza . . . had argued. Orthodox theology has denied this on the basis that God was transcendent."[18] Yet that view, too, can support the animal by the shared subordination and created status of all species. Moreover, human power, like that of God, can be turned on its head through the imperative of generosity. Just as Jesus was a servant, "whenever we find ourselves in a position of power over those who are relatively powerless our moral obligation of generosity increases in proportion. If our power over animals confers upon us any rights, there is only one: the right to serve."[19]

Oneness doctrine, for its part, can lead—especially in environmental thinking—to a questionable lumping together of the sentient and nonsentient, as in the outlook of some present-day Christians, whereby "if animals appear at all, they are viewed as part of 'earth' or 'the earth community.'"[20] Linzey criticizes this "emerging green view of 'holistic interdependence'":

> Christian tradition clearly makes a distinction between humans and animals, and also between animals and vegetables. Scholars eager to establish the pre-eminence of humans in Scripture have simply overlooked ways in which animals exist alongside humans within the covenant relationship. The Spirit is itself the "breath of life" (Gen. 1:30) of both humans and animals. The Torah delineates animals within its notion of moral community.[21]

But many environmentalists "want to exclude animals from special moral consideration."[22] Thus Bradley's belief in "the essential unity between humans, animals and the inanimate elements of creation"[23] results in an almost total absence, in his book, of any practical policy recommendations on behalf of animals, despite many sympathetic comments.

In conservative Islam, the separate, authoritarian God prevails and, outside Sufism, which itself is cautious on this point, unitary indications are, in the end, rejected: "Nor does it consider that all things are part of one reality: there is a vast gulf between creator and created."[24] The eponymous theme of submission provides cosmological support for worldly rulership and hierarchy of social status, gender and species. The early Islamic Arabs' "hegemony . . . derived meaning and purpose from the monotheistic polity which Muhammad had created . . . and the monotheist faith which he had made their own."[25] Monotheism supports power more than does polytheism because if there is only one God, then that God has all the power, from which there is no appeal.

But there is another, more pantheistic strand in Islam, in which Oneness becomes impersonal and, as it were, democratic. "Allah is / The (only) Reality," the Qur'an tells us (31:30), in which case all reality is Allah. For the medieval Arabic philosophers, influenced by Plotinus, "God is the One from which emanate all multiplicity and matter";[26] later, the Sufi Waliullah also adopted an emanationist view. Haykali's "Thou art there" describes in each line a different human, natural, or spatiotemporal thing, followed by the title words.[27]

At times, pantheistic views within Sufism have led to an amoralist tendency springing from the idea that "there is neither good nor evil, since both alike flow from God."[28] Thus the Malamatiya sect "held that the true worship of God is best proved by the contempt in which the devotee is held by his fellow-men; on this argument they justified ... the commission of the most outrageous sins."[29] Bell observes that Sufis following this tendency "restricted the consequences of their principles to the adepts."[30] Nevertheless, it is not surprising that this facet of mysticism is ignored by supporters of animal or human rights.

Despite such problems, the Oneness concept is often advanced for animal-friendly purposes. According to the Church and Society Consultation report,

> Instead of a king relating to his realm, we picture God as the creator who "bodies forth" all that is, who creates not as a potter or an artist does, but more as a mother.... The universe, including our earth and all its creatures and plants "lives and moves and has its being" in God (cf. Acts 17:28), though God is beyond and more than the universe.[31]

That the same quotation from Paul should occur here and in Spinoza (see above) dramatically illustrates the normative flexibility of the unitary approach. Vegan antivivisectionist Fadali combines the Oneness perspective with the notion of a creator God: "God's image (manifestation) is the whole universe ... every engendered creation. All are One"; "A true sense of one body with all things is the only worthy prescription to provide remedy for the primary threat to life—including our own—which is ourselves."[32]

"Intuitively," reflects the Animal Judge, "I find the move toward Oneness, despite its drawbacks, more reassuring than the adaptation of divine authoritarianism to support my case." Some activists, as well, may "find their sensibilities offended by even these less gratuitous interpretations of dominion and stewardship. These ideas are clearly rooted in a transcendent notion of God."[33] But all in all, as can be seen from chapter 6, the theistic animal supporters examined here have not placed much reliance on unitary ideas. Implications of transcendence, such as compassion and ethical prescriptions—particularly

Linzey's "moral priority of the weak"—"are the attitudes most subscribed to by Christians and will probably bring the greatest shift in the reduction of pain and death for animals without requiring Christians to accept changes that might appear too radical";[34] the same can be said of Jews and Muslims. The God of the ancient Middle East, constructed partly to justify a then apparently necessary exploitation of animals, has been given a more generous face by those of his present-day Western worshippers who see neither justice nor necessity in that exploitation.

THE EMPTINESS DOCTRINE AND THE BODHISATTVA IDEAL: SAVING THE NONBEINGS

But it is in the predominantly mystical creed of Buddhism that we find the most difficult questions arising from a doctrine of Oneness, expressed as emptiness or *sunyata*. This central teaching of later Buddhism, though clearly present in the earlier writings, is connected to animals through the absence of anthropocentrism in the culture, making possible the rejection—as expressed through the myth of karmic interchangeability—of permanent species membership. In brief, as discussed in chapter 5, the doctrine holds that all phenomena are devoid of fixed existence because of the constant fluidity of their parts. For the same reason, everything is interconnected.

Such an outlook is not exclusive to Buddhism. In the *Mahabharata*, the

> familial interconnectedness of these characters . . . reveals an underlying tenet of the Indian world view: that we are all interconnected beings and need to more fully recognize and embody this fact. Theologically, this perspective can be traced to Upanisadic monism, the notion that there is an all-pervading higher reality out of which we are born and to which we will ultimately return.[35]

Zaehner favors Ramanuja's "qualified monism" account,[36] for Hinduism combines theism with oneness. Krishna in the Bhagavad Gita identifies himself with everything natural, mythical, and abstract, using the "I am" construction. Animals are included, for instance: "Among horses know that I am

Uccaihsravas [Indra's steed] . . . among princely elephants [Indra's, called]
Airavata, among men the king" (Gita paragraph 10.27). "And what is the seed
of all contingent beings, that too am I. No being is there, whether moving or
unmoving, that exists or could exist apart from Me" (10.39); the passage concludes, "This whole universe I hold apart [supporting it] with [but] one frag-
ment [of Myself], yet I abide [unchanging]" (10.42).[37]

In Buddhism, by contrast, there is no God and all is emptiness by virtue of
impermanence. So, if suffering creatures do not even have a fixed existence
(the Oneness view), how can suffering matter and why should one do anything about it (the morally dualistic view)?

> A Bodhisattva's wisdom seems to conflict with his duty of compassion. When
> he listens to the voice of wisdom, a Bodhisattva will see to it that his mind is
> not established anywhere, that it does not dwell on anything whatsoever.
> But if he wants to benefit others, he must make an initial vow to help all
> beings. . . . This vow seems to imply that beings actually exist.[38]

What is at stake in this problem is the ability to believe in two doctrines—
emptiness and the ideal of compassion—each of which has great value in itself (for the status of animals as well as in other ways), but do not seem to be
compatible with one another.

First I want to remove the common misconception that in Buddhist theory
nothing really exists. In fact, becoming, rather than being or nonbeing is the
correct view, as Venkata Ramanan explains:

> What is meant by non-existence is becoming, change.
>
> Those who wrongly conceive sunyata lend themselves to the kind of
> negativism that denies causal continuity. . . . As the Sastra [Nagarjuna's
> Maha-prajnaparamita-sastra] would say, that which is utterly nothing is
> not even speakable. To say that this thing is not is itself to speak of its exis-
> tence.
>
> What thing can undergo change if it has no nature at all? Everything has its
> own nature but not unconditioned. . . . Things are relatively existent, sunya,
> and not nothing.[39]

So, to our problem, which comprises three questions.

(1) How can one reconcile conceptual emptiness with observable suffering
and the compassion that responds to it, as symbolized in the Bodhisattva

ideal? Two common answers are (a) parallelism, or "you need both," and (b) having compassion for deluded beings.

(a) is the answer commonly given by monks, and often found in scripture, but it is not clear why. After all, parallelism does not amount to integration, or explain why wisdom should guarantee compassion, or what compassion contributes to reaching the highest stage of enlightenment.

(b) is given by Page, echoing the "dream" image given in the Diamond Sutra and used by Nagarjuna:

> With perfected insight, we realise that all the suffering which smites us and others is . . . illusory. [But] as we would indeed awaken a child who is crying out in terror at the illusory images of a nightmare . . . , so the sole reason for the Buddha's appearance in the world is to awaken us all from the nightmare called "life" (samsara).[40]

This answer requires recognition that the illusion of suffering is itself real enough to demand action from the Bodhisattva. But that answer puts a limit on the assertion of emptiness. Recall the words of the Heart Sutra: "In this emptiness there can be no stopping [of craving], because one cannot speak of something as stopped if it never existed, or came into being, or originated."[41]

My own answer (c) is that since the concerns of individual sentient beings, for themselves and for others, motivate and contain both wisdom and compassion, only an answer weighted on the side of the latter can solve the Buddhist version of the problem of Oneness. There can be no synthesis of equal parts. As Sangharakshita puts it, despite his reduction elsewhere[42] of "suffering" as a merely pedagogic variable within the formula of the four Noble Truths: "both philosophic enquiry and religious aspiration arise out of pain or suffering, out of a feeling of profound dissatisfaction with the present state of knowledge or mode of being."[43]

Even the search for wisdom itself offers entry into a kind of well-being, achieved by seeing things differently: "Nirvana is samsara without birth and decay. The difference between them is in *our way of looking at them*; it is epistemic, not metaphysical."[44] The concept of epistemic heaven offers at least a partial answer to why wisdom is so strongly emphasized in Buddhism. Not only does it offer meditators the hope of eventual peace of mind, indeed perhaps of bliss, for themselves; but, through the prospect of identification with a whole, undivided universe, it also offers the rationale for that compassion toward other beings that brings a different kind of satisfaction.

There is also the assumption that the truth is auspicious, that knowing it will make things all right, and that it will provide solutions to tormenting problems of which one can see no way out. This may be a false assumption, but evidence for it is provided by the testimony of the Buddha and other adepts who feel that they have attained enlightenment.

(2) Does wisdom dictate amoralism? Whether or not it might be logical to derive a beyond-good-and-evil outlook from the emptiness doctrine, Nagarjuna himself treats Buddhist ethical and karmic principles as axiomatic and even uses them to support his metaphysical arguments. For example, in his rejection of the poles of being and notbeing, having first argued against absolute being, he continues: "Further, if (absolute) non-existence were true of things then there would be neither sin nor merit, neither bondage nor freedom; there would not also be the varied natures of things."[45] It is the *concepts* of good or evil, virtuous or sinful, and the attachment to them that wisdom rejects, not the reality:

> (The farer on the Great Way), the bodhisattva, comprehends the (ultimate) sameness of all deeds; and he does not take the good deed as meritorious and the evil deed as devoid of merit. (For, in the ultimate truth there is not this distinction of good and bad.) In the ultimate truth there are no deeds, good or evil. . . . Having achieved the true understanding of deeds, one neither does deeds nor desists from them (for one is devoid of clinging and so one does not consider oneself as the doer of deeds). And such a wise man always does the right deeds and never any wrong ones. This is the right deed of the bodhisattva.[46]

In this way the Bodhisattva may be seen as "beyond good and evil" and, at the same time, moral, without any paradox being involved, if he represents the perfection of morality that contains no concepts and requires no further decisions.

We see a questionable relativism in Jainism, through its "sevenfold analysis of reality that specifically disallows the holding of any extreme view. Implicit in this approach is a recognition of the limitations imposed by linguistic structures and their ultimate irrelevance in light of the task and achievement of human liberation."

According to the Jain analysis:

1. In a certain way, a thing exists.

2. In a certain way, a thing does not exist.

3. In a certain way, a thing both exists and does not exist (sequentially).

4. In a certain way, if existence and non-existence are taken simultaneously, things are inexpressible.

5. Hence, existent and inexpressible.

6. Nonexistent and inexpressible.

7. Existent, nonexistent, and inexpressible.[47]

Such paradoxical analyses are aimed partly, as indicated, at showing the inadequacy of words; but in Jainism they also serve to promote the "partial-truth" view, or "philosophy of non-absolutism, an outgrowth of the *ahimsa* doctrine, [which] would not allow a Jaina to hold an opinionated or rigid attitude about this or any other situation" (44). This view could be used to excuse the Jains' performing of animal experiments (see chapter 5). Although more humanely conducted than by anyone else, the practice does violate *ahimsa*; and the Animal Judge wonders whether nonabsolutism would be used to impair that most fundamental Jain principle, nonviolence itself. The Jains do "include within their system a provision for committing violence out of self-defense" (44), yet self-defense against an immediate threat can be seen as a form of nonviolence in that it prevents violence, while animal experiments can only tenuously and indirectly be considered self-defense against disease—a possible argument suggested by Chapple (44).

On the vivisection issue, Buddhist emptiness doctrine protects animals more effectively, since "neither scientists nor disease victims nor animals have independent self-natures. . . . All three need to be helped, not merely to live a longer or more comfortable life, but also to see their nonsubstantiality, their impermanence. For the Buddhist, avoidance of death, the telos of scientific realm, would not be the highest value" (45).

We can now look at the last question regarding Buddhism's emptiness doctrine and its relation to morality: (3) Does wisdom dictate compassion? It might dictate it negatively, in that the loss of the separate ego would remove any incentive to harm other beings. But one cannot be certain that it would lead to the incentive to help. Would the enlightened Bodhisattva necessarily (though we are assured that she would in fact) want positively to help others, rather than merely refrain, through lack of egoistic motivation, from harming them? After all, we can easily imagine the Bodhisattva, free from personal suffering because free from ego, looking down on the suffering world and saying, "It's just how things are; it'll be all the same in a hundred years." The memory of the unenlightened state would cause the Bodhisattva to *know* that others were suffering, but intellectual memory alone would not be enough to cause her to *care*. For that, some element of emotional egoism would need to remain (as suggested in the introduction, regarding the paradox of individual ego).

Which means that wisdom by itself cannot necessarily produce altruism without some element of emotionally motivated free will being grafted on to it. Although portrayed as incapable of doing evil, the Bodhisattva as a moral robot is not an inspiring image. Indeed, Buddhism acknowledges the coexistence of free will with causality—recall the Buddha's words in the monkey skin story: "If one can never generate new, fresh karma, then how could one ever have had the 'old' karma . . . ?" The Lankavatara Sutra also contains an implication of free will: "The Tathagata-garbha[48] holds within it the cause for both good and evil, and by it all the forms of existence are produced. Like an action it takes on a variety of forms, and [in itself] is devoid of an ego-soul."[49] The sutra goes on to describe how different ideas can produce different actions, thus giving wisdom primacy but acknowledging moral aims in its application.

Applying a projectionist approach to the problem of Oneness, the question to ask is not *whether* the unitary view (wisdom, in the aspect of Buddhism under discussion) is compatible with moral dualism (compassion), but *why* human beings have constructed the two in tandem, as a synthesis.

It seems that Buddhists have taken from the Oneness view its implications for kinship, ignoring its implications for indifference, thus enabling them to maintain its inseparability from compassion. We can surmise that the account of truth as comprising both wisdom and compassion has been tailored by Buddhists so as to accommodate an uncompromisingly altruistic ethic.

Vedanta tailors its metaphysics in the same way; its "central ideal . . . is Oneness. . . . Everything is that One; the differences are of degree and not of kind. . . . Vedanta entirely denies such ideas as that animals are essentially separate from men and that they were made and created by God to be used for our food."[50]

And while, seen in one way, Jainism's "world view that regards all aspects of physical reality to be imbued with multitudes of life . . . resulted in the practice of *ahimsa*" (9), in other words, that its ontology dictated its ethics, yet its practical dedication to nonviolence—allowing for the difficulties discussed earlier—is so thoroughgoing as to indicate the reverse causality: "At the heart of Jainism is the practice of *ahimsa*" (10).

Note that causality in either direction disappears in the Jain statement of the identity of wisdom and compassion: "This is the quintessence of wisdom: not to kill anything."[48]

Buddhism, influenced by Jainism and closer to it than to Hinduism, shows a somewhat watered-down version of the same belief. And we are still not told why it should be so.

Unitary accounts of reality seem inconsistent with compassionate moral precepts—these being necessarily dualistic in that they contain the desirable versus the undesirable in whatever ideological formulation. So when animal advocates react against hierarchy and soul/body dualism by turning to a doctrine of Oneness, they may find themselves up against either a collectivism that neglects sentience or an amoralism that completely defeats their purpose. As a result, theists have tended to invoke a benevolent-authoritarian God rather than "the whole" in arguing for animal rights, while when they do endorse Oneness they neglect its unfavorable implications.

The problem is most urgent in Buddhism with its teaching of "emptiness" coexisting with the Bodhisattva ideal of altruism. Here I have concluded that despite the primacy often given to "wisdom" (i.e., insight into emptiness) in the texts, its application and interpretation have been dictated by an axiomatic fidelity to the ethos of compassion.

So, in all the worldviews, when considering the parts and the whole, theorists have mostly cherry-picked according to their ethical priorities, including those affecting human-animal relations.

As stated earlier, it is possible with equal truth to assert that the world is One and that it is Many (as the mystics have recognized when struggling with the question). But the unitary perspective has a greater appeal in two ways. Philosophically—or perhaps merely aesthetically—it is tidier and more economical than any dualistic or hierarchical account. Its ethical advantages are obvious; its ethical deficit (the capacity for amoralism) can be got round through the belief that human self-interest will naturally lead to altruistic choices in the long run: in other words, that *potentially* the universe is both all one and all good.

Nevertheless, in terms of sentient well-being, it does not matter which ontology is used to support benevolence. Says the Animal Judge, "A hierarchical-minded theist who tells us we shouldn't eat animals is preferable to a mystic who tells us we can; and a mystic who says we shouldn't is preferable to an authoritarian theist who says we can." The fact of selective interpretation should make it clear that, for theologians and philosophers, morality (in the animal context or any other) has helped to shape their picture of reality. In the last chapter I discuss the possible eventual outcome of this ethical drive.

9. Animal Rights
The Next Step in Human Moral Evolution

MORAL CONFLICT HAS BEEN A RECURRING FEATURE of human experience, as people have had to choose between exploiting others (whether human or animal) or leaving them alone; between eating animals or going hungry. Even when influenced by real or perceived necessity, choices that resulted in harm to others left a residue of guilt. Religion has expressed the wish to resolve such conflict, and never more profoundly so than in the case of human-animal relations: profoundly, because the doctrines' conflict-resolving role has largely been unrecognized, with the ideas having been held responsible for the treatment of animals rather than vice versa. When the same role has been played by ideologies in regard to the treatment of humans, the strategies have been more obvious.

Over the millennia, the drive to fulfill sympathy and achieve inner peace has led to more and more benevolent policies, since aggressive justifications, evasive and superficial kindness, and apologetic rituals have all failed to solve the problem.

This has been a natural development, caused by our psychological make-up and facilitated by environmental and technological change. It is neither chance nor any necessary external design, but learning that has brought about progress. However, theists can reasonably—although not provably or disprovably—claim that God has created all these factors for the purpose of ultimate moral perfection.

Even Darwin, whose emphasis on the element of randomness in biological evolution, rather than teleology with humans as the pinnacle, is often appealed to by animal supporters,

> shared with [his fellow Victorians] an incurable optimism about moral progress. . . . "Sympathy beyond the confines of man, that is, humanity to the lower animals, seems to be one of the latest moral acquisitions. . . . This virtue, one of the noblest with which man is endowed, seems to arise incidentally from our sympathies becoming more tender and more widely diffused, until they are extended to all sentient beings."[1]

Up to now, the beneficiaries of increased benevolence have been human, as slavery, despotism, racism, and sexism were gradually (and still incompletely) abandoned. Perhaps the animals have come last because their oppression represented those "daily habits of life" (recall J. S. Mill's analysis in the introduction) that have been most difficult for humans to give up. Today, the majority of people still cling to those habits, insisting that vivisection is essential to medical progress and that meat eating is just too enjoyable to be forgone: so that animal rights, in both secular and sacred discourse, is in 2008 still a minority commitment, vilified by the British government, stigmatized as potentially "terrorist" by the American government, and rejected by many otherwise liberal opinion makers.

But the trend is away from speciesism. Religious animal advocates have promoted an evolutionary scenario, pointing to the visions of the vegetarian Eden and the peaceful kingdom not as fantasies but as aims that can be furthered by our actions now. Schwartz cites Joe Green's conclusion "that Jewish religious ethical vegetarians are pioneers of the Messianic era; they are leading lives that make the coming of the Messiah more likely."[2]

R. Abraham Kook, so prominent in this movement, "was steeped in the kabbalistic tradition and this, coupled with his reading of the works of Henri Bergson, inclined him to see an evolutionary component underlying the progress of history and human development. Every aspect of such development can be seen as a component of evolution leading to the messianic goal."[3] Animals were part of his vision: "The free movement of the moral impulse to establish justice for animals generally and the claim for their rights from mankind are hidden in a natural psychic sensibility in the deeper layers of the Torah."[4] He felt that "restrictions on eating meat, such as the kosher laws, are intended to keep alive a spirit of reverence for life among meat eaters, so that someday they may return to the vegetarian diet humans had before the Great Flood."[5]

Among Christians, Bradley asks whether the vegetarian Garden of Eden "is a goal which we are moving towards by his grace . . . ? Does it not in fact properly come at the end of the human story rather than at the beginning?"[6] while Isaiah 11, "as well as being a direct promise of what will come about in the last days . . . is also a call."[7] Linzey writes, "Gospel hope in the future is not some optional extra to moral endeavour but its essential basis. . . . I believe not only in this earth . . . but also in the *new* earth—and all the redeemed creatures, both human and animal, that will belong to it."[8]

Ahmed, in like vein, claims that "slavery and meat eating were foreseen . . . to be ending in the course of time."[9] He combines conservatism with dynamism in the statement that Muhammad's "own job, entrusted to him by the

Creator, was to put the last brick. . . . From then on mankind can progress unhindered by God."[10]

In Buddhism, the Bodhisattva ideal points to a telos affecting the entire sentient world, by contrast with the limited goal of personal salvation. Sangharakshita maintains that such a long-term goal is realizable: "that all beings are potentially Buddhas, is the logical corollary of the Bodhisattva Ideal, as universalized by the Mahayana. . . . However distant the day of Enlightenment may be, dawn it must for everyone, even if after the lapse of aeons impossible to enumerate."[11]

Thus religion confirms Best's predominantly secular animal liberationist assertion that "the next logical and necessary step in Western cultural evolution is to broaden the notion of rights to include animals."[12]

THE LONG STORY

We have looked at texts both written and unwritten, from the propitiatory rituals of subsistence hunters to the dominionist theories—modified by evasive kindness—of Middle Eastern religion, and the Buddhist principles of noninjury and compassion—modified by defensive excuses for meat eating and an invidious karmic theory.

The narrative has not been linear. Different sources have coexisted and influenced each other, as when guilt-assuaging aboriginal rites are echoed in Abrahamic rules of sacrifice and slaughter or the shamanism of hunters finds its way into the yogic values of nonverbal meditation and holistic identification with all beings. We have seen human language and reason offered as justification for the most brutal dismissal of animals' needs, while at the same time, and increasingly in the modern era, saints, mystics, popular culture, and later theology have turned for inspiration to the perspective, seen as simpler and purer, of the animal. We have also seen an interchange of Eastern nonviolence, sometimes all too passive, with Western activism.

The most damagingly aggressive stories have been the following: God made humans in his own image. Only humans have souls. God gave humans permission to eat meat—and the blind obedience exemplified by Abraham's sacrifice means, for some Jews as well as Muslims, that the permission amounts to a command, lest one usurp God's right of moral prescription. Even according to the more animal-friendly Buddhists, birth in animal form is the result of sins in a previous life. Animals cannot achieve enlightenment until they attain, with enormous difficulty, rebirth as humans.

But, into these damning accounts, the human conscience introduced evidence of its wish to behave better toward animals, so long as their habitual usage is unimpaired. Among such evasive texts, food imagery in the Bible and Qur'an, when positive, is largely vegetable. The symbolism of God or Christ as a shepherd evades the killing of animals by directing attention to the benevolent role of their temporary guardian and protector. Sympathy for the sacrificial lamb shines forth in the identification of that creature with the martyred Christ. The prophets denounce sacrifice itself, although any ethical motives on their part remain obscure. In addition, precepts of kindness to animals and stories about compassionate sages and saints are found in Judaism, Christianity, and Islam. Buddhism allows the exploitation of work animals, but warns against taking advantage of any being's inferior birth and promises karmic reward for kindness.

Defensive rituals, rules, and concepts, unlike aggressive or evasive themes, acknowledge that there is something fundamentally regrettable about killing animals, but seek to come to terms with it by various means short of abandoning the killing. I have mentioned the echoes of propitiatory rites in rules of sacrifice and of slaughter for food. In conservative thought (by contrast with the more recent teleological readings), the utopian pictures of vegetarian Eden and of the biblical and Talmudic peaceable kingdom are taken as nice but currently unattainable fantasies, reserved for the sweet by and by.

Literal defense against the feared revenge of slaughtered animals may have informed some of Buddhism's fundamental ethical principles. Meat-eating monks have defended themselves by prescribing that the meat must not come from animals killed specifically for themselves and cultivating (along with some present-day lay Buddhists) attitudes of reverence, gratitude, and goodwill that are supposed to make the act acceptable. In Buddhist countries prayers are sometimes offered up for a good rebirth for slaughtered animals.

All the worldviews have defended themselves politically against rivals and critics either by insisting that their attitudes are greener and more animal friendly than those of other creeds or by argumentatively justifying unfavorable doctrines.

The effective defense of giving up animal abuse is the strategy that emerges when rationalization fails, the conflict becomes intolerable, and spokespersons for all the worldviews insist that consistency with their prevailing values cannot be achieved until exploitation ceases. To promote change, people draw upon established bases for reinterpretation and upon theories of flux within the existing account—whether it be the changing God of Judaism and Christianity who suffers with creatures and accompanies humanity and nature in their development, the anticipated fulfillment in evolving Islam of the groundwork laid by the Prophet, or the Buddhist principle of impermanence, uniting all sentient life in the karmic stream.

According to this story, God's mercy, for all the Abrahamic religions, discredits speciesist claims, while human superiority itself is used by Linzey to promote the "moral priority of the weak" and by Webb to promote paternalistic control. In all these religions stewardship replaces dominion. Buddhist vegetarians ancient and modern argue from karmic interchangeability, from the supreme value of noninjury, from the injunction to avoid brutal professions, and from the Bodhisattva ideal of selfless compassion.

In practical terms, these changed accounts have been used to support vegetarianism and veganism and to oppose sacrifice, vivisection, hunting, and other cruel practices. There are animal rights groups within each of the worldviews.

Here, as more briefly indicated in the introduction, is why they support animal rights. Particular ideological reasons have been dealt with where they arise in the religions; the following is the common coin of the debate, though there is some overlap.

THE GOLDEN RULE; OR, THE NONINJURY PRINCIPLE

I have subtitled this section the "Noninjury Principle" partly to stress the greater importance of not causing pain, compared with causing pleasure, and partly to avoid an emphasis on Christianity. In fact, the principle is found everywhere: in Matthew 7:12, of course, and in negative form in the teachings of Hillel the Elder (ca. 70 BCE–10 CE), who endorsed an existing folk tradition.[13] Michael Mountain gives examples from other creeds:

> "Hurt not others with that which pains you yourself."
> *Udanavarga, Buddhist text.*
> "Do not unto others what you would not they should do unto you."
> *Analects, Confucian text.*

"This is the sum of duty: do nothing unto others which, if done to you, would
    cause you pain."
Mahabharata, Hindu text.
"A man should wander about treating all creatures as he himself would be
    treated."
Sutrakritanga, Jain text.
"Treat others as you would be treated. What you like not for yourself dispense
    not to others."
Abdullah Ansari, Islamic Sufi text.[14]

It is echoed in various philosophical principles, such as Kant's Categorical
Imperative—"Act only in accordance with that maxim through which you
can at the same time will that it become a universal law"—which also entails
maximum well-being. Kant's denial of the similarity to the Golden Rule[15] was
made necessary (for him) by its obviousness on the surface, which others
have noted, e.g., "the 'categorical imperative' . . . is perhaps a long-winded
way of asking us to treat others as we would have them treat us."[16] Kant himself acknowledges a relation when he says that the rule is "merely derivative
from our principle, although subject to various qualifications."[17] However, he
found problems with reciprocity, believing in punishment for lawbreakers—a
substantial derogation from the rule.

    J.S. Mill, for his part, wrote, "In the golden rule of Jesus of Nazareth, we
read the complete spirit of the ethics of utility."[18] And the idea of putting oneself in another's place occurs in Rawls's "veil of ignorance" (although he does
not apply it to moral patients—that is, beings such as animals or mentally
handicapped people who cannot reciprocate obligations and must be "treated"
in a certain way).

    The maxim that Kant called "trivial"[19] is actually quite logical, as well as
being psychologically and politically convincing. Logically, you cannot violate it without undermining your own claims to consideration. Psychologically, it appeals to the ethical reasoning of identification with others, which
runs: "If I hurt this being, he will suffer. Since I can suffer also, when I see
him suffering, I suffer in imagination. I do not want to suffer, even in imagination. I can avoid that suffering by not hurting him. So I choose not to." This
type of moral egoism was endorsed by Hobbes, when

    a poor and infirme old man craved his alms. He, beholding him with eies of
    pity . . . gave him 6d. Sayd a divine that stood by—"Would you have donne

this, if it had not been Christ's command?"—"Yea," sayd he.—"Why?" . . . "Because . . . I was in paine to consider the miserable condition of the old man;
and now my almes, giving him some reliefe, doth also ease me."[20]

Politically, the Golden Rule is inclusive. Although not generally applied to
animals, it can and to be consistent must be. It does not say "do to others what
you would have them do to you, as long as they're not weaker or less intellectual than you." Further, in not specifying benefits, it allows for identification
with beings whose particular needs may differ from your own. Here an ad-
dendum, "if you were in their place," would conform to and indeed would
follow from the principle.

The Golden Rule values the well-being of sentient individuals. By sentient
I mean having conscious preferences and aversions. And, like altruism itself,
a sentience criterion of moral value is prevalent in our culture. Suffering is
what we want to avoid; happiness what we seek; and despite the high valuation of cognition and other prestigious qualities, morality is directed toward
the more widespread characteristic of sentience, with special indignation felt
toward abuse of the weak and vulnerable. While some moral principles, such
as honor and truth, are admired for their own sake, regardless of the potential for good or bad consequences, the bulk of ethical concern is directed toward unambiguous welfare objectives.

A familiar challenge to the sentience criterion is "There are different levels
of sentience; where do you draw the line?" The British government identifies
"protected animals" as vertebrates plus the common octopus; but I would
give the benefit of the doubt to insects as well and try to avoid killing them. If
plants should be discovered to be sentient, it would pose an insuperable dilemma, since even vegans would have to kill sentient beings in order to live.
In that case, plants would in effect be animals and require to be treated as
individuals, not as parts of the ecosphere.

Another frequent claim, with regard to suffering and other mental activity, is that some supervenient human quality is needed to turn the activity
into an experience or, in common parlance, "They don't feel it in the same
way as we would." But despite the philosophical and scientific complexities
to be found in mental events, such events exist also on a very simple level. In
order to be conscious one needn't be self-conscious, but merely awake. In
order to have a perspective, one needn't have a worked-out account of reality, but merely the perceptual equipment for seeing, hearing, or otherwise
sensing the world. Nor does one need to formulate a concept of suffering in

order to suffer. Moreover, even if in some ways humans suffer more than animals because of imagination and more complex psychological needs, such as the need for dignity, in other ways animals suffer more because of their lack of cognition. When mistreated and imprisoned, they have little understanding of what has happened, no capacity to speculate on the future or to devise effective means of resistance or escape, no philosophical or religious comfort.

Against the claim that animals do not suffer significantly, there is much evidence both empirical and logical. Of course, empirical evidence about subjective states is always open to disputed interpretation by the very nature of the material: you can never get inside someone else's head. Thus, before presenting their wealth of data about animal emotion, Masson and McCarthy must devote a preface and two chapters to arguing that the data represent animal experience rather than the mechanical or evolutionary explanations offered by some scientists.[21] But the logical evidence is stronger, consisting of the fact that Descartes' heirs, the experimenters of today, themselves do experiments that would be meaningless if the animals did not suffer: you could not test an analgesic on creatures who did not display aversion to pain-causing (in human experience) stimuli and relaxation when a successful form of relief was offered. Psychologist Lorin Lindner points to psychological research in which animal suffering is "essential to the basic design of the experiment—for example, in learned helplessness studies of depression . . . in studies of sleep and sensory deprivation that often go on until the animal goes insane."[22] British government regulations, despite falling far short of welfare campaigners' wishes, at least acknowledge suffering by establishing bands of severity of the experiments.

Hume combines observation with analogical argument:

> We are conscious, that we ourselves, in adapting means to ends, are guided by reason and design, and that 'tis not ignorantly nor casually we perform those actions, which tend to self-preservation, to the obtaining pleasure, and avoiding pain. When therefore we see other creatures, in millions of instances, perform like actions, and direct them to like ends, all our principles of reason and probability carry us with an invincible force to believe the existence of a like cause. . . .
>
> . . .'Tis from the resemblance of the external actions of animals to those we ourselves perform, that we judge their internal likewise to resemble ours.[23]

In any case, the animal rights movement—in its practical campaigning, as distinct from its varied philosophical arguments—is concerned with those animals whom humans actually exploit (rather than, e.g., insects) and about whose sentience, in whatever form and to whatever extent, there is little if any debate. Similarly, the texts of the religions discussed in this book refer to the animals who are used or encountered at a particular time and place and whose capacity to suffer is acknowledged in precepts of kindness, just as modern anticruelty laws acknowledge it. (An exception might be found in the insects and "small creatures" given moral status by Jainism and Buddhism, though whether this is on grounds of sentience or merely of animal form is unclear.)

THE PRIMA FACIE ACCEPTANCE OF CONSIDERATION FOR ANIMALS

Even the most vehement speciesist literature does not generally suggest that hurting or killing animals is a good thing in itself. An exception is Francis Bacon's view that "scientific knowledge . . . of minerals and vegetables and animals—is best elicited with 'nature under constraint and vexed . . . when by art and the hand of man she is forced out of her natural state.'"[24] For Bacon, the animal within human beings was evil, and "to take hold of an animal and in the cause of science to put it to the question—to 'squeeze,' 'mold,' 'constrain,' and 'vex' it—is . . . a kind of catharsis."[25] But even Bacon was capable of describing a certain procedure as "too inhuman."[26] Aquinas held that since animals exist only to serve humanity, "it is not wrong for man to make use of them, either by killing them or in any other way whatever."[27] Yet Aquinas, too, implies awareness of a possible moral problem and on occasion expressed the more benign sentiments quoted in chapter 3. Descartes held that you cannot hurt animals, which is not the same as recommending that you do so. Kant, who saw only human beings as ends in themselves, still advanced the indirect-duties view that "tender feelings towards dumb animals develop humane feelings towards mankind,"[28] which is a positive recommendation to kindness, whatever one thinks of the reason for it. More tellingly, Kant argued that "if a man shoots his dog because the animal is no longer capable of service, he does not fail in his duty to the dog . . . but his act is inhuman and damages in himself that humanity which it is his duty to show towards mankind."[29] How could he (or Bacon) consider such acts "inhuman" without having some instinctive belief in a direct moral duty to animals?

Harm to animals, even in Western culture, is only ever condoned as a supposedly necessary evil, with human requirements seen as conferring necessity: Ruesch reminds us of "the usual sanctimonious admonition that 'the beasts should, of course, be spared unnecessary suffering,'"[30] quoting a Jesuit supporter of animal experiments; while being kind to animals is regarded as a good thing, although given low priority.

Since Cartesians maintain that animals cannot be hurt anyway (with the implication that animal death has no clear moral import since there is no sentient personality to be destroyed), they cannot be said in theory either to accept or reject the noninjury principle when applied to animals, although in practice they reject it.

REASONS GIVEN FOR ALLOWING EXCEPTIONS TO THE NONINJURY PRINCIPLE

People who do not want to apply the Golden Rule to animals, whether at all or only in particular situations, resort either to forms of perfectionism (the belief that moral priority depends on the possession of certain valued qualities) or to the next-of-kin argument. Note that these anti-animal theories are used only to justify those "daily habits of life" that require the exploitation of animals. The theories are forgotten when banning cruelty toward pets (since pet keeping would serve no purpose if it were not benevolent), but remembered when allowing cruelty to farm or laboratory animals.

PERFECTIONISM

The human qualities adduced in the perfectionist argument include reason, language, self-consciousness and even vaguer things like richness of life or having a biography. The first three are sometimes used to support Cartesianism (the first two by Descartes himself), but all such qualities are said to confer priority on humans.

Human reason, language, and self-consciousness are featured in arguments against including the interests of animals in political movements, through the contractarian view that only autonomous rational agents can attract social obligation, plus the revolutionary view that only those who can struggle on their own behalf deserve liberation. The problem with this "autonomy" criterion is that it celebrates human free will while limiting the ways in which it can be exercised. A truly autonomous agent can choose *not* to hurt moral patients.

One thing the various perfectionist claims have in common is that they are nonsequiturs: so much so that, when offered by philosophers who place a high value on rational argument, the claims only testify to the power of tradition and prejudice. Animals aren't rational, the argument runs; therefore we have a right to hurt and kill them for our benefit. Animals can't speak . . . aren't self-conscious . . . have no biography . . . can't make a contract . . . can't argue for themselves: ditto. Yet, even given that our culture values those qualities, it does not follow that we have a right to hurt and kill beings who lack them.

In the case of animals, even more than in similar human cases, perfectionism is circular as well as nonsequential: "Class A deserves more well-being because it has Quality X" and, by a happy coincidence, "Quality X confers merit because it is unique to Class A." The latter claim is not put so blatantly, but in the form "Quality X is what distinguishes us from the beasts." Eckersley refers to it as the "differential imperative": "selecting certain characteristics that are believed to be special to humans . . . as the measure of both human virtue and human superiority over other species."[31]

Both these logical flaws reflect the complacency that comes from having power. Power is sometimes acknowledged in statements such as "these are the qualities that have given us control over the earth," but it is given a moralistic tinge, perhaps influenced by biblical dominionism, and is thus different from an overt and unadorned power ethic.

Indeed, the only indisputable way in which uniquely human qualities are "superior" is that they give us superior power. Birds' flight, fishes' ability to live underwater, dogs' and horses' ability to outrun us, are all forms of superiority, but since they do not confer power as do human reason and communication, they are discounted.

THE NEXT-OF-KIN ARGUMENT

That it is only natural to give priority to our own kind is supported by evidence that people do behave in this way, but it implies two other moral principles on which the humanist might be challenged: (1) do you consider everything "natural" (however defined) to be right? and (2) would you rob or kill your human neighbor to benefit your own family or give priority to your own ethnic group in conferring fundamental rights and opportunities? To agree to (1) would require the person to approve of much behavior which he would probably denounce as "uncivilized" or even "bestial." To agree to (2) in a culture in which values of altruism prevail would be inconsistent. To be sure, in practice the treatment of other human beings, as well as of animals, often deviates from the Golden Rule, and unsound excuses may be offered. But it seems that only where species is concerned can the fact of group self-interest be advanced as a moral argument in itself.

VALUE SYSTEMS OUTSIDE THE GOLDEN RULE

Two examples are the might makes right doctrine and those forms of ecologism (it is not true of all of them) that give sentience a relatively low priority—as when Holmes Rolston writes, "The species line is quite fundamental. It is more important to protect this integrity than to protect individuals"[32] and reports with approval how U.S. environmental authorities "asked the Navy to shoot 2,000 feral goats to save three endangered plant species."[33]

Of relevance here is whether proponents of either view would be prepared to apply it equally to animals and human beings. Does the power-ethicist consider the might of the bear who eats a human being to be just as right as the might of the human being who eats a bear? Would the environmentalist, in the absence of legal constraints, be willing to kill human beings to protect endangered plant species? The questions are not rhetorical, for different replies might well be given. If the answer is no, on such grounds as are commonly given for human supremacy, then I would reply as in earlier sections to those grounds. If the answer is yes, then the conflict with the noninjury principle enters the realm of broader ethical debate, outside the question of animal rights.

This, then, is the thinking behind the evolution of modern religious animal advocates. Where are their stories leading?

A NONSPECIESIST WORLD

In what may well be the future world, it will never even occur to people to kill animals for food, scientific or medical research, or skins or other body parts, any more than to kill humans for such purposes. All these practices will be regarded as part of the barbarous past. The accepted principle will be that all sentient beings deserve equal consideration, "sentience" to be determined by commonsense observation combined with a willingness to give the benefit of the doubt where doubt exists.

People sometimes demand, "What's going to happen to all the sheep and cows if everyone goes vegetarian?" They might equally have asked, in earlier times, "What's going to happen to the freed slaves, with no home or source of livelihood?"

In practice, vegetarianism will be adopted gradually and farmers will reduce the number of animals bred for meat. But consider the unlikely prospect of an overnight transformation. If the political will were present, existing animals could be retired, and farmers' transition to vegetable growing subsidized at public expense while the breeding of animals ceased. As with slavery, there might still be hardship to animals or humans; the Inuit, for example, are always pleading hardship in the face of antifur protests. But that is no reason to continue with practices that affront morality and that, if continued, will produce far more suffering and violence than any transitional events.

In this projected world, not only will people cease to abuse animals for direct use, they will disclaim any right to kill for environmental purposes, even where it is seen to be in the interest of the species concerned or of other animal species. We would not "cull" excess human beings. So, in future, a right to kill animals might exist only as it now does vis-à-vis other humans: in self-defense.

Nor would we police nature to serve our moral aims, by trying to end animal predation. Our own responsibility toward other species must come first, with any attack on the natural evil of predation residing in the even more remote future.

Keeping pets is necessary today because of the large number of overbred, unwanted animals who would otherwise be destroyed. Also, dogs seem to enjoy human company. But, in a nonspeciesist world, people would live in environments where dogs, cats, or other anthrophiles could go as they pleased to and from a human habitation. The destruction of open space would cease as human housing was better planned with an eye to animal and human needs. There would be far fewer cars, so that towns would be safer for all species.

Outside cities the remaining natural habitats would be undisturbed and where possible restored. While, indeed, "setting aside wild areas for the preservation of species demonstrates . . . the fact that all land is subject to human management and cultivation,"[34] Webb errs, I feel, in urging us to accept, as corollaries, that "with the continuing decline of the wild, zoos will become increasingly important in the future" and, moreover, that this is beneficial, zoos being "an emblem of the coexistence of humans and animals."[35] Many people today seem to accept the naturalistic fallacy that because the wild apparently *is* turning into at best a great zoo, therefore it *should* do so. After all, we would not want to be limited to "human sanctuaries," however benevolently run, by invading Martians. So we should restrain the use of our unavoidable power and do all we can to maintain and increase whatever is left of the wilderness.

The amount of land released by the cessation of grazing would make a great difference, as would the continuing demographic transition to fewer human births (though I regard compulsory or pressured population control as cruel).

Such a world would undoubtedly be much pleasanter and healthier for humans as well as animals. But that is not the most important reason why we should give up speciesist oppression. Ultimately, true, all altruism is selfish, not merely by producing residual benefits to the altruists but also by serving their psychological needs; otherwise, by definition, they would not choose to practice it. But the propositional content of the wish (the feature suggested by Sober and Wilson to identify altruism that is not only psychologically self-serving but also objectively other-serving)[36]—in this case, "animals shall not be harmed or killed by human beings except in self-defense"—provides a necessary, sufficient, and primary motive.

The trend, in all the traditions, toward accepting this principle is making them more consistent with their prevailing values. Inconsistency, of course, can be resolved in either direction. But to resolve the relevant conflicts in favor of a ruthless and arbitrary (rather than compassionate) God, or a punitive and hierarchical (rather than egalitarian) karma, would not serve the interests of either humans or animals or the cultural and psychological objectives of any of the worldviews. It would, in fact, make nonsense of them. This is why we must argue for consistency with the good, as expressed in the empathetic mode of the human ego.

Growing support for animal rights, with its accompanying growth in ideological consistency, yields an important insight about people. Sympathy, always an important contender for primacy in the mixture that is human nature, is winning. The paradox of individual ego, by which one must have egoistic needs oneself (creating a potential for callousness and exploitation) in order to understand and sympathize with the needs of others, is leaning more and more in the direction of altruism, although the ego must always remain—except possibly (and to me inexplicably) in the experience of saints. Nowhere can this historic tendency be seen more clearly than in the move toward renouncing human advantage for the sake of that limiting case of sentient otherness but sameness, and of vulnerability, the beast. As the Animal Judge sums it up, "The combination of a relatively powerless object, animals, and a powerful supporter, the worldviews that express people's most comprehensive ethical and philosophical beliefs, is to humanity's credit and offers hope for the future of all sentient beings."

NOTES

Introduction

1. Best, "Evolve or Die."
2. Preece, *Animals and Nature*, 97.
3. Ibid., 234.
4. Ibid.
5. Webb, *On God and Dogs*, 24.
6. Ibid., 33.
7. Ibid., 34–35.
8. Flack and de Waal, "Being Nice," 67.
9. Smart, *The World's Religions*, 346.
10. Green, *Theology, Hermeneutics, and Imagination*, 92.
11. Unterman, *Jews*, 221.
12. Francione, *Introduction to Animal Rights*, xxi.
13. Singer, quoted in Dombrowski, *The Philosophy of Vegetarianism*, 15.
14. Ibid.
15. Adams, "Feeding on Grace," 155.
16. Ibid., 156.
17. Ibid., citing Warren.
18. Russell, *Unpopular Essays*, 80–87.
19. Mill, *On Liberty and the Subjection of Women*, 124.
20. Singer, *Animal Liberation*, 215–16.
21. Ibid., 214.
22. Guenther, "Animals in Bushman Thought," 2:196.
23. Webb, *On God and Dogs*, 77.
24. Harvey, "Buddhist Attitudes," 48.
25. Preece, *Animals and Nature*, 165.
26. Rifkin, *Beyond Beef*, 276.
27. Ibid., 277.
28. Preece, *Animals and Nature*, 173, quoting James Maxwell, ed., *America's Fascinating Indian Heritage* (Pleasantville, NY: Reader's Digest, 1978).
29. Preece, *Animals and Nature*, 173.
30. Patton, "Animal Sacrifice," 396.
31. Preece, *Animals and Nature*, 233.
32. Webb, *On God and Dogs*, 28.
33. Regenstein, *Replenish the Earth*, 260.
34. Bryant, "Strategies of Vedic Subversion," 195–96.
35. Ibid., 198–99.
36. Campbell, *Primitive Mythology*, 349.

37. Ibid., 292–93.
38. Lommel, *Prehistoric and Primitive Man*, 71.
39. Ibid., 17.
40. Ibid., 41.
41. Burch and Ellanna, "Introduction," 3.
42. Adams, "Feasting on Life," 44.
43. Astill, "Monkey Business."
44. Smart, *The World's Religions*, 308–9.
45. Sharp, "Dry Meat and Gender," 188.
46. Ibid., 185.
47. Hardy, *Far from the Madding Crowd*, 70–71.
48. Singer, "The Slaughterer," 214.
49. Berman, "The Dietary Laws as Atonement," 153.
50. Quoted in Berman, "The Dietary Laws as Atonement," 153–54.
51. Unterman, *Jews*, 210.
52. Grandin, "Commentary."
53. Groves, *Hearts and Minds*, 27.
54. Ibid., 49–50.
55. Rollin, *The Unheeded Cry*, 147.
56. Arluke, *Just a Dog*, 56–57.
57. Schmithausen, "Preface," 3.
58. Foltz, "Islamic Environmentalism," 249.
59. Kemmerer, *In Search of Consistency*, 360.
60. The style of Buddhist scriptural references used is *Initial* (in this case of the *Majjhima Nikaya*).volume.page. The edition used is Horner, *Middle Length Sayings (Majjhima Nikaya)*, the present reference being to vol. 1, 430.
61. Regan, *The Case for Animal Rights*, 155.
62. Ibid.
63. Kemmerer, *In Search of Consistency*, 38.
64. Waldau, *The Specter of Speciesism*, 38.
65. Adams, *The Sexual Politics of Meat*, 27.
66. Waldau, *The Specter of Speciesism*, 26.
67. Adams, *The Sexual Politics of Meat*, 22.
68. Cited in Waldau, *The Specter of Speciesism*, 34. LaFollette and Shanks have examined speciesism with reference to animal experimentation.
69. Ibid., 35. James Rachels is the author of *Created from Animals*, a study of our relationship with other species in the light of Darwinism.
70. Ibid., 27.
71. Connor, "Scientists 'Should be Allowed to Test on Apes.'"
72. Arluke, *Just a Dog*, 194.
73. See, on the date of 1970, Waldau, *The Specter of Speciesism*, 4; on the date of 1977, see Kemmerer, *In Search of Consistency*, 39.
74. Salt, "The Logic of the Larder," 187.
75. Noske, *Beyond Boundaries*, 158–60.

76. Bahro, *Building the Green Movement*, 177.
77. Palmer, *Environmental Ethics*, 207.
78. Harris, "Buddhist Environmental Ethics," 205.
79. James, *The Varieties of Religious Experience*, 115.

1. The Hebrew Bible

1. I use Hodder and Stoughton's *The Holy Bible*. The Old Testament and Hebrew Bible (*Tanakh*) are "more or less identical" except for the order of the books, according to Unterman, *Jews*, 41.

   The order of the *Tanakh* is "*Torah* (the Pentateuch), *Neviim* (Prophets), and *Ketuvim* (Hagiographa)" (ibid., 41–42). Judaism consists of these, plus the later rabbinical writings known as the Talmud which is "a philosophical law code, the Mishnah, and an extensive analysis of and commentary upon the Mishnah" (Neusner, *Foreword*, x). The Talmud's formal closure was "about 600 C.E." (ibid., x–xi).
2. Klawans, "Sacrifice in Ancient Israel."
3. Kundera, *The Unbearable Lightness of Being*, 286.
4. Murray, *The Cosmic Covenant*, 98.
5. Ibid.
6. Levinas, *Beyond the Verse*, 118.
7. Klawans, "Sacrifice in Ancient Israel," 68–69.
8. Ibid., 69.
9. Atran, *In Gods We Trust*, 74.
10. Ibid., 75.
11. *The Holy Bible*, p. 213n., says "or *Father, who bought you*"—another means of acquiring livestock.
12. Jacobs, *The Jewish Religion*, 575.
13. Quoted in Linzey, *Animal Theology*, 127.
14. Hiebert, *The Yahwist's Landscape*, 137.
15. Berman, "The Dietary Laws," 150.
16. Hyland, *God's Covenant with Animals*, 100.
17. Regenstein, *Replenish the Earth*, 54.
18. Dombrowski, *The Philosophy of Vegetarianism*, 48.
19. Murray, *Cosmic Covenant*, 100.
20. Hyland, *God's Covenant with Animals*, 75.
21. Eliade, *A History of Religious Ideas*, 1:38.
22. Swain, "The Old Testament," 76.
23. Hiebert, *The Yahwist's Landscape*, 153.
24. Schwartz, *Judaism and Vegetarianism*, 14.
25. See Schwartz, *Judaism and Vegetarianism*, 93.
26. Linzey, *Animal Theology*, 105.
27. Quoted in Eliade, *A History of Religious Ideas*, 347.
28. Kalechofsky, "In the Camp," 111–12.
29. Schwartz, *Judaism and Vegetarianism*, 80.
30. Regenstein, *Replenish the Earth*, 53.

31. Murti, "Again and Again." He refers to Hyland's article in the January/February 1998 issue of *Humane Religion*.
32. Schwartz, "*Tsa'ar ba'alei chayim*," 63.
33. Klawans, "Sacrifice in Ancient Israel," 71.
34. Quoted in Schwartz, *Judaism and Vegetarianism*, 18.
35. Ibid., 5.
36. Hyland, *God's Covenant with Animals*, 27.
37. Both quoted in Schwartz, *Judaism and Vegetarianism*, 5.
38. Regenstein, *Replenish the Earth*, 177.
39. Berry, *Food for the Gods*, 153.
40. Berman, "The Dietary Laws," 150.
41. Klawans, "Sacrifice in Ancient Israel," 67.
42. Ibid., 68.
43. Phelps, *The Longest Struggle*, 46.
44. All quoted in Schwartz, *Judaism and Vegetarianism*, 15.
45. Maimonides, *The Guide for the Perplexed*, 288.
46. Cohen, *Everyman's Talmud*, 235, referring to Exodus 20:8–10.
47. Quoted in Kalechofsky, "Introduction," 250.
48. Ibid.
49. Schwartz, *Judaism and Vegetarianism*, 9.
50. Ibid., 114.
51. Quoted in Kalechofsky, "In the Camp," 115.
52. Quoted ibid., 110.
53. Kalechofsky, "*Kashrut*," 99–100.
54. Phelps, "Special Youth Challenge Hunts."
55. Hiebert, *The Yahwist's Landscape*, 103.
56. Haykal, *The Life of Muhammad*, 58.
57. Fox, *The Unauthorized Version*, 253.
58. *The NIV Thematic Study Bible*, 1474.
59. Klawans, "Sacrifice in Ancient Israel," 70.
60. Dombrowski, *The Philosophy of Vegetarianism*, 26.
61. Hiebert, *The Yahwist's Landscape*, 97.
62. Ibid., 60.
63. Murray, *Cosmic Covenant*, 99.
64. Lommel, *Primitive and Prehistoric Man*, 10.
65. Murray, *Cosmic Covenant*, 109.
66. Ibid., 105.
67. Ibid., 109.
68. Atran, *In Gods We Trust*, 114.
69. Patton, "Animal Sacrifice," 396.
70. Berman, "The Dietary Laws," 89.
71. Raisin, "Humanitarianism," 25.
72. Regenstein, *Replenish the Earth*, 50.
73. Klawans, "Sacrifice in Ancient Israel," 65.

74. Waldau, *The Specter of Speciesism*, 211.

75. Ibid.

2. Judaism

1. Cohen, *Everyman's Talmud*, 39.

2. Ibid., 40.

3. Unterman, *Jews*, 23–24.

4. Ibid., 24–25.

5. Schwartz, *Judaism and Vegetarianism*, 92.

6. Ibid., 103–4.

7. Cohen, *Everyman's Talmud*, 67.

8. Ibid., 76.

9. Maimonides, *The Guide for the Perplexed*, 14.

10. Kabbalism is the mystical school of Judaism that arose in twelfth- and thirteenth-century Europe: "known as the Qabbalah or Tradition," its mystical tendency "had been evident in the so-called Merkavah (Chariot) mysticism of . . . Rabbi Aqiba in the first and second centuries CE. The 'chariot' refers to the chariot of fire in which the prophet Eliyyahu (Elijah) ascended to heaven"—a symbol of contemplation. Smart, *The World's Religions*, 264. Kabbalism's most important text is the thirteenth-century *Zohar*, which glitters with weird and colorful symbolism.

11. Scholem, "Kabbalah," 607.

12. Levinas, *Beyond the Verse*, 158.

13. Ibid., 159.

14. Ibid., 161.

15. Hirsch, *Rabbinic Psychology*, 64.

16. Ibid., 154.

17. Cohen, *Everyman's Talmud*, 238.

18. Ibid., 76.

19. Solomon, "Judaism," 102.

20. Spinoza, *A Spinoza Reader*, 224 (*Ethics* IV P45 and Schol.).

21. Ibid., 219 (*Ethics* IV P37 Schol. 1).

22. Jacobs, *The Jewish Religion*, 575.

23. Solomon, "Judaism," 109–10.

24. Described in Hirsch, *Rabbinic Psychology*, 109–10.

25. Cohen, *Everyman's Talmud*, 385; it is "doubtful whether the Hereafter in this passage is to be understood as the period after death or the Messianic era. The term has both connotations and they are sometimes confused" (ibid., fn.).

26. Jacobs, *The Jewish Religion*, 575.

27. Cohen, *Everyman's Talmud*, 77.

28. Schwartz, *Judaism and Vegetarianism*, 14.

29. Cohen, *Everyman's Talmud*, 77, quoting Genesis Rabbah xiv:9.

30. Ibid., 379, quoting Ecclesiastes Rabbah to iii:21.

31. Jacobs, *The Jewish Religion*, 27.

32. Dan, "In the Kabbalah," 14:615.

33. Cohen, *Everyman's Talmud*, 77.
34. Riskin, "Compassion or Concession," 43.
35. Sanhedrin 109a, quoted in Cohen, *Everyman's Talmud*, 260–61.
36. Unterman, *Jews*, 228.
37. Cohen, *Everyman's Talmud*, 90. ARN, the *Avot d'Rabbi Natan* (Fathers According to Rabbi Nathan), is a Talmudic tractate of disputed date.
38. Ibid., 302.
39. Feliks, "Apes."
40. Schwartz, *Judaism and Vegetarianism*, 22, giving the reference Shabbat 128b (ibid., 174).
41. Ibid., 15.
42. Phelps, *The Longest Struggle*, 46.
43. Schwartz, *Judaism and Vegetarianism*, 15.
44. Ibid., 16–17.
45. Unterman, *Jews*, 203; also Schwartz, *Judaism and Vegetarianism*, 17; Jacobs, *The Jewish Religion*, 28.
46. Cohen, *Everyman's Talmud*, 236; and Schwartz, *Judaism and Vegetarianism*, 17.
47. Cohen, *Everyman's Talmud*, 236.
48. Schwartz, *Judaism and Vegetarianism*, 17.
49. Solomon, "Judaism," 108.
50. Levinas, *Beyond the Verse*, 154.
51. Schwarzschild, "Noachide Laws," 12:1189.
52. Unterman, *Jews*, 10.
53. Kalechofsky, "Jewish Law and Tradition," 51.
54. Schwartz, *Judaism and Vegetarianism*, 19.
55. Riskin, "Compassion or Concession," 44.
56. Ibid., quoting Rashi.
57. Maimonides, *The Guide for the Perplexed*, 372.
58. Jacobs, *The Jewish Religion*, 28.
59. Ibid.
60. Schwartz, *Judaism and Vegetarianism*, 9.
61. Cohen, *Everyman's Talmud*, 248.
62. Kalechofsky, "*Kashrut*," 99.
63. Schwartz, *Judaism and Vegetarianism*, 22–23.
64. Tappan, "Judaism and Vegetarianism," quoting Exodus Rabbah 2:2. Also in Cohen, *Everyman's Talmud*, 235; Schwartz, *Judaism and Vegetarianism*, 13.
65. Tappan, "Judaism and Vegetarianism"; also Schwartz, *Judaism and Vegetarianism*, 22.
66. Schwartz, *Judaism and Vegetarianism*, 23, citing "Tanchuma, Noah 3; cited by Schochet, Animal Life, p. 148" (ibid., 174).
67. Cohen, *Everyman's Talmud*, 236.
68. Schwartz, *Judaism and Vegetarianism*, 23, citing "Genesis Rabbah, Noah 31:14" (ibid., 174)..
69. Schwartz, *Judaism and Vegetarianism*, 24–25.

70. Ibid., 26.

71. Ibid., 25.

72. Solomon, "Judaism," 108.

73. Cohen, *Everyman's Talmud*, 235–36; also Cantor, "Kindness to Animals," 26, and Schwartz, *Judaism and Vegetarianism*, 23–24.

74. Schwartz, *Judaism and Vegetarianism*, 24.

75. Ibid.

76. Sherira Gaon, "Sherira Gaon Defends."

77. Ibid., 16.

78. Kalechofsky, "Jewish Law and Tradition," 53.

79. Adams, "'A Very Rare and Difficult Thing,'" 591.

80. Cohen, *Everyman's Talmud*, 385.

81. Ibid., 387–88.

82. Ibid., 353.

83. Schwartz, *Judaism and Vegetarianism*, 21.

84. Regenstein, *Replenish the Earth*, 200.

85. Patton, "Animal Sacrifice," 392.

86. Webb, *On God and Dogs*, 140.

87. Schwartz, *Judaism and Vegetarianism*, 21; mentioned also by Unterman, *Jews*, 178, but without interpretation.

88. Quoted in Schwartz, *Judaism and Vegetarianism*, 21; also Aviva Cantor, "Kindness to Animals," 27.

89. Solomon, "Judaism," 106.

90. Ibid., 105.

91. Quoted ibid., 103.

92. Berry, *Food for the Gods*, 158.

93. Ibid., 150.

94. Ibid., 157.

3. Christianity

1.   Akers, *The Lost Religion of Jesus*, 17.

2.   Ibid., 157.

3.   Regenstein, *Replenish the Earth*, 181, citing the view of the Edenites, an American Christian vegetarian group.

4.   Murti, "Again and Again"; 2–3 of printout.

5.   Ibid., 3, citing Matthew 5:17–20.

6.   Ibid., 4.

7.   Ibid., 8.

8.   Young, *Is God a Vegetarian?* 3.

9.   Ibid., xix.

10. Ibid., 163.

11. Murray, *The Cosmic Covenant*, 141.

12. Ibid., 131.

13. Linzey, *Animal Theology*, 71.

14. Young, *Is God a Vegetarian?* 86.
15. Murray, *Cosmic Covenant*, 130.
16. Preece, *Brute Souls*, 154–55.
17. Young, *Is God a Vegetarian?* 8.
18. Ibid., 119.
19. Ibid., 122.
20. Webb, *On God and Dogs*, 24.
21. Kemmerer, *In Search of Consistency*, 261.
22. Webb, *On God and Dogs*, 24.
23. Jeffrey, *People of the Book*, 52–53.
24. Ibid., 56.
25. Ibid., 57.
26. Hiebert, *The Yahwist's Landscape*, 153.
27. Aquinas, "Differences," 57.
28. Summarized by Webb, *On God and Dogs*, 47.
29. Davies, "Christianity," 33.
30. Chereso, "Image of God," 7:369.
31. Quoted in Linzey, *Animal Gospel*, 58.
32. Linzey, *Animal Theology*, 51–52.
33. Ibid., 52.
34. Ibid., 142.
35. Regenstein, *Replenish the Earth*, 74.
36. Preece, *Animals and Nature*, 145.
37. Regenstein, *Replenish the Earth*, 118–19.
38. Ibid., 121.
39. Ibid., 113.
40. Quoted ibid., 114.
41. Rollin, *The Unheeded Cry*, 130.
42. Quoted in Linzey, *Animal Gospel*, 58.
43. Ibid., 61.
44. Quoted ibid., 58.
45. Linzey, *Animal Theology*, 35.
46. Akers, *The Lost Religion of Jesus*, 65.
47. Ibid., 124–25.
48. Linzey, *Animal Theology*, 132.
49. Ibid., 110.
50. Quoted in Waldau, *The Specter of Speciesism*, 213.
51. Linzey, *Animal Theology*, 133.
52. Ibid., 134; see also Young, *Is God a Vegetarian?* 10–11.
53. Ibid., 133.
54. Ibid., 120.
55. Regenstein, *Replenish the Earth*, 64.
56. Fox, *The Unauthorized Version*, 416.
57. Ibid., 76.

58. *The Holy Bible*, 69, footnote to Exod. 12.

59. Cited by Waldau, *Specter of Speciesism*, 212.

60. Akers, *The Lost Religion of Jesus*, 45.

61. Webb, *On God and Dogs*, 149.

62. Ibid., 162.

63. Ibid., 171.

64. Küng, "Belief in a Son of God," 148.

65. *New Catholic Encyclopedia*, 9:151.

66. Bradley, *God Is Green*, 75.

67. Ibid., 96.

68. Ibid.

69. Phelps, *The Longest Struggle*, 59.

70. Preece, *Brute Souls*, 131.

71. Preece, *Animals and Nature*, 125.

72. Ibid.

73. Quoted in Regenstein, *Replenish the Earth*, 13.

74. Fellowship of Life, "Thy Will Be Done?"

75. Dalrymple, *From the Holy Mountain*, 295; Moschos began his pilgrimage in 578 (ibid., 11).

76. Regenstein, *Replenish the Earth*, 57.

77. Preece, *Animals and Nature*, 127.

78. Ibid.

79. Preece, *Brute Souls*, 132.

80. Quoted in Lossky, *Mystical Theology*, 111.

81. Preece, *Animals and Nature*, xix.

82. Regenstein, *Replenish the Earth*, 58; Preece, *Brute Souls*, 335.

83. Quoted in Preece, *Brute Souls*, 335.

84. Ibid., 127.

85. Ibid., 128.

86. Classified as a heresy within Christianity because of its founder's Christian upbringing, Manichaeism was actually intended as "universalistic," embodying "the teachings of Zarathustra, the Buddha, and Jesus." (Smart, *The World's Religions*, 222.) Its "dominant doctrine, of the separation of good and evil, light and darkness, seems to have owed much more to the Zoroastrian tradition" (ibid.).

87. Preece, *Animals and Nature*, 127.

88. Kempe, *The Book of Margery Kempe*, 104. She refers to herself in the third person.

89. Linzey, *Animal Theology*, 50; Bradley, *God Is Green*, 79.

90. Preece, *Animals and Nature*, 126.

91. Regenstein, *Replenish the Earth*, 67.

92. Quoted ibid., 68.

93. Ibid., 116.

94. Ibid., 78.

95. Smart, *The World's Religions*, 323.

96. Foster, *Marx's Ecology*, 74.

97. Regenstein, *Replenish the Earth*, 87.

98. Webb, *On God and Dogs*, 33; Regenstein, *Replenish the Earth*, 87.

99. Phelps, *The Longest Struggle*, 61.

100. Regenstein, *Replenish the Earth*, 98.

101. Preece, *Animals and Nature*, 141.

102. Regenstein, *Replenish the Earth*, 88.

103. Quoted ibid.

104. Ibid., 90.

105. Preece, *Animals and Nature*, 142.

106. Regenstein, *Replenish the Earth*, 92.

107. Ibid., 110.

108. Bradley, *God Is Green*, 7.

109. Ibid., 31.

110. Preece, *Animals and Nature*, 111.

111. Ibid., 9.

112. Bradley, *God Is Green*, 2.

113. Linzey, *Animal Theology*, 6.

114. Ibid., 9.

115. Ibid., 114, 119.

116. Bradley, *God Is Green*, 3.

4. Islam

1. On the Qur'an, see Ali, *The Meaning of the Holy Qur'an*; on the Hadith, see Khan, *Summarized Sahih Al-Bukhari*.

2. Hourani, *Reason and Tradition in Islamic Ethics*, 184.

3. Ibid., 39.

4. Ibid., 123.

5. Smart, *The World's Religions*, 286.

6. Ghazali (1057–1111), quoted in Hourani, *Reason and Tradition*, 145.

7. Izzi Dien, *The Environmental Dimensions of Islam*, 146.

8. Forward and Alam, "Islam," 93.

9. Berry, *Food for the Gods*, 249.

10. Ibid., 241.

11. Quoted in Izzi Dien, *The Environmental Dimensions of Islam*, 146.

12. Ibid., 146.

13. Ibid.

14. Foltz, "Is Vegetarianism Un-Islamic?" Foltz is citing Muttaqi's view.

15. Mawdudi, *Towards Understanding Islam*, 101.

16. Haykal, *The Life of Muhammad*, 212.

17. Foltz, "Islamic Environmentalism," 257.

18. Khan, *Summarized Sahih Al-Bukhari*, book 54, chapter 10, no. 1396. Future Hadith references will be given in the text.

19. Forward and Alam, "Islam," 91.

20. Ali, *The Meaning of the Holy Qur'an*, note 770.

21. Waines, *An Introduction to Islam*, 130.
22. Varisco, *Medieval Folk Astronomy*, 7.64–65.
23. Arberry, *Sufism*, 28.
24. Hafiz, *Teachings of Hafiz*, 167.
25. Sa'di, *Sa'di*, 30.
26. Ibid., 31.
27. Ibid., 235.
28. Shah, *The Way of the Sufi*, 14.
29. Ibid., 25.
30. Quoted ibid., 310.
31. Buddhism is clear about the possibility of humans being reborn as animals; and although such rebirth is linked to behavior when in the human condition, Evans-Wentz's arguments (Evans-Wentz, *The Tibetan Book of the Dead*, 50ff) that it merely symbolizes human characteristics both in Plato and in the Tibetan Book of the Dead are unconvincing at least in regard to the Buddhist tradition.
32. Arberry, *Sufism*, 101.
33. Waines, *An Introduction to Islam*, 12.
34. Arberry, *Sufism*, 16.
35. Quoted in Shah, *The Way of the Sufi*, 62.
36. Masri, *Excerpts from the Islamic Teachings*, 4.
37. Forward and Alam, "Islam," 95.
38. az-Zaybaq, *The Animal*, 34.
39. Ibid.
40. Ibid., 34–35.
41. Quoted ibid., 35.
42. Quoted in Masri, "They Are Communities," 190.
43. Haykal, *The Life of Muhammad*, 187.
44. Ibid., 327.
45. Izzi Dien, *Environmental Dimensions*, 174, n. 24.
46. Ibid., 105.
47. Ali, *The Meaning of the Holy Qur'an*, note 1044.
48. Masri, "They Are Communities," 187.
49. Ali, *The Meaning of the Holy Qur'an*, note 1046.
50. Sa'di, *Sa'di*, 63.
51. Arberry, *Sufism*, 36.
52. Foltz, "Is Vegetarianism Un-Islamic?" 10 of printout.
53. Sa'di, *Sa'di*, 67.
54. Ibid., 87.
55. Shah, *The Way of the Sufi*, 99.
56. Sa'di, *Sa'di*, 227.
57. Ibid., 188.
58. Ibid., 125.
59. Ibid., 102.
60. Foltz, "Is Vegetarianism Un-Islamic?" 3–4 of printout.

61. Walters and Portmess, "Al-Hafiz B. A. Masri," 181.

62. az-Zaybaq, *The Animal*, iv.

63. Cook, *Muhammad*, 68.

64. Ali, *The Meaning of the Holy Qur'an*, note 977.

65. ibn Rushd, *The Distinguished Jurist's Primer*, 527.

66. Izzi Dien, *Environmental Dimensions*, 114, citing ibn Nujaym.

67. Ibid., 115, citing Bustani's *Majalla*.

68. Forward and Alam, "Islam," 94.

69. Ali, *The Meaning of the Holy Qur'an*, note 698 to 6:121.

70. ibn Rushd, *The Distinguished Jurist's Primer*, 541.

71. Ibid.

72. Ahmed, *Islam and Vegetarianism*, 13.

73. Ali, *The Meaning of the Holy Qur'an*, note 2809.

74. ibn Rushd, *The Distinguished Jurist's Primer*, 450.

75. Ibid., 516–17.

76. Foltz, *Animals in Islamic Tradition*, 26.

77. ibn Rushd, *The Distinguished Jurist's Primer*, 388.

78. Ibid.

79. Ali, *The Meaning of the Holy Qur'an*, note 684.

80. ibn Rushd, *The Distinguished Jurist's Primer*, 388.

81. Forward and Alam, "Islam," 96.

82. Masri, "They Are Communities," 188.

5. Buddhism

1. Chapple, *Nonviolence to Animals*, 9.

2. Ibid., 21.

3. Preece, *Animals and Nature*, 199.

4. Chapple, *Nonviolence to Animals*, 11.

5. Ibid., 42–43.

6. Ibid., 15.

7. Dotan, "Israel's Largest Milk Producer."

8. The Buddha's name was Siddhartha Gotama. "The Buddha" means "the one who has awoken." Skilton, *A Concise History of Buddhism*, 23.

9. *Karma* and derivatives is from the Sanskrit; the equivalent from the Pali is *kamma*. When referring specifically to texts translated from those languages, or concepts of the schools of thought using those languages, I use the corresponding spelling; but when using the term generically I use the Sanskrit, in this case *karma*, which is also in common Anglo-American use. The same procedure is followed for the words *Bodhisatta/Bodhisattva*, *dhamma/dharma*, and *nibbana/nirvana*, the first version in each case being from the Pali.

10. *The Bhagavad-Gita*, 373.

11. Preece, *Animals and Nature*, 203–4.

12. Chapple, *Nonviolence to Animals*, 11.

13. Ibid., 13.

14. Bodhisatta: in the Pali scriptures, the Buddha-to-be in a previous life, before the one in which he became enlightened.

15. The jatakas, or stories of the Buddha's previous lives, are found in an early Pali collection and a later Mahayana one (my edition being translated from Tibetan).

    The style of references that I use to the early jatakas is as follows: xxii.337 (533, 178) means book 22 (not the same as the publication volume but specified in the verso running head), original page 337 (in square brackets in the text), story number 533, publication page 178. The edition used is Cowell, *Jataka I and II, Jataka III and IV, Jataka V and VI*.

    The Jatakamala is a much shorter and more didactic Mahayana collection of jatakas. The edition used is Aryasura, *Jatakamala (The Marvelous Companion)*.

    Transmigration stories are an old Indian tradition. The jataka tales themselves "occur even in the Canonical Pitakas" (Cowell, *Jataka I and II*, xxi), "were widely known in the third century B.C." (ibid., xxii), and a form of them "was translated into Pali about 430 A.D. by Buddhaghosa" (ibid., xxiv).

16. A title of the Buddha: "one who has realised and known things as they are in reality; Perfect Being": Murti, *The Central Philosophy of Buddhism*, 350.

17. Nalagiri was an elephant whom Devadatta (the Buddha's cousin and enemy) set upon Gotama, after mistreating the animal in order to provoke the latter to murderous rage. But the compassion and goodwill radiated by the Buddha calmed the elephant.

18. Page, *Buddhism and Animals*, 99.

19. Ibid., 101.

20. Jacobsen, "Humankind and Nature in Buddhism," 385.

21. Chapple, *Nonviolence to Animals*, 44.

22. Choudhury, "Hinduism," 76.

23. Regenstein, *Replenish the Earth*, 223.

24. Chapple, *Nonviolence to Animals*, 16.

25. Bryant, "Strategies of Vedic Subversion," 198.

26. Ibid., 194.

27. Schmithausen, "The Early Buddhist Tradition."

28. Chapple, *Nonviolence to Animals*, 15.

29. Cited in Clark, *The Moral Status of Animals*, 27n.

30. *Metta* may be translated various ways; it is not as intense as "love," but indicates "friendliness," "loving-kindness," "goodwill." Because of this difficulty it is often left untranslated.

31. Schmithausen, "The Early Buddhist Tradition," 15.

32. Harvey, *An Introduction to Buddhism*, 201.

33. Keown, *Buddhism and Bioethics*, 97.

34. Ibid.

35. Ibid., 98.

36. *Vin.i.137 (Vinaya* vol. 1, 137), quoted in Keown, *Buddhism and Bioethics*, 98.

37. Ibid.

38. Ibid., 99.

39. Harvey, *An Introduction to Buddhism*, 205.

40. Ruegg, "Ahimsa and Vegetarianism," 234.

41. Ibid.

42. The later school of Buddhism, beginning to emerge "during the centuries either side of the beginning of the common era" (Skilton, *A Concise History of Buddhism*, 93), but perhaps not commonly designated as such until the fourth century CE (ibid., 94). It "regards the aspirations . . . of the non-Mahayana schools, i.e., individual liberation and arhatship, as selfish and inadequate, and replaces them with a radical emphasis upon . . . full and perfect Buddhahood attained for the sake of alleviating the suffering of all beings" (ibid., 93). *Mahayana* means "Great Way," and its supporters labeled the previous schools the "Hinayana" or "Lesser Way" (ibid.).

43. Surangama Sutra, "Prohibition Against Killing," 65.

44. Harvey, *An Introduction to Buddhism*, 204.

45. Kapleau, *To Cherish All Life*, 30.

46. Regenstein, *Replenish the Earth*, 227.

47. This verse and other references to cannibalism suggest that the culture was not that far removed from it. Cowell, *Jataka V and VI*, 248n, mentions "legends connected with cannibalism in the modern Pisaca country." The practice occurs without censure in number 193 in which the Bodhisatta and other humans eat human flesh, the future Buddha's only distinction being that he saves his own wife and even gives her his blood to drink.

48. Steele and Kaza, "Buddhist Food Practices," 54.

49. Ibid., 58.

50. Walters and Portmess, "The Dalai Lama," 87.

51. Ibid., 89.

52. Gandhi, "Diet and Non-violence," 55.

53. Chapple, "Nonviolence to Animals in Buddhism and Jainism," 51.

54. Harvey, "Buddhist Attitudes," 44.

55. Roger Corless, quoted in Regenstein, *Replenish the Earth*, 238.

56. Preece, *Animals and Nature*, x.

57. Harvey, "Buddhist Attitudes," 48.

58. From the *Vinaya: Vin.*i.137, trans. Wijayaratna, amended, quoted by Keown, *Buddhism and Bioethics*, 34; his emphasis.

59. Smart, *The World's Religions*, 70.

60. Berry, *Food for the Gods*, 46.

61. Schmithausen, "Buddhist Ecological Ethics," 21–22.

62. Suzuki, *Lankavatara Sutra*, 211.

63. Ibid., 213–14.

6. Change and the Effective-Defensive Strategy

1. Atran, *In Gods We Trust*, 277.

2. Ibid., 249.

3. Jacob Neusner, "Foreword," x.

4. Ibid., xxxv–xxxvi.
5. Ahmed, letter to Tappan, December 14, 1998, 2.
6. VegetarianIslam.
7. Foltz, *Animals in Islamic Tradition*, 125.
8. Ibid., 42.
9. Izzi Dien, *The Environmental Dimensions of Islam*, 17–18.
10. Akers, *The Lost Religion of Jesus*, 79.
11. Regenstein, *Replenish the Earth*, 43.
12. Masri, "Animals in Islam I."
13. Masri, *The Islamic Code of Animal-Human Relationships*, 5.
14. Bryant, "Strategies of Vedic Subversion," 195.
15. Ibid., 199.
16. Page, *Buddhism and Animals*, 123.
17. Kapleau, *To Cherish All Life*, 39–40.
18. Cohen, *Everyman's Talmud*, 3.
19. Davies, *An Introduction to the Philosophy of Religion*, 84.
20. Webb, *On God and Dogs*, 45.
21. Akers, *The Lost Religion of Jesus*, 182, referring to *Recognitions* 1.36.
22. Ibid., 129.
23. Linzey, *Animal Theology*, 60.
24. Ibid., 106.
25. Lossky, *The Mystical Theology of the Eastern Church*, 98.
26. Mawdudi, *Towards Understanding Islam*, 59n.
27. Shah, *The Way of the Sufi*, 281.
28. Ahmed, letter to Tappan, December 14, 1998, 2.
29. Ferguson, "Muslims Urge Stop."
30. Foltz, *Animals in Islamic Tradition*, 45–46.
31. Ibid., 46.
32. Skilton, *A Concise History of Buddhism*, 31.
33. Keown, *Buddhism and Bioethics*, 29.
34. Chapple, *Nonviolence to Animals*, 46.
35. Schwartz, *Judaism and Vegetarianism*, 3.
36. Ibid., 98.
37. Schwartz, *Judaism and Vegetarianism*, 88.
38. Unterman, *Jews*, 64.
39. Ahmed, letter to Tappan, July 1, 1998, 1.
40. Ibid., 2.
41. Schwartz, *Judaism and Vegetarianism*, 30.
42. Friedrich, "Pig Roast in Wyoming."
43. Ahmed, letter to Tappan, December 14, 1998, 2.
44. Tappan, "Islam and Vegetarianism," 3.
45. Young, *Is God a Vegetarian?* 58.
46. Ibid., 12.
47. Swinburne, *Providence and the Problem of Evil*.

48. Cohen, *Everyman's Talmud*, 18.

49. Ibid., 236.

50. Quoted in Schwartz, *Judaism and Vegetarianism*, 1.

51. Quoted in ibid., 2.

52. Ibid., 64.

53. Kalechofsky, "*Kashrut*," 97.

54. Ibid.

55. Solomon, "Judaism," 106.

56. Ibid., 107.

57. Ibid.

58. Quoted in Regenstein, *Replenish the Earth*, 192.

59. Cohen, *Everyman's Talmud*, 210.

60. Ibid., 211–12.

61. Riskin, "Compassion or Concession," 44.

62. Kalechofsky, "Introduction," 2.

63. Church and Society Consultation, *Liberation of Life*, 3.

64. Davies, "Christianity," 36.

65. Ibid., 35.

66. Ford, "Pantheism vs. Theism," 294.

67. Quoted in Regenstein, *Replenish the Earth*, 116.

68. Ibid., 117.

69. Linzey, *Animal Theology*, 25.

70. Ibid., 69.

71. Morton, *Shelley and the Revolution in Taste*, 136, quoting Shelley's *Vindication of Natural Diet*.

72. Bradley, *God Is Green*, 57.

73. Ibid., 59.

74. Linzey, *Animal Theology*, 126.

75. Ibid., 127.

76. Ibid., 32.

77. Dombrowski, *Hartshorne*, 8.

78. Davies, "Christianity," 51–52.

79. Ferguson, "Inhumane Animal Slaughter."

80. Foltz, *Animals in Islamic Tradition*, 142.

81. Abou El-Fadl, "The Lord of the Essence."

82. Kemmerer, *In Search of Consistency*, 353, quoting Haq. Kemmerer uses the word *anymals* to indicate the variety of nonhuman species.

83. az-Zaybaq, *The Animal*, 26–27.

84. Foltz, *Animals in Islamic Tradition*, 33.

85. Kemmerer, *In Search of Consistency*, 348 and 349, quoting Ozdemir.

86. Foltz, *Animals in Islamic Tradition*, 96.

87. Ibid., 4.

88. Quoted in ibid., 57.

89. Ibid., 96.

90. Ibid., 95.
91. Ibid., 120.
92. Ferguson, "Inhumane Animal Slaughter."
93. Foltz, *Animals in Islamic Tradition*, 122.
94. *Viceregent/viceregency* is often given as *vicegerent/vicegerency* in the literature.
95. Izzi Dien, *The Environmental Dimensions of Islam*, 75.
96. Naseef, "The Muslim Declaration on Nature," 13.
97. Khalid, "Islam, Ecology, and the World Order," 20.
98. Ibid., 21.
99. Ibid., 28
100. Dutton, "Islam and the Environment," 70–71.
101. Jacobsen, "Humankind and Nature in Buddhism," 384.
102. Schmithausen, "The Early Buddhist Tradition," 16.
103. Ibid.
104. Quoted in Preece, *Animals and Nature*, 202
105. Chapple, *Nonviolence to Animals*, 4, quoting the Acaranga Sutra.
106. Skilton, *A Concise History of Buddhism*, 65.
107. Schmithausen, "Buddhist Ecological Ethics," 17.
108. Smart, *The World's Religions*, 92. The idea is similar to the transmigrational totemism of the Itza' Maya, some of whom "say their name is howler monkey . . . because they were howler monkeys before; the spider monkey . . . is Tesukun (another family)." Atran, *In Gods We Trust*, 85.
109. Keown, *Buddhism and Bioethics*, 184.
110. Harvey, *An Introduction to Buddhism*, 199.
111. Sumedho, *Cittaviveka*, 58.
112. FWBO, *The FWBO Puja Book*, 18.
113. Harvey, *An Introduction to Buddhism*, 199.
114. Aryasura, *Jatakamala*, 220.
115. Ibid., 224.
116. Ibid., 226.
117. de Silva, "Environmental Ethics," 179.
118. Harvey, *An Introduction to Buddhism*, 204.
119. Manu, "The Sin of Killing," 42.
120. *The Bhagavad-Gita*, 186; 4.13 of the *Gita*.
121. Ibid., 285; 9.30 of the *Gita*.
122. Preece, *Animals and Nature*, 201.
123. Cowell, *Jataka III and IV*, 10.
124. Choudhury, "Hinduism," 74. The understanding of rebirth in Hinduism is different from that of Buddhism, however, since Hindus believe in a specific, though transmigrating, soul for each individual, while for Buddhists all identity is in flux. The Buddhist account of rebirth of individuals is for this reason quite incoherent, posing perhaps the greatest difficulty encountered by Western converts; I have never heard a satisfactory explanation of it from monks.
125. Chapple, *Nonviolence to Animals*, 12.

126. Conze, *Buddhist Scriptures*, 20 and 24–26.

127. Chapple, "Nonviolence to Animals in Buddhism and Jainism," 53.

128. Tiyavanich, *Forest Recollections*, 80.

129. Quoted in Sangharakshita, *A Survey of Buddhism*, 396.

130. Suzuki, *Lankavatara Sutra*, 218.

131. Ibid.

132. Quoted in Page, *Buddhism and Animals*, 173; also in Sangharakshita, *Survey of Buddhism*, 402.

133. Sumedho, *Cittaviveka*, 19.

134. Chapple, *Nonviolence to Animals*, 114.

135. Ibid.

136. Berman, "The Dietary Laws," 151.

137. Webb, *On God and Dogs*, 31.

138. Ibid., 31.

139. Preece, *Animals and Nature*, 127.

140. Regenstein, *Replenish the Earth*, 141.

141. Linzey, *Animal Theology*, 136.

142. Akers, *The Lost Religion of Jesus*, 53.

143. PETA Europe, "2008's Sexiest Vegetarian Celebrity"

144. Solomon, "Judaism," 109.

145. Berry, *Food for the Gods*, 159.

146. Solomon, "Judaism," 109.

147. Schwartz, *Judaism and Vegetarianism*, 141.

148. Ibid., 142.

149. Ibid., 144.

150. Dotan, "Israel's Largest Milk Producer."

151. Regenstein, *Replenish the Earth*, 196.

152. Ibid., 202.

153. Cohen, *Everyman's Talmud*, 237.

154. Ibid., 237n.

155. Quoted in Schwartz, *Judaism and Vegetarianism*, 20.

156. Solomon, "Judaism," 111.

157. Kalechofsky, *Judaism and Animal Rights*.

158. Cramer, "The Inconsistency of Animal Experimentation," 322.

159. Schwartz, *Judaism and Vegetarianism*, 104.

160. Menache, "A Jewish Intuition About Animal Research," 334–35.

161. Ibid., 336.

162. Mendelsohn, "Foreword to Slaughter of the Innocent," 262.

163. Spira, "Animal Rights," 338.

164. Cohen, *Everyman's Talmud*, 107.

165. Ibid., 105.

166. Ibid., 82.

167. Akers, *The Lost Religion of Jesus*, 212. The next several page references to Akers will be given in the text.

168. Webb, *On God and Dogs*, 146.

169. Ibid., 147.

170. Sixth-century traveler John Moschos, quoted in Dalrymple, *From the Holy Mountain*, 294.

171. Ibid., 295.

172. Linzey, *Animal Theology*, 136.

173. Regenstein, *Replenish the Earth*, 179.

174. Linzey, *Animal Theology*, 136.

175. Ibid., 180.

176. Webb, *On God and Dogs*, 34.

177. Ibid., 35.

178. Quoted in Regenstein, *Replenish the Earth*, 115.

179. *Animal Times*.

180. Regenstein, *Replenish the Earth*, 81.

181. McCarthy, "'Cloistered' Chickens."

182. Chapple, *Nonviolence to Animals*, 18.

183. VegetarianIslam.

184. Fadali, *Animal Experimentation*, 199; Masri, "Animals in Islam II."

185. VegetarianIslam.

186. Masri, "Animals in Islam II."

187. Foltz, *Animals in Islamic Tradition*, 122.

188. Foltz, "Is Vegetarianism UnIslamic?" 9 of printout.

189. Dalrymple, *From the Holy Mountain*, 191.

190. Masri, "Animals in Islam II."

191. Ferguson, "Inhumane Animal Slaughter."

192. Shah, *The Way of the Sufi*, 240; a slightly different version is also cited by Foltz, "Is Vegetarianism UnIslamic?" 10.

193. Tutuncuoglu, "The Past and Current Situation."

194. Editors' introductory note to Rumi, "The Men Who Ate the Elephant," 173.

195. Ibid., 173–74.

196. Ibid., 174.

197. Monastra, "Who Says Muslims?"

198. Foltz, "Is Vegetarianism UnIslamic?" 1 of printout.

199. Ibid., 2 of printout.

200. Akers, *The Lost Religion of Jesus*, 212.

201. Monastra, "Who Says Muslims?"

202. Khan, *Summarized Sahih Al-Bukhari*, no. 1923.

203. Forward and Alam, "Islam," 92; Masri, "Animals in Islam I."

204. Ahmed, *Islam and Vegetarianism*, 15.

205. Masri, "Animals in Islam I."

206. Quoted in Regenstein, *Replenish the Earth*, 259.

207. Masri, "Animals in Islam II."

208. Ibid.

209. Harvey, *An Introduction to Buddhism*, 29.

210. Gombrich, "Recovering the Buddha's Message," 12.
211. Quoted ibid., 17.
212. Quoted ibid., 18.
213. Zaehner, *Bhagavad-Gita*, 192–95; 424–33 of the *Gita*.
214. Sangharakshita, *Survey of Buddhism*, 424.
215. Chapple, *Nonviolence to Animals*, 25.
216. Ibid., 26.
217. Ibid., 25–26.
218. Harvey, *An Introduction to Buddhism*, 76.
219. Choudhury, "Hinduism," 76.
220. Chapple, *Nonviolence to Animals*, 16.
221. Manu, "The Sin of Killing," 41.
222. Akaranga Sutra, "To Harm No Living Being," 45.
223. Ruegg, "Ahimsa and Vegetarianism," 234.
224. Ibid., 235.
225. Harvey, "Buddhist Attitudes," 39.
226. Chapple, *Nonviolence to Animals*, 29.
227. Suzuki, *Lankavatara Sutra*, 212.
228. Chapple, *Nonviolence to Animals*, 26.
229. Ruegg, "Ahimsa and Vegetarianism," 236.
230. Ibid., 237.
231. Linzey, "Interfaith Service."
232. http://www.serv-online.org.
233. Preece, *Animals and Nature*, xxv.
234. Harvey, "Buddhist Attitudes," 45.
235. Berry, *Food for the Gods*, 44.
236. Preece, *Animals and Nature*, 20.
237. Ibid., 201.
238. Foltz, *Animals in Islamic Tradition*, 85.
239. Ibid., 197.
240. Clifton, "Indian Diets."
241. Fadali, *Animal Experimentation*, 202–4.
242. Preece, *Animals and Nature*, 216.
243. Ibid., 217.
244. Ibid., 213.
245. Schwartz, *Judaism and Vegetarianism*, 97.
246. Harvey, "Buddhist Attitudes," 46.
247. Sumedho, *Now Is the Knowing*, 17.
248. Page, *Buddhism and Animals*, 181.
249. Ibid., 180.
250. Ibid., 180–81.
251. Chapple, *Nonviolence to Animals*, 30.
252. Preece, *Animals and Nature*, 206.
253. Quoted in Eller, "The Impact of Christianity," 102.

254. "Attitudes Towards Vegetarianism"; also Phelps, *The Longest Struggle*, 307–8.

255. Clifton, "Indian Diets."

256. "Stop This Monkey Business."

7. Seeing as a Whole

1. Cohen, *Everyman's Talmud*, 24.

2. Levinas, *Beyond the Verse*, 119.

3. Ibid., 120.

4. Scholem, "Kabbalah," 569–70.

5. Quoted in Levinas, *Beyond the Verse*, 164.

6. Linzey, *Animal Theology*, 68–69.

7. Dombrowski, *Hartshorne*, his chapter 4 throughout.

8. Quoted ibid., 65.

9. Ibid., 89.

10. Izzi Dien, *The Environmental Dimensions of Islam*, 12.

11. Ali, *The Meaning of the Holy Qur'an*, n. 1132.

12. Corbin, *Creative Imagination*, 68.

13. "7. What we cannot speak about we must pass over in silence." Wittgenstein, *Tractatus Logico Philosophicus*, 87.

14. Quoted in Shah, *The Way of the Sufi*, 72–73.

15. Ibid., 114.

16. Tiradhammo, "Joy in Spiritual Practice," 94.

17. Moore, "A Defence of Common Sense," 37.

18. Aryasura, *Jatakamala*, 200.

19. Suzuki, *Lankavatara Sutra*, 123–24.

20. Ibid., 124.

21. Smart, *The World's Religions*, 39.

22. Quoted in Arberry, *Sufism*, 54–55.

23. Asher, *Rare Earth*, 246.

24. Regenstein, *Replenish the Earth*, 75.

25. Quoted in Preece, *Brute Souls, Happy Beasts, and Evolution*, 168.

26. Ibid.

27. Preece, *Animals and Nature*, 138.

28. Hirsch, *Rabbinic Psychology*, 61.

29. Ibid., 244.

30. "Pope Concedes Souls to Animals."

31. Regenstein, *Replenish the Earth*, 78.

32. Ibid., 87.

33. Webb, *On God and Dogs*, 33.

34. Ibid.

35. Ibid., 94.

36. Quoted ibid., 44.

37. Masri, *The Islamic Code of Animal-Human Relationships*, 3.

38. Webb, *On God and Dogs*, 173.

39. Solomon, "Judaism," 104.

40. Jacobs, *The Jewish Religion*, 27.

41. Solomon, "Judaism," 105.

42. Hardy, *The Complete Poetical Works of Thomas Hardy*, 206, *Tess of the d'Urbervilles*, 138.

43. Davies, "Christianity," 39.

44. Izzi Dien, *The Environmental Dimensions of Islam*, 69.

45. Sa'di, *Sa'di*, 97.

46. Hakim Sanai, quoted in Shah, *The Way of the Sufi*, 109.

47. Waliullah, *Sufism and the Islamic Tradition*, 49.

48. Masri, *The Islamic Code of Animal-Human Relationships*, 6.

49. Fadali, *Animal Experimentation*, 197.

50. Ahmed, letter to Tappan, December 14, 1998, 2.

51. Page, *Buddhism and Animals*, 103.

52. Kane, *Wisdom of the Mythtellers*, 44.

53. Choudhury, "Hinduism," 75.

54. Cohen, *Everyman's Talmud*, 289.

55. Ibid., 280.

56. Ibid.

57. Dalrymple, *From the Holy Mountain*, 306, quoting Fr. Theophanes of Mar Saba monastery.

58. Haykal, *The Life of Muhammad*, 346.

59. Ibid., 171–72.

60. Mernissi, *The Veil and the Male Elite*, 106.

61. *The NIV Thematic Study Bible*, 1471.

62. Hirsch, *Rabbinic Psychology*, 201.

63. Atran, *In Gods We Trust*, 172.

64. Corbin, *Creative Imagination*, 51.

65. Shah, *The Way of the Sufi*, 270.

66. Quoted ibid., 101.

67. Khan, *Summarized Sahih Al-Bukhari*, bk. 40, ch. 4, no. 1076. I am giving Hadiths by book, chapter, and number, but editor's comments by page.

68. Ibid.

69. Ibid., 506n.

70. Ibid., 507.

71. Quoted in Shah, *The Way of the Sufi*, 185.

72. Foltz, *Animals in Islamic Tradition*, 132.

73. Ibid., 141.

74. Sangharakshita, *A Survey of Buddhism*, 302.

75. Green, *Theology, Hermeneutics, and Imagination*, 1.

76. Hafiz, *Teachings of Hafiz*, 157.

77. Ali, *The Meaning of the Holy Qur'an*, n. 2349.

78. Ibid., n. 2350.

79. Ibid., n. 2336.

80. Sa'di, *Sa'di*, 30.

81. Ibid., 132.

82. Foltz, *Animals in Islamic Tradition*, 133.

83. Ali, *Qur'an*, n. 2334.

84. Regenstein, *Replenish the Earth*, 37.

85. Cohen, *Everyman's Talmud*, 236–37.

86. Dalrymple, *From the Holy Mountain*, 186.

87. Ibid.

88. Shah, *The Way of the Sufi*, 163, quoting a member of the Naqshbandi Order.

89. Ibid., 202–3.

90. Quoted in Foltz, "Is Vegetarianism Un-Islamic?" 5 of printout.

91. Foltz, *Animals in Islamic Tradition*, 52.

92. Kassam, "The Case of the Animals Versus Man," 165.

93. Ibid.

94. Foltz, *Animals in Islamic Tradition*, 53.

95. See chapter 5, n. 14, for an explanation of jataka references.

8. The Problem of Oneness

1. Cohen, *Everyman's Talmud*, 40–41.

2. Unterman, *Jews*, 104.

3. Smart, *The World's Religions*, 264.

4. Scholem, "Kabbalah," 569.

5. Ibid.

6. Solomon, "Judaism," 102–3.

7. Scholem, "Kabbalah," 606. Hasidism: "A movement founded in Eastern Europe (Ukraine and Southern Poland) in the late eighteenth century, with an emphasis on mysticism." Smart, *The World's Religions*, 265.

8. Scholem, "Kabbalah," 603.

9. Ibid., 603.

10. Spinoza, *A Spinoza Reader*, 16.

11. Ibid., 59.

12. Levinas, *Beyond the Verse*, 166.

13. Ibid.

14. Dombrowski, *Hartshorne*, 89.

15. Sprigge, *The Vindication of Absolute Idealism*, 157.

16. Dombrowski, *Hartshorne*, 27. According to Scholem, the term dates from the early nineteenth century, when it "was coined to distinguish such a view from pure pantheism" (Scholem, "Kabbalah,", 603).

17. Dombrowski, *Hartshorne*, 107.

18. Davies, "Christianity," 36.

19. Linzey, *Animal Theology*, 38.

20. Palmer, "Animals in Christian Ethics," 163.

21. Linzey, *Animal Gospel*, 37–38.

22. Ibid., 37.

23. Bradley, *God Is Green*, 20.

24. Forward and Alam, "Islam," 81.

25. Cook, *Muhammad*, 85–86.

26. Craig, *The* Kalam *Cosmological Argument*, 16.

27. In Shah, *The Way of the Sufi*, 268.

28. Hafiz, *Teachings of Hafiz*, 68.

29. Arberry, *Sufism*, 70.

30. Hafiz, *Teachings of Hafiz*, 74 (translator's note).

31. Church and Society Consultation, *Liberation of Life*, 5.

32. Fadali, *Animal Experimentation*, 216.

33. Tappan, "Christianity and Vegetarianism," 5.

34. Ibid.

35. Chapple, *Nonviolence to Animals*, 76.

36. *The Bhagavad-Gita*, 8.

37. Ibid., 297–302.

38. Conze, *Buddhist Wisdom Books*, 76.

39. Venkata Ramanan, *Nagarjuna's Philosophy*, 176.

40. Page, *Buddhism and Animals*, 194. For the "dream" image, see Conze, *Buddhist Wisdom Books*, 68 and 70.

41. Conze, *Buddhist Wisdom Books*, 123.

42. Sangharakshita, *A Survey of Buddhism*, 107ff.

43. Ibid., 111.

44. Murti, *The Central Philosophy of Buddhism*, 163.

45. Nagarjuna, quoted in Venkata Ramanan, *Nagarjuna's Philosophy*, 175.

46. Ibid., 190; Venkata Ramanan's brackets.

47. Chapple, *Nonviolence to Animals*, 87. Further references will appear in parentheses in text.

48. The Tathagatagarbha, "the 'womb' or 'embryo' of the Tathagata, the seed of Buddhahood that lies in all beings" (Skilton, *A Concise History of Buddhism*, 131), but in this passage given a meaning almost encompassing the entire universe.

49. Suzuki, *Lankavatara Sutra*, 190.

50. Vivekananda, "Oneness Includes All Animals," 50.

51. Sutrakrtanga, quoted in Smart, *The World's Religions*, 69.

9. Animal Rights

1. Webb, *On God and Dogs*, 119.

2. Schwartz, *Judaism and Vegetarianism*, 112.

3. Unterman, *Jews*, 81.

4. Kook, "A Firm and Joyous Voice of Life," 118.

5. Regenstein, *Replenish the Earth*, 195.

6. Bradley, *God Is Green*, 65.

7. Ibid., 69.

8. Linzey, *Animal Gospel*, 152.

9. Ahmed, letter to Tappan, December 14, 1998.

10. Ibid., July 1, 1998, 2.

11. Sangharakshita, *A Survey of Buddhism*, 266.

12. Best, "Evolve or Die," outlining some ideas in his forthcoming book, *Animal Liberation and Moral Progress: The Struggle for Human Evolution* (Rowman and Littlefield, 2009).

13. *Encyclopaedia Hebraica*, "Hillel," 484.

14. Mountain, "Dogma and Catechism," 171.

15. Kant, *The Moral Law*, 97n.

16. Vesey and Foulkes, *Dictionary of Philosophy*, 161.

17. Kant, *The Moral Law*, 97n.

18. Quoted by Bok in Honderich, *The Oxford Companion to Philosophy*, 321.

19. Kant, *The Moral Law*, 97n.

20. Kemp, *Ethical Naturalism*, 21, quoting Aubrey.

21. Masson and McCarthy, *When Elephants Weep*.

22. Lorin Lindner, "To Love Like a Bird," 56.

23. Hume, "Of the Reason of Animals," 69.

24. Klug, "Laboratory Animals," 273.

25. Ibid., 275.

26. Ibid., 276.

27. Quoted in Linzey, *Animal Theology*, 14.

28. Quoted in Regan, *The Case for Animal Rights*, 178.

29. Ibid.

30. Ruesch, *Slaughter of the Innocents*, 317, quoting a Jesuit supporter of animal experiments.

31. Eckersley, "Socialism and Ecocentrism," 283.

32. Rolston, "Duties to Endangered Species," 72.

33. Ibid., 67.

34. Webb, *On God and Dogs*, 182.

35. Ibid.

36. Sober and Wilson, "Summary of *Unto Others*," 198.

GLOSSARY

ahimsa   The ancient Indian principle of not causing harm to any living being.

anicca (Pali)/*anitya* (Sanskrit)   Impermanence; one of the Three Marks of Existence in Buddhism, the others being *DUKKHA* and *ANATTA*.

anatta (Pali)/*anatman* (Sanskrit)   Insubstantiality, the lack of permanent identity of all things including the self; another of Buddhism's Three Marks of Existence.

Aryans   Warlike, nomadic Euro-Asian people who invaded India to usher in the Vedic age.

Bhagavad Gita   The most read and most revered book of the MAHABHARATA. Arjuna does not want to fight his relatives, but KRISHNA explains why he must, for reasons both ethical (as construed within the caste system) and metaphysical.

Bodhisatta (Pali)/*Bodhisattva* (Sanskrit)   The future historical Buddha in one of his earlier lives. Or, any person seeking enlightenment or eventual Buddhahood.

bourn(e)   In writings on Buddhism, refers to the state into which a person is reborn, such as human, animal, hungry ghost, etc.

Brahma   1. In Hinduism, absolute reality, to which the adherent seeks to return from the world of bondage and illusion. 2. The name of a Buddhist god.

Brahmans   The Hindu and proto-Hindu priestly and scholarly caste.

Buddhaghosa   Theravadan Buddhist commentator of the fifth century.

dana   Offerings made to Buddhist monks by laypeople.

dhamma (Pali)/*dharma* (Sanskrit)   A word with many meanings, such as absolute reality, truth as expounded by the Buddha, or individual things. The intended meaning is usually evident from the context.

dukkha (Pali)/*duhkha* (Sanskrit)   Another of Buddhism's Three Marks of Existence, it means "unsatisfactoriness," sometimes translated as "suffering" or "ill." But it can refer to happiness as well, since happiness is accompanied by the fear of loss.

Ebionites   Early "Jewish Christians," as defined by Akers, who regarded Jesus as a human being, born normally but adopted by God to be the Jewish Messiah. They believed in following the Jewish law, but their ideas were overcome by those of Pauline Christianity.

Edenites   A modern American Christian vegetarian society.

Gotama/Gautama   The historical Buddha's family name, his first name being Siddhartha.

Hadith   The sayings of Muhammad, their chains of transmission carefully noted for authenticity, which is however often challenged to support doctrinal positions. They are also known as Traditions.

Hafiz   Khajeh Shamseddin Mohammad Hafiz Shirazi, 1310/25–1388/89, important Persian poet. There is dispute as to whether his worldly subject matter is meant literally or is spiritually symbolic. He is sometimes classified as a SUFI.

halal   Permissible according to Islamic law, especially with reference to meat, which must be of certain types and slaughtered with certain rituals reflecting certain principles. The opposite is *haram*, forbidden.

Hasidism   A mystical Jewish school of thought, originating in the late eighteenth century in Eastern Europe.

Hekhalot   Jewish esoteric literature of the Talmudic era.

Ibn 'Arabi   Muhyiddin Ibn 'Arabi, 1165–1240, a mystical Islamic philosopher and exponent of SUFISM.

ijtihad   In Islam, original interpretation of legal problems left uncertain in the Qur'an, HADITH, or *ijma* (scholarly legal consensus).

'Isa   Transliteration of the Arabic name for Jesus.

jatakas   Tales of the Buddha's former lives, when he was still a BODHISATT(V)A.

Jatakamala   A later, Mahayana collection of jatakas, much shorter than the original collection, and emphasizing moral lessons to be gained from the stories.

jhana (Pali)/*dhyana* (Sanskrit)   The state of meditative absorption, occurring in four progressive stages.

Kabbalism or Kabbalah   Jewish mystical teaching, given its name ("that which is received" in Hebrew) by Ibn Gabriol in the eleventh century.

kamma (Pali)/*karma* (Sanskrit)   The Buddhist principle of cause and effect running throughout reality; in moral teaching, good or bad activity resulting in reward or punishment; the results themselves, as in "He has created good/bad karma."

kashrut/kasher (kosher)   The Jewish food laws especially regarding types, rituals, and principles of slaughter, and preparation of animal products.

Krishna   The Hindu god VISHNU in another form.

Mahabharata   A post-Vedic epic which is Hinduism's foundational text.

Mahayana Buddhism   A school of Buddhism commonly identified by that name by the fourth century CE, although it emerged earlier. It sees the earlier stress on individual enlightenment as selfish and promotes instead the ideal of the BODHISATTVA, who seeks enlightenment with the ultimate aim of liberating all other sentient beings. Mahayana means Great Way, by contrast with the pejorative label Hinayana, Small or Lesser Way, applied to the earlier schools.

Maimonides   The philosopher R. Moses Ben Maimon, 1135–1204. His *Guide to the Perplexed* seeks to reconcile Aristotelian rationalist philosophy with the Bible as revelation.

Manichaeanism   A religion founded in the third century CE by the Persian philosopher Mani. He followed Christ, but his teaching contained strands from other religions. St. Augustine was originally a Manichaean, and his rejection of it was accompanied by a rejection of the ascetically based vegetarianism that it endorsed.

metta (Pali)/*maitri* (Sanskrit)   The Buddhist principle, difficult to translate, of friendliness, lovingkindness, or goodwill that Buddhists are enjoined to direct toward all beings.

Midrash   Rabbinical reflections, observations, and moral tales that illuminate and interpret biblical texts.

Mishnah   The Mishnah, composed by Judah the Prince (135–219 CE), is a law code on which other sections of the TALMUD provide interpretation.

muhrim   A Muslim on pilgrimage.

Mu'tazilites   A ninth-century school of Islam, endorsing a Greek-derived rationalism by contrast with orthodox Islamic legalism.

Nagarjuna   The great Buddhist metaphysician, ca. 150–250 CE, who fully developed the concept of emptiness, or *sunyata*, already implicit in Buddhist thought, thus founding the Madhyamaka (Middle School) branch of MAHAYANA BUDDHISM.

nirvana   The state of the enlightened being who has overcome attachment, especially to the sense of self, and whose status after physical death is declared to be beyond explanation. It may be popularly thought of as a place, but is rather a condition. Although on the surface the opposite of SAMSARA, in mystical thought it is the same.

Pali   The language of the earlier Buddhist scriptures.

Rumi   Jalal al-Din Rumi (1207–1273), the best-known Sufi poet and mystic.

Sa'di/Sa'adi   Mosleh a-Din Sa'adi Shirazi (1210–1290), important Persian Sufi poet and prose writer.

samsara   Reality as experienced by the unenlightened; the ordinary world.

Sangha   The community of Buddhist monks and nuns.

Sanskrit   The language of the VEDAS, the Hindu epics, MAHAYANA BUDDHIST texts, and the writings of NAGARJUNA.

sefirot   In Kabbalist teaching, the many and varied emanations of God.

shechitah   In Judaism, the laws of ritual slaughter.

Shi'ah/Shi'ism   The minority tradition within Islam. Shi'ites believe that Muhammad's nephew Ali should be recognized as the Prophet's chosen successor to lead the Muslim community, rather than Muhammad's associates Abu Bakr, Umar, Uthman and Ali.

Sufism   The mystical strain of Islam, emphasizing the oneness of God with all things and the possibility of direct union with God. Its practitioners have been more favorable to vegetarianism than followers of mainstream Islam.

sunna   Correct Islamic practice, as codified in the HADITH.

Sunni   The majority division of Islam. Its most technical dispute with SHI'AH is over the legitimate successors to the Prophet, the Sunni view being that the first four caliphs, rather than Muhammad's nephew Ali, should be so regarded. Sunnites tend toward greater orthodoxy and legalism than Shi'ites.

sutta (Pali)/*sutra* (Sanskrit)   Indian religious text, of variable length; in Buddhism, traditionally the words of the Buddha.

Talmud   The MISHNAH and midrashim (MIDRASH), composed by the rabbis from about the second century to 600 CE, which, together with the *TANAKH*, comprise Judaism.

Tanakh   The Hebrew Bible, the same as the Old Testament but with the books in a different order: The word combines the initials of *Torah*, the first five books of the Bible, *Neviim*, the prophets, and *Ketuvim*, or the hagiographa.

tasmiyah   Pronouncement of the name of Allah just before slaughtering an animal: a condition of the meat's being HALAL.

Tathagata   A Sanskrit title of the Buddha, indicating a perfect being who has attained complete insight into reality.

tathagatagarbha   A Sanskrit term indicating the potential Buddhahood in every being.

Temple   Usually refers to the Second Temple, which, after the destruction of the First Temple in 586 BCE, was completed in 516 BCE. Destroyed by the Romans in 70 CE, it was the site of animal sacrifice.

Tetragrammaton   The Hebrew name of God, consisting of four Hebrew letters, and written in English as Yahweh or Jehovah. By tradition, Jews are not supposed to pronounce the name.

Theravada Buddhism   "Teaching of the Elders"; a school of earlier or Hinayana (see under MAHAYANA) Buddhism.

Upanishads   The last and most visionary part of the VEDAS, conveying the idea of a godhead both within and above the world.

Vedanta   Religion based on the VEDAS, but emphasizing its metaphysic of oneness rather than its promotion of sacrifice. It was popularized in the late nineteenth century by Vivekananda, an opponent of meat eating.

Vedas   The earliest Indian religious literature, consisting of the Rg, Yajur, Sama, and Atharva Vedas. The Vedic period occurred sometime between 2500 and 600 BCE. Alongside metaphysical and religious ideas, the Vedas promote and prescribe the details of animal sacrifice.

Vinaya   The rules of monastic discipline, codified as the *patimokkha*, containing 227 rules. The Vinaya is one of the three "baskets," or groups of texts, in the Buddhist canon.

Vishnu   A Hindu god sometimes appearing in animal form in the religious texts.

BIBLIOGRAPHY

Abou El-Fadl, Khaled. "The Lord of the Essence: A Fatwa on Dogs." In *The Search for Beauty in Islam: A Conference of the Books*, chapter 80. www.scholarofthehouse.org/tloofesfaond.html.

Adams, Carol J. *The Sexual Politics of Meat: A Feminist-Vegetarian Critical Theory.* New York: Continuum International, 1999.

—— "Feasting on Life." *Ecotheology* 9 (July 2000): 38–48.

—— "Feeding on Grace: Institutional Violence, Christianity, and Vegetarianism." In K.S. Walters and L. Portmess, eds., *Religious Vegetarianism from Hesiod to the Dalai Lama*, 148–67. Albany: State University of New York, 2001.

—— "A Very Rare and Difficult Thing: Ecofeminism, Attention to Animal Suffering, and the Disappearance of the Subject." In Paul Waldau and Kimberley Patton, eds., *A Communion of Subjects. Animals in Religion, Science, and Ethics*, 591–604. New York: Columbia University Press, 2006.

Ahmed, Rafeeque. *Islam and Vegetarianism.* London: R. Ahmed, 1997.

—— Letter to R. Tappan, July 1, 1998

—— Letter to R. Tappan, December 14, 1998.

Akaranga Sutra. "To Harm No Living Being." In K.S. Walters and L. Portmess, eds., *Religious Vegetarianism from Hesiod to the Dalai Lama*, 43–46. Albany: State University of New York, 2001.

Akers, Keith. *The Lost Religion of Jesus.* New York: Lantern, 2000.

Ali, A.Y. *The Meaning of the Holy Qur'an.* Beltsville, MD: Amana, 1409/1989.

Animal Times (June/July 1994), 11.

Aquinas, Thomas. "Differences Between Rational and Other Creatures." In T. Regan and P. Singer, eds., *Animal Rights and Human Obligations*, 56–59. Englewood Cliffs, NJ: Prentice-Hall, 1976.

Arberry, A.J. *Sufism.* London: Unwin/Mandala, 1990.

Arluke, A. *Just a Dog.* Philadelphia: Temple University Press, 2006.

Aryasura. *Jatakamala (The Marvelous Companion).* Trans. anon., based on Joseph Speyer (English, 1895) and Vidya Karasimha (Tibetan, eighth century). Berkeley: Dharma, 1983.

Asher, M. *Rare Earth.* London: HarperCollins, 2002.

Astill, J. "Monkey Business." *Guardian*, July 4, 2001, G2 section, pp. 2–4.

Atran, Scott. *In Gods We Trust: The Evolutionary Landscape of Religion.* Oxford: Oxford University Press, 2002.

"Attitudes Towards Vegetarianism—U.K." London: Mintel International Group Ltd., Sept. 1, 2006. Summarized by Market Research.com: www.marketresearch.com/map/prod/1353078.html

Bahro, Rudolf. *Building the Green Movement.* London: Heretic, 1986.

Berman, L.A. "The Dietary Laws as Atonement for Flesh-eating." In Roberta Kalechofsky, ed., *Judaism and Animal Rights*, 150–64. Marblehead, MA: Micah, 1992.

Berry, Rynn. *Food for the Gods: Vegetarianism and the World's Religions*. New York: Pythagorean, 1998.

Best, Steven. "Evolve or Die: Can We Shed Our Moral Primitivism Before It's Too Late?" http://www.bestcyrano.org/THOMASPAINE/?p=713.

The Bhagavad-Gita. Trans. R.C. Zaehner. Oxford: Oxford University Press, 1973.

Bloom, Harold. *The Book of J*. Trans. David Rosenberg. New York: Vintage, 1991.

Bradley, Ian. *God Is Green*. London: Darton, Longman and Todd, 1990.

Bryant, Edwin. "Strategies of Vedic Subversion: The Emergence of Vegetarianism in Post-Vedic India." In Paul Waldau and Kimberley Patton, eds., *A Communion of Subjects. Animals in Religion, Science, and Ethics*, 193–203. New York: Columbia University Press, 2006.

Burch, E.S. Jr., and L.J. Ellanna. "Introduction.'" In E.S. Burch Jr and L.J. Ellanna, eds., *Key Issues in Hunter-Gatherer Research*, 1–8. Oxford: Berg, 1994.

Campbell, Joseph. *Primitive Mythology*. New York: Penguin Arkana, 1991.

Cantor, Aviva, with Barry Rosen and Hillel Besdin. "Kindness to Animals." In Roberta Kalechofsky, ed., *Judaism and Animal Rights*, 26–32. Marblehead, MA: Micah, 1992.

Chapple, Christopher. "Nonviolence to Animals in Buddhism and Jainism." In K. Kraft, ed., *Inner Peace, World Peace*, 49–62. Albany: State University of New York Press: 1992.

——*Nonviolence to Animals, Earth, and Self in Asian Traditions*. Albany: State University of New York Press, 1993.

Chereso, C.J. "Image of God." In *New Catholic Encyclopedia*, 7:369. New York: McGraw-Hill, 1967.

Choudhury, A.R. "Hinduism." In J. Holm, with J. Bowker, ed., *Attitudes to Nature*, 53–78. London: Pinter, 1994.

Church and Society Consultation of the World Council of Churches, Geneva. *Liberation of Life*. Annecy: World Council of Churches, 1988.

Clark, S.R.L. *The Moral Status of Animals*. Oxford: Clarendon, 1977.

Clifton, Merritt. "Indian Diets and the Future of Animal Welfare." *Animal People*, March 2007. Transmitted by Eileen Weintraub <eileenweintraub@comcast.net> to Society of Ethical and Religious Vegetarians e-mail forum.

Cohen, A. *Everyman's Talmud*. New York: Schocken, 1995.

Connor, Steve. "Scientists 'Should Be Allowed to Test on Apes.'" *The Independent*, June 3, 2006. www.findarticles.com/p/articles/mi_qn4158/is_20060603/ai_n16460017

Conze, Edward. *Buddhist Scriptures*. London: Penguin, 1959.

—— *Buddhist Wisdom Books (The Diamond Sutra and the Heart Sutra)*. London: Unwin, 1988.

Cook, M. *Muhammad*. Oxford: Oxford University Press, 1983.

Corbin, H. *Creative Imagination in the Sufism of Ibn 'Arabi*. Trans. Ralph Manheim. London: Routledge and Kegan Paul, 1969.

Cowell, E.B., ed. *Jataka I and II*. Trans. R. Chalmers (vol. 1), trans. W.H.D. Rouse (vol. 2). Oxford: Pali Text Society, 1995.

——*Jataka III and IV*. Trans. H.T. Francis and R.A. Neil (vol. 3), W.H.D. Rouse (vol. 4). Oxford: Pali Text Society, 1995.

—— *Jataka V and VI*. Trans. H. T. Francis (vol. 5). Trans. E. B. Cowell and W. H. D. Rouse (vol. 6). Oxford: Pali Text Society, 1995.

Craig, W. L. *The* Kalam *Cosmological Argument*. London: Macmillan, 1979.

Cramer, M. "The Inconsistency of Animal Experimentation with a Jewish Way of Life." In Roberta Kalechofsky, ed., *Judaism and Animal Rights*, 319–23. Marblehead, MA: Micah, 1992.

The Dalai Lama. "Compassion for All Sentient Beings." In K. S. Walters and L. Portmess, eds., *Religious Vegetarianism from Hesiod to the Dalai Lama*, 87–91. Albany: State University of New York Press, 2001.

Dalrymple, William. *From the Holy Mountain*. London: Flamingo, 1998.

Dan, Y. "In the Kabbalah." In *Encyclopaedia Judaica*, 14:615–16. Jerusalem: Encyclopaedia Judaica/Keter, 1971.

Davies, B. *An Introduction to the Philosophy of Religion*. Oxford: Oxford University Press, 1982.

Davies, D. "Christianity." In J. Holm, with J. Bowker, eds., *Attitudes to Nature*, 28–52. London: Pinter, 1994.

Dombrowski, D. A. *The Philosophy of Vegetarianism*. Amherst: University of Massachusetts Press, 1984.

—— *Hartshorne and the Metaphysics of Animal Rights*. Albany: State University of New York Press, 1988.

Dotan, D. "Israel's Largest Milk Producer Now Marketing Soy Drink." E-mail transmitted through Emanuel Goldman and Maynard Clark to Veg-Biz@EnviroLink.org and other contacts of the Society of Ethical and Religious Vegetarians, September 21, 2003.

Dutton, Yasin. "Islam and the Environment: A Framework for Enquiry." In Harfiyah Abdel Haleem, ed., *Islam and the Environment*, 56–74. London: Ta-Ha, 1998.

Eckersley, Robyn. "Socialism and Ecocentrism: Toward a New Synthesis." In Ted Benton, ed., *The Greening of Marxism*, 272–97. New York: Guilford, 1996.

Eliade, M. *A History of Religious Ideas*. Vol. 1. London: Collins, 1979.

Eller, C. "The Impact of Christianity on Buddhist Nonviolence in the West." In K. Kraft, ed., *Inner Peace, World Peace*, 91–110. Albany: State University of New York Press, 1992.

Evans-Wentz, W. Y., ed. *The Tibetan Book of the Dead*. Trans. Lama Kazi Dawa-Samdup. Oxford: Oxford University Press, 1960.

Fadali, Moneim A. *Animal Experimentation: A Harvest of Shame*. Los Angeles: Hidden Springs, 1996.

Feliks, J. "Apes." In *Encyclopaedia Judaica*, 3:175. Jerusalem: Encyclopaedia Judaica/Keter, 1971.

Fellowship of Life. "Thy Will Be Done?" Bangor, Gwynedd: Fellowship of Life, undated.

Ferguson, Barbara. "Muslims Urge Stop to Inhumane Animal Slaughter." *Arab News*, May 3, 2006. Transmitted by Eileen Weintraub <eileenweintraub@comcast.net> to Society of Ethical and Religious Vegetarians e-mail forum, 7 May, 2006.

Flack, J. C. and F. B. M. de Waal. "Being Nice Is Not a Building Block of Morality." In L. D. Katz, ed., *Evolutionary Origins of Morality*, 67–77. Thorverton: Imprint Academic, 2002.

Foltz, Richard C. "Is Vegetarianism Un-Islamic?" *Studies in Contemporary Islam* 3.1: 39–54. http://www.islamicconcerns.com/IsVegetarianismUnIslamic.asp.

—— "Islamic Environmentalism: A Matter of Interpretation." In R.C. Foltz, F.M. Denny, and A. Baharuddin, eds., *Islam and Ecology: A Bestowed Trust*, 249–79. Cambridge: Harvard University Press, 2003.

——*Animals in Islamic Tradition and Muslim Cultures.* Oxford: Oneworld, 2006.

Ford, L. S. "Pantheism vs. Theism: A Re-appraisal." *Monist*, 80.2: 286–306.

Forward, M., and M. Alam. "Islam." In J. Holm, with J. Bowker, eds., *Attitudes to Nature*, 79–100. London: Pinter, 1994.

Foster, J.B. *Marx's Ecology. Materialism and Nature.* New York: Monthly Review Press, 2000.

Fox, R.L. *The Unauthorized Version.* London: Viking, 1991.

Francione, Gary L. *Introduction to Animal Rights: Your Child or the Dog?* Philadelphia: Temple University Press, 2000.

Friedrich, B. "Pig Roast in Wyoming." E-mail to serveg@yahoogroups.com and other contacts of the Society of Ethical and Religious Vegetarians, August 26, 2003.

FWBO (Friends of the Western Buddhist Order). *The FWBO Puja Book.* Glasgow: Windhorse, 1990.

Gandhi, M. "Diet and Non-violence." In K.S. Walters and L. Portmess, eds., *Religious Vegetarianism from Hesiod to the Dalai Lama*, 53–55. Albany: State University of New York Press, 2001.

Gombrich, Richard. "Recovering the Buddha's Message." In D.S. Ruegg and L. Schmithausen, eds., *Earliest Buddhism and Madhyamaka*, 5–23. Leiden: Brill, 1990.

Grandin, Temple. "Commentary: Behavior of Slaughter Plant and Auction Employees Towards the Animals." www.grandin.com/references/behavior.employees.html. From *Anthrozoos* 1.4 (1988): 205–13.

Green, G. *Theology, Hermeneutics, and Imagination.* Cambridge: Cambridge University Press, 1999.

Groves, J. McA. *Hearts and Minds.* Philadephia: Temple University Press, 1997.

Guenther, M. "Animals in Bushman Thought, Myth and Art." In T. Ingold, D. Riches, and J. Woodburn, eds., *Hunters and Gatherers*, 2:192–202. Oxford, DC: Berg, 1997.

Hafiz (Khajeh Shamseddin Mohammad Hafiz-e Shirazi). *Teachings of Hafiz.* Trans. Gertrude Bell. London: Octagon, 1979.

Hardy, Thomas. *Far from the Madding Crowd.* London: Macmillan, 1974.

—— *Tess of the d'Urbervilles.* London: Macmillan, 1975.

—— *The Complete Poetical Works of Thomas Hardy.* Ed. S. Hynes. Vol. 2. Oxford: Clarendon, 1987.

Harris, I. "Buddhist Environmental Ethics and Detraditionalization: The Case of EcoBuddhism." *Religion* 25.3 (July 1995): 199–211.

Harvey, Peter. *An Introduction to Buddhism.* Cambridge: Cambridge University Press, 1990.

—— "Buddhist Attitudes to and Treatment of Non-human Nature." *Ecotheology* 4 (January 1998): 35–50.

Haykal, M. H. *The Life of Muhammad.* Trans. Ismail R. A. Al Faruq. London: Shorouk International, 1983.

Hiebert, Theodore. *The Yahwist's Landscape: Nature and Religion in Early Israel.* New York: Oxford University Press, 1996.

"Hillel the Elder." In *Encyclopaedia Judaica,* 8:482–85. Jerusalem: Encyclopaedia Judaica/Keter, 1971.

Hirsch, W. *Rabbinic Psychology.* London: Goldston, 1947.

The Holy Bible. London: Hodder and Stoughton, 1997.

Honderich, T. *The Oxford Companion to Philosophy.* Oxford: Oxford University Press, 1995.

Horner, I. B., trans. *Middle Length Sayings (Majjhima Nikaya).* Vol. 1. London: Luzac, 1954.

—— *Middle Length Sayings (Majjhima Nikaya).* Vol. 3. London: Luzac, 1959.

Hourani, G. F. *Reason and Tradition in Islamic Ethics.* Cambridge: Cambridge University Press, 1985.

Hume, David. "Of the Reason of Animals." In T. Regan and P. Singer, ed., *Animal Rights and Human Obligations,* 69–71. Englewood Cliffs, NJ: Prentice-Hall, 1976.

Hyland, J. R. *God's Covenant with Animals: A Biblical Basis for the Humane Treatment of All Creatures.* New York: Lantern, 2004.

Izzi Dien, M. *The Environmental Dimensions of Islam.* Cambridge: Lutterworth, 2000.

Jacobs, L. *The Jewish Religion: A Companion.* Oxford: Oxford University Press, 1995.

Jacobsen, K. A. "Humankind and Nature in Buddhism." In E. Deutsch and R. Bontekoe, eds., *A Companion to World Philosophies,* 381–91. Malden, MA: Blackwell, 1997.

James, William. *The Varieties of Religious Experience.* New York: Triumph, 1991.

Jeffrey, David Lyle. *People of the Book: Christian Identity and Literary Culture.* Grand Rapids, MI: Eerdsman/Institute for Advanced Christian Studies, 1996.

Kalechofsky, Roberta. "In the Camp of *Kivrot-Hata'avah.*" Additional essay included in Richard H. Schwartz, *Judaism and Vegetarianism,* 110–16. Marblehead, MA: Micah, 1988.

—— "Introduction: The Way We Are Now." In R. Kalechofsky, ed., *Judaism and Animal Rights,* 249–60. Marblehead, MA: Micah, 1992.

—— "Jewish Law and Tradition on Animal Rights." In R. Kalechofsky, ed., *Judaism and Animal Rights,* 46–58. Marblehead, MA: Micah, 1992.

—— "*Kashrut:* A Provegetarian Bias in Torah." In K. S. Walters and L. Portmess, eds., *Religious Vegetarianism from Hesiod to the Dalai Lama,* 97–104. Albany: State University of New York Press, 2001.

Kalechofsky, Roberta, ed. *Judaism and Animal Rights.* Marblehead, MA: Micah, 1992.

Kane, S. *Wisdom of the Mythtellers.* Peterborough, Ontario: Broadview, 1994.

Kant, Immanuel. *The Moral Law; or, Kant's Groundwork of the Metaphysic of Morals.* Ed. and trans. H. J. Paton. London: Hutchinson, 1956.

Kapleau, Philip. *To Cherish All Life.* Rochester, NY: Zen Center, 1981.

Kassam, Z. "*The Case of the Animals Versus Man:* Towards an Ecology of Being." In Paul Waldau and Kimberley Patton, eds., *A Communion of Subjects: Animals in Religion, Science, and Ethics,* 160–69. New York: Columbia University Press, 2006.

Kemmerer, Lisa. *In Search of Consistency: Ethics and Animals.* Leiden: Brill, 2006.

Kemp, J. *Ethical Naturalism: Hobbes and Hume.* London: Macmillan, 1970.

Kempe, Margery. *The Book of Margery Kempe.* Trans. Barry Windeatt. London: Penguin, 1994.

Keown, D. *Buddhism and Bioethics.* Basingstoke: Macmillan, 1995.

Khalid, Fazlun. "Islam, Ecology, and the World Order." In Harfiyah Abdel Haleem, ed., *Islam and the Environment,* 16–31. London: Ta-Ha, 1998.

Khan, M. M. *Summarized Sahih Al-Bukhari.* Riyadh: Dar-us-Salam, 1994.

Klawans, Jonathan. "Sacrifice in Ancient Israel: Pure Bodies, Domesticated Animals, and the Divine Shepherd." In Paul Waldau and Kimberley Patton, eds., *A Communion of Subjects: Animals in Religion, Science, and Ethics,* 65–80. New York: Columbia University Press, 2006.

Klug, Brian. "Laboratory Animals, Francis Bacon and the Culture of Science." In R. Kalechofsky, ed., *Judaism and Animal Rights,* 264–81. Marblehead, MA: Micah, 1992.

Kook, Abraham Isaac. "A Firm and Joyous Voice of Life." In K. S. Walters and L. Portmess, eds., *Religious Vegetarianism from Hesiod to the Dalai Lama,* 118–21. Albany: State University of New York Press, 2001.

Kundera, Milan. *The Unbearable Lightness of Being.* Trans. Michael Henry Heim. London: Faber and Faber, 1985.

Küng, Hans. "Belief in a Son of God?" In P. Burns and J. Cumming, ed., *The Bible Now,* 143–51. Dublin: Gill and Macmillan, 1981.

Lankavatara Sutra. "Cherish each being like an only child." In K. S. Walters and L. Portmess, eds., *Religious Vegetarianism from Hesiod to the Dalai Lama,* 66–74. Albany: State University of New York Press, 2001.

Levinas, Emmanuel. *Beyond the Verse: Talmudic Readings and Lectures.* Trans. G. D. Mole. London: Athlone, 1994.

Lindner, Lorin. "To Love Like a Bird." In Michael Tobias and Kate Solisti-Mattelon, eds., *Kinship with the Animals,* 53–63. Hillsboro, OR: Beyond Words, 1998.

Linzey, Andrew. *Animal Theology.* London: SCM Press, 1994.

——*Animal Gospel.* Louisville, KY: Westminster John Knox, 2000.

——"Interfaith Service in Celebration of Animals." E-mail transmitted by Joe Schmoe via Sue Grisham to *serveg@yahoogroups.com* and other contacts of the Society of Ethical and Religious Vegetarians, April 30, 2004.

Lommel, Andreas. *Prehistoric and Primitive Man.* New York: McGraw-Hill, 1966.

Lossky, V. *The Mystical Theology of the Eastern Church.* Trans. Fellowship of St. Albans and St. Sergius. Cambridge: Jas Clarke, 1991.

McCarthy, C. "'Cloistered' Chickens." *National Catholic Reporter,* April 6, 2007. Transmitted by Bruce Friedrich, brucef@peta.org, to Society of Ethical and Religious Vegetarians e-mail forum, April 5, 2007.

Maimonides, Moses. *The Guide for the Perplexed.* Trans. M. Friedlander. New York: Dover, 1956.

Manu. "The Sin of Killing." In K. S. Walters and L. Portmess, eds., *Religious Vegetarianism from Hesiod to the Dalai Lama,* 40–42. Albany: State University of New York Press, 2001.

Masri, al-Hafiz B.A. "Animals in Islam I." www.themodernreligion.com/misc/an/an1 .htm, 2002. Excerpts from *Animals in Islam*. Chippenham, Wilts: Rowe, 1989.

—— "Animals in Islam II." www.themodernreligion.com/misc/an/an2.htm, 2002. Excerpts from *Animals in Islam*. Chippenham, Wilts: Rowe, 1989.

—— *Excerpts from the Islamic Teachings on Animal Welfare*. Birmingham/London: Islamic Foundation for Ecology and Environmental Sciences/World Society for the Protection of Animals, n.d.

—— *The Islamic Code of Animal-Human Relationships*. Horsham, W. Sussex: RSPCA, n.d.

—— "They Are Communities Like You." In K.S. Walters and L. Portmess, eds., *Religious Vegetarianism from Hesiod to the Dalai Lama*, 181–91. Albany: State University of New York Press, 2001.

Masson, Jeffrey M., and Susan McCarthy. *When Elephants Weep*. London: Vintage, 1996.

Mawdudi, A. A'la. *Towards Understanding Islam*. Leicester: Islamic Foundation, 1980.

Menache, Andre. "A Jewish Intuition about Animal Research." In Roberta Kalechofsky, ed., *Judaism and Animal Rights*, 334–36. Marblehead, MA: Micah, 1992.

Mendelsohn, R.S. "Foreword to Slaughter of the Innocent." In Roberta Kalechofsky, ed., *Judaism and Animal Rights*, 261–63. Marblehead, MA: Micah, 1992.

Mernissi, Fatima. *The Veil and the Male Elite*. Reading, MA: Addison-Wesley, 1991.

Mill, John Stuart. *On Liberty and the Subjection of Women*. Ware, Herts: Wordsworth, 1996.

Monastra, Yahya. "Who Says Muslims Can't Be Vegetarian?" http://members.aol.com/ yahyam/muslim_vegetarian.html, 2000.

Moore, G.E. "A Defence of Common Sense." In *Philosophical Papers*, 32–59. London: Allen and Unwin, 1959.

Morton, Timothy. *Shelley and the Revolution in Taste*. Cambridge: Cambridge University Press, 1994.

Mountain, M. "Dogma and Catechism." In M. Tobias and K. Solisti-Mattelon, eds., *Kinship with the Animals*, 169–77. Hillsboro, OR: Beyond Words, 1998.

Murray, Robert. *The Cosmic Covenant: Biblical Themes of Justice, Peace, and the Integrity of Creation*. Piscataway, NJ: Tigris, 2007.

Murti, T.R.V. *The Central Philosophy of Buddhism*. London: Unwin Hyman, 1987.

Murti, Vasu. "Again and Again." E-mail to Society of Ethical and Religious Vegetarians forum, June 1, 2006.

Naseef, Abdullah Omar. "The Muslim Declaration on Nature." In Harfiyah Abdel Haleem, ed., *Islam and the Environment*, 12–13. London: Ta-Ha, 1998.

Neusner, Jacob. "Foreword." In A. Cohen, *Everyman's Talmud*, ix–xxviii. New York: Schocken, 1995.

New Catholic Encyclopedia. Vol. 9. New York: McGraw-Hill, 1967.

The NIV Thematic Study Bible. Ed. A.E. McGrath. 1st ed. London: Hodder and Stoughton, 1996.

Noske, Barbara. *Beyond Boundaries*. Montreal: Black Rose, 1997.

OIPA (International Organization for Animal Protection). "Stop This Monkey Business in Nepal." www.oipa.org/vivisection/alerts/nepal.html.

Page, Tony. *Buddhism and Animals*. London: UKAVIS, 1999.

Palmer, Clare. *Environmental Ethics and Process Thinking*. Oxford: Clarendon, 1998.

—— "Animals in Christian Ethics." *Ecotheology* 7.2 (January 2003): 163–85.

Patton, Kimberley. "Animal Sacrifice: Metaphysics of the Sublimated Victim." In Paul Waldau and Kimberley Patton, eds., *A Communion of Subjects. Animals in Religion, Science, and Ethics*. 391–405. New York: Columbia University Press, 2006.

PETA (People for the Ethical Treatment of Animals). "2008's Sexiest Vegetarian Celebrity—Who Gets Your Vote?" E-mail from PETA Europe (newsmanager@peta. org.uk), May 29, 2008.

Phelps, Norm. "Special Youth Challenge Hunts." E-mail to serveg@yahoogroups.com, Society of Ethical and Religious Vegetarians forum, September 8, 2003.

—— *The Longest Struggle. Animal Advocacy from Pythagoras to PETA*. New York: Lantern, 2007.

"Pope Concedes Souls to Animals." *Agscene* no. 100 (September/October 1990): 23.

Preece, Rod. *Animals and Nature*. Vancouver: UBC Press, 1999.

—— *Brute Souls, Happy Beasts, and Evolution: The Historical Status of Animals*. Vancouver: UBC Press, 2005.

Rachels, James. *Created from Animals*. Oxford: Oxford University Press, 1991.

Raisin, J.S. "Humanitarianism of the Laws of Israel." In Roberta Kalechofsky, ed., *Judaism and Animal Rights*, 17–25. Marblehead, MA: Micah, 1992.

Regan, Tom. *The Case for Animal Rights*. London: Routledge, 1988.

Regenstein, Lewis G. *Replenish the Earth*. New York: Crossroad, 1991.

Rifkin, Jeremy. *Beyond Beef*. London: Thorsons, 1992.

Riskin, S. "Compassion or Concession." In Roberta Kalechofsky, ed., *Judaism and Animal Rights*, 43–45. Marblehead, MA: Micah, 1992.

Rollin, B. E. *The Unheeded Cry*. Oxford: Oxford University Press, 1990.

Rolston, Holmes, III. "Duties to Endangered Species." In R. Elliot, ed., *Environmental Ethics*, 60–75. Oxford: Oxford University Press, 1995.

Ruegg, David Seyfort. "Ahimsa and Vegetarianism in the History of Buddhism." In S. Balasooriya, A. Bareau, R. Gombrich, S. Gunasingha, U. Mallawarachchi, and E. Perry, eds., *Buddhist Studies in Honour of Walpola Rahula*, 234–41. London/Sri Lanka: Gordon Fraser/Vimamsa, 1980.

Ruesch, Hans. *Slaughter of the Innocent*. Hartsdale, NY: Civitas, 1983.

Rumi, Jalal al-Din. "The Men Who Ate the Elephant." In K.S. Walters and L. Portmess, eds., *Religious Vegetarianism from Hesiod to the Dalai Lama*, 173–74. Albany: State University of New York Press, 2001.

ibn Rushd. *The Distinguished Jurist's Primer*. Trans. I. A. K. Nyazee. Reading: Garnet, 2000.

Russell, Bertrand. *Unpopular Essays*. London: Allen and Unwin, 1950.

Sa'di (Musharrif Od-din Muslih Od-din). *Sadi: The Rose-Garden*. Ed. and trans. E. B Eastwick. London: Octagon, 1979.

Salt, Henry. "The Logic of the Larder." In T. Regan and P. Singer, eds., *Animal Rights and Human Obligations*, 185–89. Englewood Cliffs, NJ: Prentice-Hall, 1976.

Sangharakshita. *A Survey of Buddhism*. Boulder/London: Shambhala/Windhorse, 1980.

Schmithausen, Lambert. "Preface." In D.S. Ruegg and L. Schmithausen, eds., *Earliest Buddhism and Madhyamaka*, 1–3. Leiden: Brill, 1990.

—— "The Early Buddhist Tradition and Ecological Ethics." *Journal of Buddhist Ethics* 4:1–74.

Scholem, G. "Kabbalah." In *Encyclopaedia Judaica*, 10:490–653. Jerusalem: Encyclopaedia Judaica/Keter, 1971.

Schwartz, Richard H. *Judaism and Vegetarianism*. Marblehead, MA: Micah, 1988.

—— "*Tsa'ar ba'alei chayim*—Judaism and Compassion for Animals." In Roberta Kalechofsky, ed., *Judaism and Animal Rights*, 59–70. Marblehead, MA: Micah, 1992.

Schwarzschild, S.S. "Noachide Laws." In *Encyclopaedia Judaica*, 12:1189–90. Jerusalem: Encyclopaedia Judaica/Keter, 1971.

Shah, Idries. *The Way of the Sufi*. London: Penguin Arkana, 1990.

Sharp, H.S. "Dry Meat and Gender: The Absence of Chipewyan Ritual for the Regulation of Hunting and Animal Numbers." In T. Ingold, D. Riches, and J. Woodburn, eds., *Hunters and Gatherers*, 2:183–91. Oxford: Berg, 1997.

Sherira Gaon. "Sherira Gaon Defends the Rights of Animals." In Roberta Kalechofsky, ed., *Judaism and Animal Rights*, 15–16. Marblehead, MA: Micah, 1992.

de Silva, P. "Environmental Ethics: A Buddhist Perspective." In Charles Wei-hsun Fu and Sandra A. Wawrytko, eds., *Buddhist Ethics and Modern Society*, 173–84. Westport, CT: Greenwood, 1991.

Singer, Isaac Bashevis. "The Slaughterer." In *Collected Stories*, 207–16. London: Penguin, 1984.

Singer, Peter. *Animal Liberation*. London: Pimlico, 1995.

Skilton, Andrew. *A Concise History of Buddhism*. Birmingham: Windhorse, 1997.

Smart, Ninian. *The World's Religions*. Cambridge: Cambridge University Press, 1992.

Sober, E., and D.S. Wilson. "Summary of *Unto Others: The Evolution and Psychology of Unselfish Behaviour*." In L.D. Katz, ed., *Evolutionary Origins of Morality*, 185–206. Thorverton: Imprint Academic, 2002.

Solomon, N. "Judaism." In J. Holm, with J. Bowker, eds., *Attitudes to Nature*, 101–31. London: Pinter, 1994.

Spinoza, Baruch. *A Spinoza Reader*. Ed. and trans. E. Curley. Princeton: Princeton University Press, 1994.

Spira, Henry. "Animal Rights—Fighting to Win." In Roberta Kalechofsky, ed., *Judaism and Animal Rights*, 337–40. Marblehead, MA: Micah, 1992.

Sprigge, T. *The Vindication of Absolute Idealism*. Edinburgh: Edinburgh University Press, 1983.

Steele, K., and S. Kaza. "Buddhist Food Practices and Attitudes Among Contemporary Western Practitioners." *Ecotheology* 9 (July 2000): 49–67.

Sumedho. *Cittaviveka*. Petersfield, Hants: Sangha, Chithurst Forest Monastery, 1983.

—— *Now Is the Knowing*. Bangkok: Mrs. Thiwasree Piyaphan, n.d.

Surangama Sutra. "Prohibition Against Killing." In K.S. Walters and L. Portmess, eds., *Religious Vegetarianism from Hesiod to the Dalai Lama*, 64–65. Albany: State University of New York Press, 2001.

Suzuki, D.T., trans. *Lankavatara Sutra*. London: Routledge and Kegan Paul, 1932.

Swain, L. "The Old Testament in the History of Israel." In P. Burns and J. Cumming, eds., *The Bible Now*, 73–85. Dublin: Gill and Macmillan, 1981.

Swinburne, Richard. *Providence and the Problem of Evil*. Oxford: Clarendon, 1998.

Tappan, Robert. "Christianity and Vegetarianism." In *Feeding the Children of Abraham*. http://www.jesusveg.com/5.html, 1998.

—— "Islam and Vegetarianism." In *Feeding the Children of Abraham*. http://www.jesusveg.com/6.html, 1998.

—— "Judaism and Vegetarianism." In *Feeding the Children of Abraham*. http://www.jesusveg.com/4.html, 1998.

Tiradhammo. "Joy in Spiritual Practice." In Amaravati Sangha, ed., *Seeing the Way*, 90–95. Hemel Hempstead: Amaravati, 1989.

Tiyavanich, K. *Forest Recollections: Wandering Monks in Twentieth-Century Thailand*. Honolulu: University of Hawaii Press, 1997.

Tutuncuoglu, Ibrahim. "The Past and Current Situation of Vegetarianism in Turkey." *European Vegetarian Union News* 4 (1998) and 1 (1999). http://www.european-vegetarian.org/evu/english/news/news991/situation.html.

Unterman, Alan. *Jews: Their Religious Beliefs and Practices*. London: Routledge, 1990.

Varisco, D.M. *Medieval Folk Astronomy and Agriculture in Arabia and the Yemen*. Aldershot, Hants: Ashgate/Variorum, 1997.

VegetarianIslam. Digest 128, e-mail forum, May 29, 2001.

Venkata Ramanan, K. *Nagarjuna's Philosophy as Presented in the Maha-Prajnaparamita Sastra*. Delhi: Motilal Banarsidass, 1978.

Vesey, G., and P. Foulkes. *Dictionary of Philosophy*. Enderby, Leicester: Bookmart, 1999.

Vivekananda. "Oneness Includes All Animals." In K.S. Walters and L. Portmess, eds., *Religious Vegetarianism from Hesiod to the Dalai Lama*, 50–52. Albany: State University of New York Press, 2001.

Waines, D. *An Introduction to Islam*. Cambridge: Cambridge University Press, 1995.

Waldau, Paul. *The Specter of Speciesism: Buddhist and Christian Views of Animals*. Oxford: Oxford University Press, 2002.

Waliullah, D. B. Fry, and J. N. Jalbani. *Sufism and the Islamic Tradition: The Lamahat and Sata'at of Shah Waliullah of Delhi*. Trans. G.N. Jalbani. London: Octagon, 1980.

Walters, K. S., and L. Portmess. "The Dalai Lama." In K. S. Walters and L. Portmess, eds., *Religious Vegetarianism from Hesiod to the Dalai Lama*, 87. Albany: State University of New York Press, 2001.

—— "Al-Hafiz B. A. Masri." In K. S. Walters and L. Portmess, eds., *Religious Vegetarianism from Hesiod to the Dalai Lama*, 181. Albany: State University of New York Press, 2001.

Webb, Stephen H. *On God and Dogs: A Christian Theology of Compassion for Animals*. New York: Oxford University Press, 2002.

Wittgenstein, Ludwig. *Tractatus Logico Philosophicus*. London: Routledge, 2001.

Young, Richard Alan. *Is God a Vegetarian? Christianity, Vegetarianism, and Animal Rights*. Chicago: Open Court, 1999.

az-Zaybaq, M. *The Animal: Its Particulars and Its Rights Within Islam*. Ed. and trans. G.A.F. Al-Baraqawi and S.A. Carlo. Jeddah: Abul-Qasim, 2001.

INDEX

Abarbanel, Isaac, 141
Aboriginals, 7–8, 10, 11
Abraham, 27, 31, 52, 58, 113, 141, 146, 179, 217; in Islam, 95, 96, 97–98
Abstinence, 162
Abulafia, Abraham, 182
Activism, 180, 217; vs. quietism, 177–78
"Act to prevent the cruel and improper Treatment of Cattle" (Martin), 91
Adams, Carol J., 11, 18, 82, 85
Addams, Charles J., 97
Afterlife, 53, 58, 69
Aggression strategy for conflict resolution, 6–7, 21, 26, 40, 51, 217; in Buddhism, 116–19; in Christianity, 74–80; in Hebrew Bible, 27–33; in Islam, 96–101; in Judaism, 53–59
Agriculture, 3, 85
Ahmed, Bina, 139, 150, 153
Ahmed, Rafeeque, 134, 139, 141, 142, 216
Akbar (Moghul emperor), 169, 174
Akers, Keith, 71, 72, 73, 81, 84–85, 135, 163, 166
Alam, M., 97, 110, 112, 171
Albo, Joseph, 145, 146, 163
Ali, A.Y., 99, 106, 110, 111
Altruism, 14, 17, 26, 213, 226, 228, 229
America (Jesuit magazine), 79
Androcles, 87
Angell, George T., 91
Animal(s): advocacy, 9, 89; anti, rationalism, 52; authority over, 33; Bodhisattva, 159–60; Buddhism and, 115–16; Catholic Church and cruelty toward, 78–80; Catholic Church and hostility toward, 71; children and, 7, 13–14; in Christianity, 84; Christianity and consideration for, 71, 74; Christianity and kindness to, 80, 81, 86–89, 90, 93; cognition of, 189–90;

communication of, 189; consideration for, 223–24; demons and, 59; denigration of, 99; divine/human concern for, 39–41; domestication of, 12, 48; emotion, 222; free, 32, 120, 192, 194; as guides/messengers, 22, 23, 25, 26, 185, 190–200, 201; Hinduism and knowledge of, 190; human beings equated with, 46; identification with, 116, 120; Islam and kindness to, 102–4, 107, 153; Jesus and, 192–93; Judaism and cruelty toward, 57, 69; Judaism and kindness to, 60, 61, 62, 63, 64, 69; kept, 29, 32, 34, 107, 120; kinship with, 34, 86–87; liberation, 178; morality and, 117; mystical experience and, 195–96; naming of, 33, 48; nativity and, 86; prayer and, 187–90, 196, 201; protection/care for, 174; Protestant Church and kindness to, 90–91; rebirth as, 115, 117, 123, 155; religious sense of, 188, 189, 190; saints' kindness to, 87–89, 93, 167; as signs, 151–53, 182; soul, 4, 57–58, 79, 135, 185–87, 201; speech and, 193; spiritual attainment of, 180, 185–90; as teachers of morality, 196–200; as teachers of wisdom, 193–95; titles in *Qur'an*, 109; Torah and consideration for, 60–61; as vegetarians, 48; welfare, 89, 91, 93; welfare vs. liberation, 7; working, 40–41, 46, 107, 116, 131, 218; worth of, 41; *see also* Insects; Pets; Primates; Sheep; *specific animals*
Animal experimentation, 6, 7, 13, 54, 78, 79, 121, 129,

164–65, 211, 222; *see also* Vivisection
Animal Judge, 2, 21, 22–23, 47, 65, 74, 119, 121, 125, 128, 129, 161, 206, 213, 229; function of, 22
Animal Nepal, 179
Animal perspective, 22–23, 185–201, 217
Animal rights, 2, 3, 17, 18, 21, 89, 163, 219; Buddhism and, 178; Christianity and, 149; inclusion of, 217; Islam and, 139, 150, 177; oneness and, 24; opposition to, 216; in *Qur'an*, 106; support for, 133, 228
Anthropocentrism, 2, 24, 53, 68, 78, 207
Antimaterialism, 76
Antirationalism, 181–85; *see also* rationalism
Apocalypse, 194
Aquinas, Thomas, 77, 88, 223
Arberry, A.J., 100
Aretaism, 65
Aristotle, 76, 77
Arluke, A., 13
Aryans, 122, 257
Asceticism, 69; vegetarianism and, 73, 76, 86, 97, 161–63
Asharism, 96
Asia for Animals, 179
Asoka (Emperor), 174
Atheism, 203
Atonement, 85
Atran, Scott, 30, 134
Augustine (Saint), 77, 88
Authoritarianism, 46, 53, 96, 206
Authority, 2, 195; of God, 27, 45, 95, 205; over animals, 33
Autonomy, 224

Bacon, Francis, 223
Bands of Mercy, 91
Baptism, 85
Barth, Karl, 99
Basil (Saint), 88, 149
Bell, 100, 206
Bellarmine, Robert, 185

Mahayana Buddhism
(*continued*)
Bodhisattva ideal and,
24, 159, 217; emptiness
doctrine and, 24; karma
and, 159; meat eating
and, 175, 176;
vegetarianism and, 125,
129, 176
Maimonides, 37, 39, 41, 54,
56, 58, 60, 62, 141, 147,
258
Majjhima Nikaya, 117, 129,
130
Manichaeanism, 239n86
Manichaeans, 76, 161, 162,
258
Mannin, Ethel, 126
Martin, Richard, 91
Masri, al-Hafiz B.A., 95,
101, 102, 106, 108–9, 113,
135–36, 169, 171, 172, 187,
189
Masson, Jeffrey M., 222
Meat eating, 4, 5, 7, 27, 38,
53, 142, 216; Buddhism
and, 116, 118–19, 125, 126,
131, 136, 218; Christianity
and, 31, 72, 81, 82, 163;
climate and, 129;
dominion and, 47; the
Fall and, 148–49; health
and, 164; Hinduism and,
174–75; Islam and, 31, 95,
96–97, 101–2, 108, 171;
Judaism and, 12, 31, 44,
57, 58, 63; justification
for, 30; Laws of Manu on,
122; Mahayana
Buddhism and, 175, 176;
New Testament and, 75;
postflood permission for,
30–31, 56–57; sacrifice
and, 31–32, 34;
wrong-doing and, 42, 43;
see also Vegetarianism
Meditation, 178, 182, 183,
217; *jhana/dhyana* and,
258
Menache, Andre, 165
Mendelsohn, Robert, 165
Mernissi, Fatima, 192
Messengers, animals as, 22,
23, 25, 26, 185, 190–200,
201
Metaphysics, 2, 3, 212
Methodist Church, 187
Metta/maitri
(lovingkindness), 123,
131, 155, 243n30, 258
Micah Press, 164
Midrash, 61, 64, 134, 141,
258
Mill, John Stuart, 7, 220
Mindfulness, 161
Miracles, 191–92

Mishnah, 59, 62, 147,
233n1, 259
El-Misri, 100
Mistranslation, 135–36
Molari, Carlo, 186
Monastra, Yahya, 171
Money, 154–55
Mongolia, 129
Monotheism, 202, 205
Moore, G. E., 183
Morality, 1, 2, 18, 24, 35,
205, 214, 221, 224;
animals as teachers of,
117, 196–200; Buddhism
and, 173; building blocks
of, 3; change and
evolution of, 16–17;
conflict, 9, 215; equality
and, 19; evil and, 142,
143, 144, 206; evolution
of, 25, 180, 215–17;
priority and, 21;
responsibility and, 55;
surrendering judgment
of, 96; wisdom and, 210
Moral Philosophy
(Rickaby), 79
Moses, 15, 30, 34, 45, 63
Mother, child bond, 37–38,
47, 103
Mountain, Michael, 219
Muhaiyaddeen, Bawa, 171
Muhammad, 95, 100, 102,
113, 191–92
Muhrim, 112, 259
Muntzer, Thomas, 90
Murray, Robert, 28, 73–74
Murti, Vasu, 72
Mu'tazilites, 259
Mystical experience,
animals and, 195–96
Mysticism, 78, 99, 181, 204,
207
Myths, 7–8; exculpatory, 10

Nagarjuna, 195, 208, 209,
210, 259
Name giving, 181; to
animals, 33, 48;
dominion through, 33
Nasef, Abdullah Omar, 154
Nativity, 85, 93; animals
and, 86
Nature: of God, 203;
harmony with, 167;
higher/lower human, 87;
love of, 151
Necessity(ies): exploitation
and, 14, 200; killing and,
1, 5, 6, 8, 14, 51, 95, 109,
110, 111, 112, 114, 116, 128,
129, 132, 142, 169; of life,
172
New International Bible, 36
New Testament, 3, 71, 80,
93, 166; meat eating and,

75; *see also Christian
Bible*
Next-of-kin claim, 21–22,
224, 225–26
Nirvana, 140, 209, 259
Noachide laws, 38, 61, 164,
171
Nonexistence, 208, 210
Noninjury (*ahimsa*), 9, 115,
120, 122, 123, 128, 130,
131–32, 156–58, 162, 169,
211, 212, 217, 257;
Christianity and,
219–21; exceptions given
to, rule, 224–26; Islam
and, 220
Nonintention, 128–29
Noske, Barbara, 23
Nursi, 151, 153

Obedience, 27, 58, 62, 79,
85, 113, 146, 217
Old Testament, 55, 135
Oneness: animal rights
and, 24; Buddhism and,
209; Christianity and,
204–5; God and, 202,
203, 206; Hinduism and,
207–8; Islam and, 205–6;
Judaism and, 202–4;
problems of, 24–25, 202,
213; Sufism and, 205–6;
Vedanta and, 212
Ontology, 179, 212;
dynamic, 137
Opportunity, 143
Oppression, 19, 173, 196;
equality and, 7; of human
beings, 6, 7; of women, 7
Order of the Cross, 167

Padmapurana, 155
Page, Tony, 119, 136, 177,
178, 209
Paley, William, 167
Pali, 17, 117, 118, 125, 137,
158, 242n9, 259; Jatakas,
119, 156, 157, 159, 160
Panentheism, 201, 203,
204
Pantheism, 201, 203, 204,
206
Passover, 81, 140
Patton, Kimberley, 9
Paul (Saint), 71, 72, 93;
influence of, 74–75
Paul VI (Pope), 89
Peace, 66, 145, 180; inner,
215
People for the Ethical
Treatment of Animals
(PETA), 139, 150, 168
Pereq Shirah, 188, 189
Perfectionism, 21, 22, 93,
224–25; in Islam,
98–100

GPSR Authorized Representative: Easy Access System Europe, Mustamäe tee
50, 10621 Tallinn, Estonia, gpsr.requests@easproject.com

www.ingramcontent.com/pod-product-compliance
Lightning Source LLC
Chambersburg PA
CBHW032120020426
42334CB00016B/1014